Pursuing Social Holiness

Pursuing Social Holiness

*The Band Meeting in Wesley's Thought
and Popular Methodist Practice*

KEVIN M. WATSON

OXFORD
UNIVERSITY PRESS

OXFORD
UNIVERSITY PRESS

Oxford University Press is a department of the University of Oxford.
It furthers the University's objective of excellence in research, scholarship,
and education by publishing worldwide.

Oxford   New York

Auckland   Cape Town   Dar es Salaam   Hong Kong   Karachi
Kuala Lumpur   Madrid   Melbourne   Mexico City   Nairobi
New Delhi   Shanghai   Taipei   Toronto

With offices in

Argentina   Austria   Brazil   Chile   Czech Republic   France   Greece
Guatemala   Hungary   Italy   Japan   Poland   Portugal   Singapore
South Korea   Switzerland   Thailand   Turkey   Ukraine   Vietnam

Oxford is a registered trademark of Oxford University Press
in the UK and certain other countries.

Published in the United States of America by
Oxford University Press
198 Madison Avenue, New York, NY 10016

Watson, Kevin M.
Pursuing social holiness: the band meeting in Wesley's thought and popular Methodist practice /
Kevin M. Watson.
pages cm
Includes bibliographical references and index.
ISBN 978-0-19-933636-4 (hardcover : alk. paper)—ISBN 978-0-19-933637-1 (ebook) 1. Holiness—
Methodist Church. 2. Methodist band meetings. 3. Wesley, John, 1703-1791. I. Title.
BX8349.H64W38 2013
262'.72–dc23   2013020358

1 3 5 7 9 8 6 4 2
Printed in the United States of America
on acid-free paper

To Doug and Scott

CONTENTS

ACKNOWLEDGMENTS

I have spent the better part of the last five years studying the ways that early Methodists pursued holiness together in community. This project began as my dissertation at Southern Methodist University (SMU). The revisions occurred when I was a faculty member in the School of Theology at Seattle Pacific University (SPU). Both during the initial work and the revisions that led to the present volume, I often reflected on the ways that this book is itself the product of the investment and support of a community. At SMU, Ted A. Campbell, William J. Abraham, Elaine A. Heath, and Richard P. Heitzenrater, who were the members of my dissertation committee, were expert guides who provided correction and redirection as needed, without imposing their own agendas on my work. I am especially indebted to Ted, who particularly invested in this work as my advisor.

Thanks are also due to Tom Albin, who generously shared his expertise in early Methodist spirituality. John Walsh graciously gave me his permission to use the material from the Samuel Roberts manuscript, which is in his private collection, and to include the entire account of the band meeting in an appendix. The board of directors for *The Bicentennial Edition of the Works of John Wesley* granted permission to publish the "Rules of the Band Societies" and "Directions given to the Band Societies" as appendices. Randy Maddox shared a forthcoming article with me that contained a fascinating modification, or forerunner, of the "Rules of the Band Societies." I would like to express my gratitude to the two anonymous readers who reviewed the original manuscript for this book and provided valuable feedback. Cynthia Read was an expert guide throughout the acquisitions process, and Charlotte Steinhardt and the rest of the staff at Oxford University Press were a delight to work with.

A research trip to the Methodist Archives at the University of Manchester was indispensable to this book. My research there would not have been nearly as fruitful without the expert guidance of Gareth Lloyd, Peter Nockles, and the wonderful staff of the Special Collections at the University of Manchester.

Gareth regularly pointed me to exactly the right source at several key points throughout my research. The trip to Manchester would not have been possible without the generosity of Elroy and Vickie Wisian Ministries, Inc., as well as the continued support of A Foundation for Theological Education (AFTE), which continues to provide a supportive scholarly community that I am humbled and grateful to be associated with.

I am grateful for the support of all my colleagues at SPU. Daniel Castelo, Douglas M. Strong, and Robert W. Wall were particularly generous in giving their time to discuss the book, providing helpful guidance as I worked toward publication. I hope that this history can be of service to SPU as it continues to articulate its distinctiveness as a church-related university of the Free Methodist Church.

Finally, I would like to thank my family. My parents, Matt and Tellia, have been a constant source of love and support. I am thankful to be their son. I also thank my children: Bethany, James, and Eden. In different ways, each of them has reminded me that as interesting as the history of early Methodism is, their lives are infinitely more so. They helped me live in the present while studying the past. Above all, I thank my wife, Melissa, whose love, support, patience, and encouragement were vital to this project. For many reasons, this book would not have been possible without her.

ABBREVIATIONS

AM: *The Arminian Magazine* (Wesley and WMC [GBr], 1778–97).

EMV: Early Methodist Volume, British Methodist Archives, John Rylands Library, Special Collections, University of Manchester.

Letters (Telford): *The Letters of John Wesley*, A. M., ed. John Telford, 8 vols. (London: Epworth Press, 1931; reprint, 1960).

MAM: Methodist Archives, John Rylands University Library of Manchester.

PWHS: *Proceedings of the Wesley Historical Society* (1897–).

Works: *The Works of John Wesley*; begun as *The Oxford Edition of the Works of John Wesley* (New York: Clarendon Press; Oxford University Press, 1975–83); continued as *The Bicentennial Edition of the Works of John Wesley* (Nashville, TN: Abingdon, 1984–), 18 of 35 vols. published to date.

Works, Jackson: *The Works of John Wesley*, ed. Thomas Jackson, 14 vols. (London: 1872; reprints Grand Rapids, MI: Zondervan, 1958, and Peabody, MA: Hendrickson Publishers, 1984).

A note on manuscript material: Quotations from manuscripts are transcribed by the author. Every effort was made to ensure that the transcriptions in the body of the book and in the appendices are accurate. Spellings and punctuation were retained from the original, in part because one of the major goals of this book is to introduce readers to the early Methodist people as they were. I have chosen to preserve their "voices," choosing particularly not to add polish in spelling, grammar, or phrasing when it was not in the original.

Pursuing Social Holiness

Introduction

When James Hall published his spiritual autobiography in 1793, he wrote: "what greatly helped me forward in the ways of God, were our band meetings."[1] These small group meetings were a particular "help" because the members of Hall's band had a common focus and commitment: "It was our only desire to live to the glory of God, and to help each other forward in true Religion. The Lord remarkably crowned our little meetings with his presence and blessing. Our souls increased daily in love and unity. We enjoyed a heaven upon earth."[2] Hall's account illustrates the power of the band meeting in the Wesleyan movement. These groups were the primary venue in which early Methodists sought to grow in holiness and where they learned experientially that people are most likely to increase in their love of God and neighbor when they are in community with others. Thus, Hall writes not only of his individual spiritual development, but of *our* souls increasing daily in love and unity. *We* enjoyed a heaven upon earth."[3] This kind of fellowship sustained Methodism and provided an embodiment of a new kind of social intimacy in the rapidly changing context of eighteenth-century British society.

Accounts by early Methodists such as James Hall offer a concrete expression of John Wesley's (1703–91) emphasis on the centrality of holiness for the Christian life. The importance of holiness featured prominently in Wesley's sermons, *Journals*, and letters. In the 1765 sermon "The Scripture Way of Salvation," for example, Wesley insisted that sanctification was by faith and that if it was by faith, something did not need to happen *before* sanctification: "If you seek it by faith, you may expect it *as you are*: and if as you are, then expect it *now*."[4] That sanctification was by faith, however, did not mean that the believer should simply wait passively for God to give the gift of sanctification. Wesley was convinced that there was an array of practices that God had made available to people who

---

[1] James Hall, "An Account of Mr. James Hall, Written by Himself," in *The Arminian Magazine* 16 (1793): 287; henceforth *AM*.

[2] Ibid.

[3] Emphasis mine.

[4] John Wesley, "The Scripture Way of Salvation," in *The Works of John Wesley*, vols. 1–4, *Sermons*, ed. Albert C. Outler (Nashville, TN: Abingdon, 1984–85), 2: 169; henceforth Wesley, *Works* (italics in original quotation).

were pursuing holiness, where they would reliably encounter the Holy Spirit. In particular, Wesley was convinced that growth in holiness was most likely to occur within the context of a supportive community.

Part of John Wesley's significance for the history of Christianity, then, is his contribution to the ongoing efforts of the Church to utilize the gift of community for Christian formation, or growing in love of God and neighbor. Wesley was the principal architect of a particularly influential approach to Christian communal formation in the eighteenth century. In 1739, Wesley argued that people could not become holy in isolation from other Christians and that the idea of "holy solitaries" was as inconsistent with Scripture as the idea of "holy adulterers." Wesley continued, in a frequently quoted, but often misunderstood phrase, "The gospel of Christ knows of no religion, but social; no holiness but social holiness."[5] Wesley was convinced that solitary religion was dangerous because people do not become holy in isolation from others; rather, they are more likely to lose their faith entirely.[6] Wesley was influential not only because of his recognition of the importance of community for growth in holiness, but also because of his ability to bring together various approaches to communal Christian formation into one practical method that helped people avoid the snare of solitary religion and enabled them to grow in holiness. Thus, the "method" that John Wesley developed from 1738 through the beginning of the 1740s concretely expressed his conviction that holiness is necessarily social—that is, a holy life can only be lived out among the company of other Christians, not alone.

As Wesley developed a distinctly Methodist approach to Christian communal formation, two weekly meetings became the major focal points of his approach to social holiness: the band meeting and the class meeting. The band meeting was the part of Wesley's approach to communal formation that was most focused on ongoing growth in holiness. Wesley was first introduced to the band meeting in 1738 by the Moravians, who provided much of the initial blueprint for the Fetter Lane Society.[7] Yet even after Wesley's separation from the Moravians in the Fetter Lane Society, he continued to organize his followers into bands. In Wesley's version, the band meeting had five to seven members and was

[5] Wesley, "Preface," *Hymns and Sacred Poems*, 1739, in *The Works of John Wesley*, Jackson edition, 14 vols. (Grand Rapids, MI: Zondervan, 1958), 14: 321; henceforth Wesley, *Works*, Jackson. On the ways that Wesley's use of "social holiness" is often misunderstood, see Andrew C. Thompson, "From Societies to Society: The Shift from Holiness to Justice in the Wesleyan Tradition," *Methodist Review: A Journal of Wesleyan and Methodist Studies* 3 (2011): 141–172, http://www.methodistreview.org/ (accessed July 10, 2012).

[6] E.g., see Wesley, *Journal* for August 25, 1763, in *Works*, vols. 18–24; *Journals and Diaries*, eds. W. Reginald Ward and Richard P. Heitzenrater (Nashville, TN: Abingdon, 1988–2003), 21: 424.

[7] The Fetter Lane Society was the group of Moravians and Anglicans that Wesley was involved with after his return from Georgia in 1738. His involvement in the Fetter Lane Society was an important precursor of his famous experience at Aldersgate Street on May 24, 1738. For more on the Fetter Lane Society, see chapter 1, "Oxford Methodism Encounters Moravianism: The Development of the Fetter Lane Society."

divided by gender and marital status. There were several prerequisites for joining a band meeting. Prospective members were expected to have previously experienced justification by faith and to have assurance of their adoption as children of God. Further, as was repeatedly emphasized in the "Rules of the Band Societies," each participant had to want the rest of the group to speak directly to their lives; everyone had to be willing to be told of their "faults" and "whatsoever we think, whatsoever we fear, whatsoever we hear, concerning you."[8] The basic format of the band meeting consisted of confessing specific sins, recounting any temptations that were experienced, and explaining how one was "delivered" from them.

The rationale most frequently cited for the band meeting was James 5:16, "Confess your faults one to another, and pray one for another that ye may be healed."[9] In "A Plain Account of the People Called Methodists" (1749), Wesley also noted that Methodists expressed a practical need for "closer union" and "pour[ing] out of their hearts without reserve, particularly with regard to the sin which did still 'easily beset' them" as the initial prompt for band meeting.[10] By Wesley's account, the results were impressive. Members prayed for healing for the "faults they had confessed—and it was so. The chains were broken, the bands were burst in sunder, and sin had no more dominion over them."[11]

The second piece of early Methodist communal formation was the class meeting, which was intended to have roughly seven to twelve people in each group (though classes were often much larger in practice). Each class was guided by a leader who was responsible for convening the class weekly, receiving contributions for relief of the poor, inquiring into the spiritual lives of each member, and offering spiritual guidance and direction as needed.[12] Wesley quickly recognized the strategic importance of the class meeting, making it a basic requirement for membership in early Methodism. In other words, at the most foundational level, a Methodist was someone who attended a weekly class meeting.

The class meeting was the part of Wesley's "method" that ensured that every Methodist was part of a small group. According to Wesley in "A Plain Account of the People Called Methodists," the class meeting provided a form of quality control as the leader of each class made "a particular inquiry into the behaviour of those whom he saw weekly."[13] As a result of this inquiry, "many disorderly walkers were detected. Some turned from the evil of their ways. Some were

---

[8] Wesley, "Rules of the Band Societies," in *Works* 9, *The Methodist Societies: History, Nature, and Design*, ed. Rupert E. Davies (Nashville, TN: Abingdon, 1989), 78; henceforth Wesley, "Rules of the Bands."

[9] Cited in "Rules of the Bands," in *Works* 9: 77.

[10] Wesley, "A Plain Account of the People Called Methodists," in *Works* 9: 266; henceforth Wesley, "Plain Account."

[11] Wesley, "Plain Account," 9: 268.

[12] This summary of the basic tasks of a class leader is dependent on John Wesley, "The Nature, Design, and General Rules of the United Societies," in *Works* 9: 70; henceforth Wesley, "General Rules."

[13] Wesley, "Plain Account," 9: 261.

put away from us."[14] Thus, the class meeting provided a way to detect hypocrisy and an unwillingness to keep Methodist discipline. According to Wesley, the class meeting also provided a profound introduction to "Christian fellowship" as Methodists began "to bear one another's burdens" and "speak the truth in love" in the context of their classes.[15] In class meetings, Methodists began to learn how to give voice to their experiences of God, particularly their searches for peace with God through justification by faith.

Because the class meeting became a basic requirement for membership in early Methodism, it has often been given more attention by historians of early Methodism than the band meeting. Yet, Wesley became so convinced of the importance of the band meeting for the pursuit of holiness that even after attendance at a weekly class meeting became a requirement for Methodists, he continued to insist on the value of the bands. In a series of letters to Edward Jackson in the last decade of his life, John Wesley repeatedly emphasized the importance of the band meeting for Methodism. In 1781, Wesley urged Jackson to be "diligent in restoring the bands" because "no Society will continue lively without them."[16] Thus, even though the band meeting was considered indispensable, it was nonetheless difficult to sustain. Seven years later, Wesley commended Jackson for upholding Methodist discipline by "denying tickets to all that have neglected meeting their classes.... You cannot be too exact in this."[17] Wesley continued by encouraging Jackson "to exhort all the believers that are in earnest or *would be* in earnest to meet in band."[18] In 1790, this time with more evident frustration, Wesley again wrote to Jackson, "It is no wonder many of the Societies should be in poor condition, considering what poor care has lately been taken of them."[19] Though this letter does not mention the band meeting explicitly, it is likely, based on his prior correspondence, that Wesley was connecting the "poor condition" of the Methodist societies to Jackson's failure to reinstate band meetings in the circuits he was traveling.

Why did Wesley connect the band meeting to the "liveliness" of Methodist societies and the earnestness of individual Methodists, especially if, as the previous comments from Wesley suggest, bands were difficult to sustain? Wesley's letters to Jackson reveal that Wesley himself was aware of the decline of the band

[14] Ibid.

[15] Ibid., 262. Wesley is quoting Galatians 6:2 and Ephesians 4:15.

[16] Wesley, letter to Edward Jackson, January 6, 1781, in John Telford, ed., *The Letters of John Wesley*, 8 vols. (London: Epworth Press, 1931), 7: 47; henceforth *Letters* (Telford).

[17] Wesley, letter to Edward Jackson, October 24, 1788, in *Letters* (Telford), 8: 98–99. Tickets were given every quarter to each person who regularly attended their class meetings. For a period of time, Methodists had to display their class meeting tickets in order to be admitted to the regular meetings of the Society.

[18] Ibid., 99 (emphasis original).

[19] Wesley, letter to Edward Jackson, January 2, 1790, in *Letters* (Telford), 8: 195.

meeting toward the end of his life. In the same letter from 1788, for example, Wesley noted the difficulty of maintaining band meetings: "the bands in every place need continual instruction; for they are continually flying in pieces."[20] Why was Wesley, who was often content to adopt and deploy what worked, so invested in struggling to maintain groups that seemed to be falling apart?

The basic argument of this study is that Wesley frequently urged his traveling preachers to tend to existing bands and restore ones that had disintegrated because of his conviction that the band meeting was the most important context within early Methodism focused on growth in holiness. And holiness was Wesley's highest priority—theologically and practically. Thus, Wesley implored Edward Jackson to urge all "believers" who were "in earnest or *would be* in earnest to meet in band" because the band meeting was strategically situated to address the ongoing need for believers' growth in holiness and their moving toward perfection, for which the class meeting was inadequate. In Wesley's conception, the band meeting was the engine of holiness, the part of his method that was designed to help Methodists, by the grace of God, to grow increasingly into the image of Christ. As such, an analysis of the band meeting is of particular significance for an adequate appreciation of Wesley's understanding of holiness, communal formation, and the way he brought the two together in his use of the phrase "social holiness."

Toward the end of his life, Wesley wrote of the necessity for Methodism to cling to the "doctrine, spirit, and discipline" that gave it its original power, if it were to continue as a dynamic, spirit-filled expression of Christianity. Interestingly, Wesley wrote that he was not concerned that Methodism would simply disappear as a religious movement, in either Europe or America. Rather, he worried that it would "only exist as a dead sect, having the form of religion without the power."[21] Wesley's struggle to preserve the classes and bands, then, can be further understood as an expression of his conviction that they were the key to Methodist discipline.[22]

In "A Plain Account of Christian Perfection," Wesley emphasized the importance of the classes and bands even more clearly: "Never omit meeting your Class or Band; never absent yourself from any public meeting. These are the very sinews of our Society."[23] Again, in a letter to Thomas Maxfield in 1762, Wesley chastised him for "slighting any, the very least rules of the bands or Society" and for "appointing such meetings as hinder others from attending either the

---

[20] Ibid., 99.

[21] Wesley, "Thoughts upon Methodism," in *Works* 9: 527.

[22] The "General Rules" were a significant piece of early Methodist discipline as well. All Methodists were expected to keep all three rules, which were "do no harm," "do all the good that you can," and "attend upon the ordinances of God." Wesley, "General Rules," 9: 69–73.

[23] Wesley, "A Plain Account of Christian Perfection As Believed and Taught by the Reverend Mr. John Wesley, From the Year 1725, to the Year 1777," in Wesley, *Works*, Jackson, 11: 433; henceforth Wesley, "A Plain Account of Christian Perfection."

public preaching or their class or band." Wesley was concerned because he felt that deemphasizing public preaching, the classes, or the bands would "dissolve our Society by cutting the sinews of it."[24] Wesley's equation of the classes and bands with the "sinews" of Methodism points to just how important he was convinced that these groups were for bringing the Methodist conception of the Way of Salvation to life in the experience of individual Methodists.[25] If Methodist preaching or doctrine were severed from the classes and bands, the movement would be immobilized.

The potency of the phrase "sinews of Methodism" has often caught the attention of scholars. However, this phrase has most frequently been used in reference to the importance of the classes, while largely ignoring the significance of the bands. In his study of the class meeting, for example, David Lowes Watson titled one chapter "The Development of the Class Meeting: The Sinews of Methodism." In that chapter, he used the phrase to refer solely to the class meeting.[26] Similarly, in his biography of Francis Asbury, John Wigger wrote that "Methodists themselves referred to class meetings as the 'soul' or 'sinews' of Methodism."[27] The problem with the usage of this phrase solely in reference to the class meeting is that it is more specific than Wesley's own use of the term.

Because of his focus on the class meeting, David Lowes Watson underappreciated the band meeting, seeing its primary significance as serving as a precursor for the classes. In summarizing Wesley's break from the Moravians in the Fetter Lane Society, Watson described the separation as creating room for Wesley "to work with the emerging Methodist societies more directly, and in due course to adopt what became the basic structural unit of the movement—the class meeting."[28] Viewing the Wesleyan bands as primarily an early failure of Methodism that served as a prelude to the class meetings does not account for Wesley's continued and ongoing advocacy of the band meeting in Methodism throughout his life, and especially after the development of the classes.

Beyond the role of the band meeting in Wesley's practical theology, his consistent advocacy of the importance of the band meeting raises questions about what was happening on the ground in popular eighteenth-century Methodism. Were the bands "continually flying in pieces" as Wesley's 1788 letter to Edward Jackson stated? Or were they simply ignored and overlooked in popular practice?

[24] Wesley, letter to Thomas Maxfield, November, 2, 1762, in *Letters* (Telford), 4: 193.

[25] "Way of Salvation" refers to Wesley's summary of the Christian life, with particular emphasis on repentance, justification by faith, the new birth, and growth in holiness. "Scripture Way of Salvation" is often seen as the key summary of the Way of Salvation, in Wesley, *Works* 2: 153–169.

[26] David Lowes Watson, *The Early Methodist Class Meeting*, 107.

[27] John Wigger, *American Saint: Francis Asbury and the Methodists* (New York: Oxford University Press, 2009), 33.

[28] David Lowes Watson, 87.

To date, historians of early Methodism have typically either studied John Wesley or other early Methodist leaders on their own terms, or they have studied popular religious experience on its own terms.[29] A conviction that informs this book is that both John Wesley and popular Methodism can be better understood by considering each in light of the other. Thus, this is both a study of Wesley's conception of the band meeting and a study of the actual popular practice of the band meeting among early Methodists. Studying the band meeting from both perspectives allows for a textured account of early Methodist communal formation and provides an assessment of the extent of John Wesley's influence in popular practice.

Indeed, it is quite difficult, if not impossible, to understand either Wesley or popular Methodism independently of one another. Wesley was not preaching or writing primarily for posterity. As a key leader in the eighteenth-century Evangelical Revival, he was trying to "reform the nation, and in particular the Church, to spread scriptural holiness over the land."[30] Put differently, he was trying to convince people to allow God to change their lives, accept his account of the good life, and then embrace the "method" for working toward that kind of life. A basic measure of the success of his own ministry, then, was the extent to which those under his care actually professed to have experienced saving faith leading to growth in holiness. Because Wesley's conception of holiness was aimed at the transformation of actual lives, the success of his ministry was dependent on corresponding evidence (or fruit) of transformation. In her study of the role of gender and emotion in early Methodism, Phyllis Mack noted that "historians have long noticed how attentively people listened to John and Charles Wesley (1707–88), but they have rarely noticed how attentively John and Charles Wesley listened to them."[31] One of the key reasons the Wesleys listened to lay Methodists so carefully was because they felt called by God to "spread scriptural holiness" as broadly and deeply as they could.

The women and men who heard John Wesley preach, sang Charles Wesley's hymns, and wrote letters to either of the brothers were paying attention to the Wesleys' message because they were increasingly aware of a variety of options in the growing religious marketplace. They made decisions about whether to

[29] Randy Maddox, *Responsible Grace: John Wesley's Practical Theology* (Nashville, TN: Kingswood, 1994); and Kenneth J. Collins, *The Theology of John Wesley: Holy Love and the Shape of Grace* (Nashville, TN: Abingdon, 2007) are the standard surveys of Wesley's theology. Phyllis Mack, *Heart Religion in the British Enlightenment: Gender and Emotion in Early Methodism* (New York: Cambridge University Press, 2008); and D. Bruce Hindmarsh, *The Evangelical Conversion Narrative: Spiritual Autobiography in Early Modern England* (New York: Oxford University Press, 2005) are two excellent studies of eighteenth-century Methodist experience.

[30] Wesley, "Minutes of Several Conversations between the Reverend Mr. John and Charles Wesley, and Others," in *Works* 10: 845.

[31] Mack, *Heart Religion in the British Enlightenment*, 22.

associate themselves most closely with John Wesley's understanding of free grace, or George Whitefield's (1714–70) Calvinist understanding of election. They decided whether to remain in the Fetter Lane Society or walk out with Wesley when he read the letter announcing his separation. Individuals who responded to the Wesleyan message, then, did so because something in that message resonated with them, and they decided to follow the Wesleys.

Francis Asbury provides one example of a young man in eighteenth-century Britain self-consciously engaging and evaluating the varieties of Christianity available to him. In his adolescence, Asbury made judgments and exercised preference for one particular form of Christianity over others. When Asbury was thirteen years old, he "grew dissatisfied with the preaching at St. Margarets," which was the Anglican Church closest to his childhood home.[32] As a result, Asbury began attending All Saints, in West Bromwich, where Edward Stillingfleet was vicar and was preaching a message sympathetic to Methodism. As Asbury became more interested in evangelical piety, his mother directed him to a gathering of Methodists in Wednesbury, where he heard John Fletcher and Benjamin Ingham preach. In a later reflection on this gathering of Methodists, Asbury showed that he was evaluating and comparing these different congregations and preachers: "I soon found this was not the Church—but it was better."[33]

In early Methodism, John Wesley not only preached in order to awaken people to their need for salvation; he also cast a vision for the Christian life. Sometimes, his audience responded by embracing his message and method (as exemplified by Asbury), at other times, by modifying it, and occasionally, by rejecting it altogether. Just as early Methodists were aware of increased variety and options within Christianity, Wesley was also aware that there were other messages and visions for the Christian life that were in various degrees of competition with his own.

From a broader angle of vision, the widespread agreement on the value of band meetings within the Evangelical Revival, even among those who disagreed deeply about other things, suggests that the form of community that the band meeting offered was of particular significance in its eighteenth-century context.[34] Wesley's conception of "social holiness" provided a new kind of social

[32] Wigger, *American Saint*, 27.

[33] Francis Asbury, *The Journal and Letters of Francis Asbury*, 3 vols., ed. Elmer T. Clark (Nashville, TN: Abingdon, 1958), 1: 721. Quoted in Wigger, *American Saint*, 28. In this context, by "Church," Asbury was referring to the established Church of England.

[34] George Whitefield and John Wesley, e.g., disagreed on election and predestination. They both agreed on the importance of the band meeting, however. When Whitefield invited Wesley to come to Bristol in March, 1739, to continue the work that he had begun there, he specifically indicated that many in Bristol were "ripe for bands." Whitefield, letter to Wesley, March 22, 1738–39, in *The Works of John Wesley*, vol. 25, *Letters I 1721–1739*, ed. Frank Baker (Oxford, UK: Clarendon Press, 1980), 25: 612.

intimacy as the beginnings of industrialization transformed English society, resulting in the disruption and loss of previous norms of village and urban life. The significance of early Methodist communal formation has been noted in previous scholarship on eighteenth-century British social life. Elie Halévy famously argued that Methodism, primarily through its highly organized approach to small groups, was the reason for "the extraordinary stability which English Society was destined to enjoy throughout a period of revolutions and crises."[35] Indeed, for Halévy, the conditions for revolution were strongly present as England's

> political institutions were such that society might easily have lapsed into anarchy had there existed in England a bourgeoisie animated by the spirit of revolution. And a system of economic production that was in fact totally without organization of any kind would have plunged the kingdom into violent revolution had the working classes found in the middle class leaders to provide it with a definite ideal, a creed, a practical programme. But the elite of the working class, the hard-working and capable bourgeois, had been imbued by the evangelical movement with a spirit from which the established order had nothing to fear.[36]

For Halévy, then, revolution did not occur in England because one of the legacies of the Wesleyan revival was a new social organization that evolved into one of the norms of nineteenth-century English society. As a result, Halévy concluded that "in the vast work of social organization which is one of the dominant characteristics of nineteenth-century England, it would be difficult to overestimate the part played by the Wesleyan revival."[37]

In the work of E. P. Thompson, the role of early Methodist communal formation was described in consistently negative (and colorful) ways. For Thompson, Methodism functioned as a place where "energies and emotions which were dangerous to social order, or which were merely unproductive . . . were released in the harmless form of sporadic love-feasts, watch-nights, band-meetings or revivalist campaigns."[38] Despite Thompson's Marxist distaste for Methodism, he nevertheless largely agreed with Halévy on Methodism's significance in the development of new forms of community on the eve of the Industrial Revolution. For Thompson, "it remains both true and important that Methodism, with its open chapel doors, did offer to the uprooted and abandoned people of the Industrial

---

[35] Elie Halévy, *A History of the English People in the Nineteenth Century: England in 1815*, trans. E. I. Watkin and D. A. Barker (New York: Barnes and Noble, 1961), 387.

[36] Ibid., 424–425.

[37] Ibid., 425.

[38] E. P. Thompson, *The Making of the English Working Class* (New York: Pantheon Books, 1964), 368.

Revolution some kind of community to replace the older community-patterns which were being displaced."[39] In a way that Halévy had not seen as clearly, Thompson noted the intrinsic significance of these new forms of community for the folks who participated in them, even if Thompson ultimately found them to be largely tragic because they restrained the revolutionary urges of the working class.

More recently, David Hempton has helped the conversation move beyond Halévy and Thompson. Hempton recognized that there is "general agreement among historians that Halévy exaggerated both the fragility of England's *ancien régime* and the power of evangelicalism to save it from its inner contradictions."[40] Despite the recent consensus that Halévy's thesis was overstated, Hempton still agreed with Halévy and Thompson that Methodism was an important influence in providing new forms of social organization. Thus, "evangelical religion" helped to forge "a rough harmony of values between the pragmatic and moralistic middle classes and the skilled and respectable sections of the English working classes who were notorious in Europe for their solid virtue and capacity for organization."[41] And though the complexities of popular evangelicalism cannot be reduced to "a single cohesive theory about religion and the evolution of the British state," Hempton described Methodism's division into societies, classes, and bands in a subsequent publication as "a riot of association in the age of associations."[42] Methodist classes and bands were "the places, par excellence, where the Methodist message moved from print to voice, from individualism to community, from cognition to emotion, and from private to public."[43] Wesley's vision for "social holiness," through small groups like classes and bands, provided the key context where the Methodist message came to life. These structures created community at a time when previous social forms were being disrupted or lost.

A previously unpublished manuscript by an alienated early Methodist named Samuel Roberts illustrates how comprehensive these forms of community could be in the lives of Methodists. It also shows how interwoven the connection was between John Wesley, other leaders, and the average members of bands and class meetings, and it reveals the great lengths to which Wesley would go in order to get through to his audience. After describing in detail the organization and conduct of an average band meeting, including a dialogue between the band leader and the members of the band, Roberts described the way that the band

[39] Ibid., 379.

[40] David Hempton, *The Religion of the People: Methodism and popular religion c. 1750–1900* (London: Routledge, 1996), 166.

[41] Ibid.

[42] Hempton, *Religion of the People*, 178; Hempton, *Methodism: Empire of the Spirit* (New Haven, CT: Yale University Press, 2005), 78.

[43] Hempton, *Methodism: Empire of the Spirit*, 79.

leaders would meet with John Wesley or another traveling preacher: "When Mr westlay Comes. then ye Clasleader. & band leaders. is Descorst to in this Meathod...by this Inquiry ye Preacher knowns. how to Auder his Descorse to ye People ather in ye Private Sociatys. or in ye Meeting of Bands."[44] Roberts also described a dialogue between Wesley and the band leaders, where Wesley was trying to learn what the specific needs of the members of a Methodist society (a group of Methodists in a particular location) were. Wesley then used these conversations in the exhortation that he later gave to the society as a whole, weaving the concerns he heard from the band leaders into his exhortation. Though Roberts's account is complicated by the strongly anti-Methodist tone that suffused his 200-page manuscript, he nonetheless appeared to add as much texture and detail regarding the way that actual Methodist societies functioned as he could, in order to make his critique of Methodism that much more credible. Despite his evident distaste for Wesleyan Methodism, Roberts gives a glimpse of Wesley's thorough and determined efforts to reach laypeople. For example, if he thought it would help, Wesley was willing to ask small group leaders about what individuals in their groups were struggling with in order to reach those people when he spoke to the entire society. Roberts's description of Wesley's conversation with band leaders and Wesley's subsequent use of these examinations as a means of making his exhortation more penetrating amplify Mack's comment that the Wesleys listened to early Methodists. In fact, Roberts's account suggests that Wesley listened attentively to Methodists because of his desire to convince them to listen to him and follow him.

Another previously unpublished manuscript that is of particular value for the study of early Methodism is the final excerpt of William Seward's (d. 1740) manuscript diary, housed at Chetham's Library in Manchester. Seward, who has been referred to as the first Methodist martyr, was initially one of John and Charles Wesley's adherents. In this manuscript, however, Seward described a rift in his relationship with the Wesleys, particularly due to a disagreement with Charles. In addition to revealing crucial details of the power dynamics in the early Methodist movement, Seward's manuscript diary also pointed to the significance of the band meeting in early Methodism. Despite his falling-out with the Wesleys, Seward continued to urge those under his influence to form band meetings: "We [Seward and Howell Harris, another evangelical leader] Exhorted them to Meet in Band, publick & private 5 or 6 in a Band."[45] Seward's diary confirms the presence of leaders in early Methodist band meetings and suggests that Wesley's standard for only allowing those who could testify that they had

---

[44] Samuel Roberts, manuscript volume privately owned by Dr. John Walsh of Jesus College, Oxford. A transcription of Roberts's account of the band meeting can be found in appendix F.

[45] William Seward, manuscript diary, September 14, 1740 (Chetham's Library, Manchester, UK, ref. A.2.116).

already experienced justification and the new birth was not an inviolable rule, as Seward wrote that the bands should contain "none...but Such who know their Sins are forgiven or are Earnestly Seeking forgiveness."[46] Aside from revealing the details of the practice of band meetings, Seward's diary also shows the extent of Wesley's influence, as well as the intricacies of the revival. On the one hand, even after separating from the Wesleys, Seward continued to value and recommend the band meeting. And yet, on the other hand, the details of Seward's use of the bands also shows that Wesley's understanding of the bands was not always put into practice exactly as he had intended. At times, his articulation was generally accepted by Methodists, but their practice bore the fingerprints of the women and men who actually met together weekly in the groups.

Previous scholars have noted the impressive volume of Wesley's correspondence with individual Methodists at nearly every level of the movement.[47] Yet, the volume of manuscript material from other early Methodists, of which the Roberts and Seward manuscripts are but two examples, has not been emphasized or studied as carefully. The popular Methodist experience has not received sustained and careful scholarly attention to the degree that the study of John Wesley has as an object of intellectual history. The works of D. Bruce Hindmarsh and Phyllis Mack are recent exceptions to this rule.[48] Their work demonstrates the possibility and fruitfulness of studying the lived experience of popular Methodists. Hindmarsh focused one chapter of his *The Evangelical Conversion Narrative* (2005) on the ways that lay Methodists described their own conversions. He wrote that Methodist "lay converts responded very early with their own narratives, expressed in their own terms."[49] Though the chapter was not focused on the band meeting itself, Hindmarsh noted the significance of the bands in popular Methodism. Methodists often "turned not to journals to give voice to their experience, but to oral testimony in band meetings or to familiar letters written to the very Methodist preachers whose message had first awakened and converted them."[50] Hindmarsh then highlighted one of the many manuscript sources that preserved these experiences, a collection of 151 letters written to Charles Wesley from 1738 through 1788 that has come to be referred to as the Early Methodist Volume. This collection is of particular value for the

---

[46] Ibid.

[47] For the most recent discussion, see Ted A. Campbell, "John Wesley as diarist and correspondent," in *The Cambridge Companion to John Wesley*, eds. Randy L. Maddox and Jason E. Vickers (New York: Cambridge University Press, 2010), 129–143.

[48] Another exception that focuses on the context of Methodism in America is Lester Ruth, *A Little Heaven Below: Worship at Early Methodist Quarterly Meetings* (Nashville, TN: Kingswood Books, 2000). See also Leslie F. Church, *The Early Methodist People* (London: Epworth Press, 1948); and *More about the Early Methodist People* (London: Epworth Press, 1949).

[49] Hindmarsh, *The Evangelical Conversion Narrative*, 130.

[50] Ibid.

study of the popular Methodist experience of the band meeting, since nineteen of the letters contain references to the band meeting.[51]

To date, Phyllis Mack's monograph has made the most extensive use of extant primary source material from early Methodists. In her *Heart Religion in the British Enlightenment: Gender and Emotion in Early Methodism*, Mack noted the "Fletcher-Tooth Collection," the archive of Mary Bosanquet Fletcher's unpublished writing and correspondence that "reaches from floor to ceiling in the storeroom of the John Rylands University Library in Manchester, perhaps the largest existing (and largely unexplored) archive of an early modern religious woman."[52] Like the Early Methodist Volume, the Fletcher-Tooth Collection contains numerous references to band meetings.

The Methodist Archives in Manchester contain dozens of manuscript journals, diaries, and letters from early Methodist traveling preachers and laywomen and laymen beyond the Early Methodist Volume and the Fletcher-Tooth Collection. A significant amount of this material contains references to bands. As I pored over these manuscripts at the John Rylands Library, Deansgate at the University of Manchester, I found numerous references by early Methodists to their participation in band meetings, as well as many more detailed descriptions. These sources demonstrate that the band meeting was an established piece of lived Methodist experience, particularly at the very beginning of Methodism, though references continue to be found throughout John Wesley's life and after his death. The popular Methodist experience also shows that the band meeting was largely organized according to John Wesley's ideal conception, with some notable exceptions. For example, the bands almost always had leaders, as did the class meetings. The most significant deviation from Wesley's advocacy for the bands was the extent to which the band meeting declined over Wesley's lifetime. I argue that the difficulty of sustaining the band meeting points to a deeper inability of Wesley's vision of holiness and entire sanctification to be practiced within popular Methodism. In other words, Wesley worried about bands "flying in pieces" because he was convinced that this was evidence of a fraying of Methodism's audacious vision for the possibilities of perfectly loving God and neighbor in this life.

In addition to John Wesley's own writings, this book is informed by numerous previously unpublished primary source manuscripts, in order to (1) understand the band meeting completely, from as many perspectives as possible, (2) consider

[51] The Early Methodist Volume is housed at the Methodist Archives in the Special Collections of the University of Manchester at the John Rylands University Library.

[52] Mack, *Heart Religion in the British Enlightenment*, 22. Andrew Goodhead's *A Crown and a Cross: The Rise, Development, and Decline of the Class Meeting in Eighteenth-Century England* (Eugene, OR: Wipf and Stock, 2010) also contains frequent references to early Methodist popular accounts. However, Goodhead's use of this material is at times problematic, particularly his determination that material on the early Methodist band meeting could be used to describe and explain the early Methodist class meeting. Goodhead, 168.

the actual lived experience of popular Methodists, and (3) explore the extent of harmony or dissonance between John Wesley's ideal of how things *should* have worked in Methodism and how they *actually* worked. In order to explore these three aspects of early Methodism, this study is organized as follows.

I argue that Wesley synthesized distinctive insights of Moravian and Anglican piety in the early Methodist band meeting, that the bands were the key locus of John Wesley's efforts to organize social holiness, and that Wesley's conception of the band meeting was largely (but not uniformly) practiced in the early Methodist experience of the bands. In order to demonstrate these arguments, this work is presented in two parts.

The first part (chapters 1 through 3) focuses primarily on John Wesley's conception of communal formation, particularly Wesley's conception of the band meeting. The first chapter situates the bands in the broader historical context. The forerunners of the Methodist bands are considered, starting with the influence of Continental Pietism, especially as mediated through the *collegia pietatis* and the Moravian *Banden*. The influence of Methodism's Anglican context is also explored, with particular focus on the importance of the Anglican Religious Societies for John Wesley's formation. The chapter concludes by describing the development of the Fetter Lane Society, which brought together people from both Anglican and Moravian backgrounds in the late 1730s.

The second chapter describes Wesley's general theology and method of discipleship. The chapter first demonstrates the central role of holiness in Wesley's theology, as well as the significance of his insistence that holiness is necessarily social. The chapter then describes the various structures of Wesley's method for communal Christian formation, particularly focusing on the society, class, and band meetings.

Chapter 3 narrows the focus to consider the particular influence of Anglican and Pietistic practice on Wesley's conception of the band meeting. The influence of both is seen in Wesley's "Rules of the Band Societies," which was the key document that he wrote describing how a Wesleyan band meeting ought to function. The key argument of this chapter is that, in his conception of the band meeting, Wesley brought together the Moravian understanding of the need for justification by faith and the witness of the Spirit with the Anglican understanding of the importance of a disciplined practice of the means of grace for growth in holiness.[53] The chapter concludes by arguing that, largely due to this synthesis,

---

[53] Richard P. Heitzenrater has noted the frequency with which theologians refer to "grace" and take for granted that the definition is obvious to all, noting that "a large proportion of writers, from biblical times to the present, use the term 'grace' without providing a careful philosophical or theological definition." Heitzenrater, "God with Us: Grace and the Spiritual Senses in John Wesley's Theology," in *Grace upon Grace: Essays in Honor of Thomas A. Langford*, Robert K. Johnston, L. Gregory Jones, and Jonathan R. Wilson, eds. (Nashville, TN: Abingdon, 1999), 89. This study defines grace, as Heitzenrater does in his essay, as "the active presence or power of God." Ibid., 92.

the band meeting was the ideal location for the pursuit of holiness in Wesley's "method."

The second part (chapters 4 and 5) considers the reception of the band meeting in early Methodism, with a focus on the extent to which Wesley's synthesis of Moravian and Anglican piety was expressed in Methodist bands. Chapter 4 considers the extent to which Wesley's conception of the band meeting was practiced in popular Methodism from 1738 through the mid-1760s. The chapter starts by studying the practice of early Methodist bands in the period before the advent of the class meeting. The chapter then considers the reception of the band meeting in the first two decades after the class meeting became a mandatory weekly meeting for Methodists. In order to facilitate comparison between these periods, the two parts of this chapter are similarly organized. First, the organization and conduct of the band meetings are described. Then, the extent to which actual bands expressed each side of Wesley's synthesis of Moravian and Anglican piety is considered. In general, I find that Wesley's understanding of the band meeting was indeed largely practiced at the popular level of early Methodism.

The final chapter examines the Methodist experience of the band meeting from the 1760s through the beginning of the nineteenth century. This chapter is also divided into two main chronological sections. The first section studies the band meeting from the 1760s through the mid-1780s. The second section focuses on the period from the later 1780s through the beginning of the nineteenth century. This chapter also includes a discussion of the primary source material related to the select society, often referred to as the select band, a group that particularly focused on the pursuit of entire sanctification or Christian perfection. The chapter concludes with a brief discussion of the evidence for the continued presence of some band meetings in the first half of the nineteenth century. It is suggested that nineteenth-century references to bands evidence a transition to prayer meetings, which were becoming more popular during this period.

This first full account of the importance of band meetings in early Methodism will help round out our understanding of eighteenth-century spirituality and provide a detailed test case of Wesley's influence on early Methodist popular practice. This study also helps to situate early Methodism more fully within its historical context by parsing the ways that Anglicanism and Pietism influenced John Wesley and his development of a disciplined pursuit of social holiness.

1

Forerunners of the Early Methodist Band Meeting

*In the 1670s, Philipp Jakob Spener (1635–1705) established the *collegia pietatis*, or "gatherings for piety," at nearly the same time Anthony Horneck (1641–97) developed a similar approach to the communal pursuit of piety through the Religious Societies within the Anglican context. Half a century later, in the late 1720s, on the Continent, a revival occurred at Herrnhut that resulted in the creation of the *Banden*, which were small groups where people unburdened themselves and revealed the true states of their souls in order to become more disciplined in their pursuit of holiness. Concurrently, a small group of particularly earnest Anglicans began gathering together at Oxford University in order to hold one another accountable for the disciplined practice of the Christian life. This organization eventually was recognized as the beginning of Methodism; Wesley himself would later refer to this group as the "first rise of Methodism."[1] The Oxford Methodists adopted the general approach of the Religious Societies, though they were even more disciplined in their practice of the Christian life, particularly through spiritual conversation and confession of sins.

These parallel traditions were joined together when John and Charles Wesley first encountered Moravians on a missionary trip to Georgia, and later in London. An ongoing scholarly debate has centered on the question of the fundamental identity of the Fetter Lane Society, which was the primary place where these two traditions came together in London. Arguments about whether Fetter Lane was more essentially Moravian or Anglican miss the most crucial point: The creation of the Fetter Lane Society in May of 1738 marked a pivotal initial effort to bring together the similar, yet distinct, approaches of the Anglican Religious Societies, particularly as expressed by the Oxford Methodists and the Moravian *Banden*. Though this early

---

* An early draft of parts of this section appeared in Kevin M. Watson, "Forerunners of the Early Methodist Band Meeting," *Methodist Review* 2 (2010): 1–31.

[1] John Wesley, "A Short History of the People Called Methodists," in *Works 9*: 430 (henceforth Wesley, "Short History").

attempt to combine the contributions of Anglicanism and Moravianism at Fetter Lane ultimately created more tension than the Society could hold, Fetter Lane, nevertheless, marked a key stage in the development of the Methodist "method" and involved a critical step in Wesley's efforts to bring the best of the Anglican Religious Societies and the Moravian *Banden* into a new synthesis.[2] During his time in the Fetter Lane Society, Wesley was both influenced by Peter Böhler (1712–75) and other Moravians and began to conceive of his own version of the bands.

The Beginnings of the *Collegia Pietatis* and the Anglican Religious Societies

The 1670s were a decade that experienced an increase in the importance of small groups for Christian formation and the pursuit of holiness, particularly within Lutheran Pietism and Anglicanism. In 1670, Philipp Jakob Spener began organizing Christians together in small groups, which became known as *collegia pietatis*. As the *collegia* became more generally known and spread to cities outside of Spener's immediate influence, another group of conventicles, the Religious Societies, began to appear in England.

Philipp Jakob Spener and the *Collegia Pietatis*

Pietism proper has often been seen to begin with Philipp Jakob Spener.[3] Johannes Wallmann, in particular, has argued that Pietism began with Spener, because he articulated the key emphases of Pietism: "the development of the conventicle movement, the *ecclesiola in ecclesia*; the chiliastic hope for 'better times;' and pronounced emphasis upon Bible reading and study."[4] Spener's development of the conventicle movement, particularly through the *collegia pietatis*, was a key predecessor of the Wesleyan band meeting.[5]

---

[2] The Fetter Lane Society would ultimately divide in July, 1740, when John Wesley and his followers formally left Fetter Lane and joined the Foundery Society. See Wesley, *Journal* for July 20–23, 1740, in *Works* 19: 161–163.

[3] Academics continue to debate the boundaries of Pietism. In *The Pietist Theologians*, Carter Lindberg summarized the debate, which primarily centers on "the temporal and geographical boundaries of Pietism." Lindberg pointed to Johannes Wallmann and Martin Brecht as the recent leaders of this debate. Brecht has argued for a broad understanding of Pietism that begins with Johan Arndt (1555–1621) and continues into the twentieth century. For the purposes of this study, Wallmann's understanding of Pietism will be accepted because his conception of Pietism helps focus attention on the development of conventicles. See Carter Lindberg, ed., *The Pietist Theologians: An Introduction to Theology in the Seventeenth and Eighteenth Centuries* (Malden, MA: Blackwell, 2005), 2–3.

[4] Ibid., 2.

[5] The influences and origins of Spener's *collegia pietatis* have been disputed just as the boundaries and origins of Pietism itself are a source of disagreement. Theodore G. Tappert revealed that "attempts have been made to show the dependence of these [*collegia pietatis*] on the house meetings

In his introduction to *Pia Desideria* (1675), Theodore G. Tappert cited Spener's first reference to the value of small group meetings aimed at fostering holiness.[6] This excerpt is worth quoting at some length, because of the insight it provides into the benefits Spener believed would come from *collegia pietatis* and the reasons he thought such groups were necessary:

> How much good it would do if good friends would come together on a Sunday and instead of getting out glasses, cards, or dice would take up a book and read from it for the edification of all or would review something from sermons that were heard! If they would speak with one another about the divine mysteries, and the one who received most from God would try to instruct his weaker brethren! If, should they be not quite able to find their way through, they would ask a preacher to clarify the matter! If this should happen, how much evil would be held in abeyance, and how the blessed Sunday would be sanctified for the great edification and marked benefit of all! It is certain, in any case, that we preachers cannot instruct the people from our pulpits as much as is needful unless other persons in the congregation, who by God's grace have a superior knowledge of Christianity, take the pains, by virtue of their universal Christian priesthood, to work with and under us to correct and reform as much in their neighbors as they are able according to the measure of their gifts and their simplicity.[7]

In 1670, in an effort to bring this vision into reality, Spener began to organize people into *collegia pietatis*, or "gatherings for piety." Ted A. Campbell discussed the rapid growth of these groups, which by 1682 "had grown so large...that local authorities allowed Spener the use of one of the city churches for their meetings."[8] Indeed, with the passage of time, Spener became more and more

of Jean de Labadie (1610–1674) in Geneva, the 'prophesyings' of the Puritans in England, or similar assemblies among the Reformed in the Netherlands and among Lutherans in various parts of Germany." Ultimately, Tappert concluded, "there is no evidence to prove such dependence." He did concede that the *collegia pietatis* were not entirely new, and they could be seen to be in conformity with groups such as Labadie's. W. R. Ward, on the other hand, saw the *collegia pietatis* "as an elite society" that was similar to the groups that had already been gathered by Jean de Labadie, though Spener's groups would include a broader membership. Theodore G. Tappert, "Introduction" to Philipp Jakob Spener, *Pia Desideria*, trans. Theodore G. Tappert (Philadelphia: Fortress Press, 1964), 13–14; W. R. Ward, *The Protestant Evangelical Awakening* (Cambridge, UK: Cambridge University Press, 1992), 57.

[6] Philipp Jakob Spener, *Pia Desideria*, trans. Theodore G. Tappert (Philadelphia: Fortress Press, 1964), 13.

[7] Ibid.

[8] Ted A. Campbell, *The Religion of the Heart: A Study of European Religious Life in the Seventeenth and Eighteenth Centuries* (Columbia, SC: University of South Carolina Press, 1991), 84. At the same time, the *collegia* were also spreading to cities beyond Frankfurt as "Spener was becoming recognized as the leader of a widespread religious movement." Ibid.

convinced that the *collegia pietatis* would be instrumental in any renewal of the church. In *Pia Desideria*, Spener further articulated the belief that "if several persons in each congregation can be won for these ... activities ... together with such other things as, especially, fraternal admonition and chastisement ... a great deal would be gained and accomplished ... and finally the church would be visibly reformed."[9] In this passage, Spener seems to have seen the *collegia pietatis* as the yeast that would spread throughout the church, causing it to rise.[10]

What exactly happened in these small groups? F. Ernest Stoeffler has described the early *collegia pietatis* as meetings that Spener opened with a prayer. After the prayer, an edifying passage was read and discussed. The discussion was not meant to be technical or academic; rather, it was focused on the things that would lead to the edification of those who were present. After 1675, the readings came exclusively from the Bible.[11] In the 1677 tract *The Spiritual Priesthood*, Spener described (and defended) the *collegia pietatis*, stating: "It cannot be wrong if several good friends sometimes meet *expressly to go over a sermon* together and recall what they heard, *to read in the Scriptures*, and *to confer* in the fear of the Lord how they may put into practice what they read."[12]

The *collegia pietatis* are a key place to start in the search for forerunners of the early Methodist band meeting, because the *collegia* and the influence of Philipp Jakob Spener (which increased substantially with his publication of *Pia Desideria*) gave rise to the practice of gathering together committed disciples in order to provide further instruction and encouragement in their Christian discipleship. Though Spener was not working in a contextual vacuum himself, his efforts were significant in contributing to the spread, within the larger church, of smaller groups particularly focused on growth in holiness.

And yet, the primary significance of the *collegia pietatis* may be that they set the precedent of small groups being a valuable tool for those who want to make a serious commitment to their discipleship. In other words, the *collegia pietatis* were not direct or unmediated predecessors of the early Methodist band meeting. They involved reading a passage and discussing it, an element not found in the Methodist bands. Moreover, they did not specifically practice communal confession of sins, which was at the heart of the Methodist bands. However, the spread of the *collegia pietatis* was a crucial step toward the development of the Methodist

---

[9] Spener, 95.

[10] See Matt. 13:33. Tappert brought this imagery to mind in his introduction to *Pia Desideria*: "If the church was to be renewed, he [Spener] felt, a beginning would have to be made with the remnant of true Christians in every congregation. These had to be gathered and edified in private meetings in order that they might become a leaven to leaven the whole lump." Spener, 19.

[11] This summary of the early *collegia pietatis* is dependent on F. Ernest Stoeffler, "The Rise of Evangelical Pietism," in *Studies in the History of Religions*, vol. 9 (Leiden, DE: E. J. Brill, 1965), 237.

[12] Philipp Jakob Spener, "The Spiritual Priesthood: Briefly described according to the word of God in seventy questions and answers," in *Pietists: Selected Writings*, Peter C. Erb, ed. (Mahwah, NJ: Paulist Press, 1983), 63 (italics original).

bands, because Spener's small groups were important predecessors of both the Anglican Religious Societies and the Moravian *Banden*. The *collegia* influenced the Religious Societies through Anthony Horneck, who was raised in the context of Continental Pietism and returned to Germany in 1670, the year Spener's small groups began. On the Continent, the spread of the *collegia pietatis* affected Pietism itself, as they were influential in paving the way for the system of small groups for piety that the Moravians would develop at Herrnhut in the late 1720s.

Anthony Horneck and the Anglican Religious Societies

Though it would not be immediately obvious, Continental Pietism would have a nearly instant impact on Anglicanism in Britain. The Anglican Religious Societies were created in 1678 or 1679 when Anthony Horneck "began actively to encourage the piety of some of the young men who heard him preach by organizing them into societies."[13] Scott Kisker has argued that it is ultimately "not clear where Horneck got the idea for the societies."[14] However, the Religious Societies were influenced from the beginning by Pietism. Kisker saw Horneck as a crucial transitional figure between Pietism and Anglicanism, arguing that "Anthony Horneck is key for Pietism's migration into Restoration Anglicanism, and thus to . . . later movements."[15] Yet, the impact of Pietism on Horneck does not mean that the Religious Societies were simply an English brand of Pietism. Horneck was truly an Anglican, in large part, according to Kisker, because his "time at Oxford [in the 1660s] made him an Anglican."[16] Other scholars have argued that the Religious Societies were also influenced by the conventicles of English dissent and nonconformity, thus further emphasizing the unique contribution of the English context to the creation of the Religious Societies.[17]

The Religious Societies that Horneck developed were organized by drawing up a list of rules that would govern them. The rules of Horneck's Societies show "the development of a truly Anglican Pietism."[18] The influence of Pietism is seen in the societies' decision to remain within the established church, which

---

[13] Scott Thomas Kisker, *Foundation for Revival: Anthony Horneck, the Religious Societies, and the Construction of an Anglican Pietism* (Lanham, MD: Scarecrow Press, 2008), 68. John Spurr dated the beginning of the Religious Societies to "1678 or 1679" in "The Church, the societies and the moral revolution of 1688," in John Walsh, Colin Haydon, and Stephen Taylor, eds. *The Church of England c. 1689–c. 1833: From Toleration to Tractarianism* (Cambridge, UK: Cambridge University Press, 1993), 131. John S. Simon surveyed John Wesley's relationship to the Religious Societies in *John Wesley and the Religious Societies* (London: Epworth Press, 1921). See esp. 9–27, 194–200, and 322–334. See also John S. Simon, *John Wesley and the Methodist Societies* (London: Epworth Press, 1923).

[14] Kisker, 68.

[15] Ibid., xxiv.

[16] Ibid., 43.

[17] John Spurr, "The Church, the societies and the moral revolution in 1688," 136.

[18] Kisker, 70.

for Anglicanism at the time represented a "radical innovation."[19] Yet, the very desire of the societies to be firmly planted within the established church further contributed to their being authentically Anglican. One rule of the Religious Societies, for example, limited membership to those who were members of the Church of England. The Anglican identity of the Religious Societies was further reinforced by another rule requiring that an Anglican priest lead each society.[20]

Richard Kidder's (1633–1703) and Josiah Woodward's (1660–1712) published versions of the rules for the Religious Societies in 1698, despite some disparity, reveal that "the ultimate purpose of these societies was holiness."[21] Conceding that the rules could at times "sound very moralistic," Kisker nevertheless argued that "following the moral law was not merely outward, not separate from individual spiritual experience."[22] In particular, Kisker appealed to Kidder's ninth rule to show that the Religious Societies focused on both the inner and outer conditions of their members. The ninth rule reads: "After all is done, if there be time left, they may discourse each other about their spiritual concerns; but this shall not be a standing Exercise, which any shall be obliged to attend unto."[23] Although this rule does affirm the possibility of "discourse about spiritual concerns," it was not considered to be essential, since making such conversation an obligatory "standing exercise" was explicitly forbidden by the same rule.

Woodward's account of the Religious Societies may actually make a stronger case for Kisker's argument that they were not "separate from individual spiritual experience." In Woodward's version of the rules of the Religious Societies, the third rule described a weekly meeting "to encourage each other in *practical Holiness*, by discoursing on Spiritual Subjects, and reading God's Holy Word; and to pray to *Almighty God*, and praise his Name together."[24] Whereas Kidder's ninth rule specifically forbid making conversations about spiritual concerns a "standing exercise," Woodward seemed to understand "discoursing on spiritual subjects," along with reading Scripture and praying, to be constitutive of the exercise of encouraging one another in "practical holiness." Woodward further revealed that those who participated in the Religious Societies "better discover'd their own Corruptions, the Devil's Temptations, and how to countermine his *Subtle Devices*; as to which each Person communicated his *Experiences* to the

---

[19] Ibid.

[20] Ibid., 71.

[21] Ibid., 72. For Kidder and Woodward's rules, see Kisker, appendix A, 207–208, and appendix B, 209–212. For the original sources, see Richard Kidder, *The Life of the Reverend Anthony Horneck* (London: n.p., 1698); Josiah Woodward, *An Account of the Rise and Progress of the Religious Societies in the City of London* (London: RA Simpson, 1698). The emphasis on holiness is seen in the first rule of both documents.

[22] Kisker, 73.

[23] Kidder, 14.

[24] Woodward, 121 (emphasis original).

rest."[25] Ultimately, the accounts of both Woodward and Kidder suggest that the deepest focus of the Religious Societies was on "practical holiness," which was seen to be best pursued through a disciplined practice of the means of grace. "Spiritual discourse" was sometimes seen as an asset in this approach, but it was not the main focus.

As a result, Anthony Horneck and the Religious Societies that he helped create should be seen as important forerunners of the early Methodist band meeting. The connection between the Religious Societies and John Wesley is further confirmed by the fact that John Wesley's father Samuel (1666–1735) started a Religious Society at Epworth in 1701.[26] The Religious Societies were part of John Wesley's world for as long as he could remember. The impact of the Religious Societies on Wesley's leadership of Methodism can also be seen in one of the foundational documents of early Methodism, "The Nature, Design, and General Rules of the United Societies" (1743).[27] The body of the "General Rules" consisted of a list of rules that was remarkably similar in organization to the rules of the Religious Societies. In both the earlier lists of rules and in Wesley's version, there were negative rules that prohibited certain actions, as well as positive rules that guided one in expressing love of God and neighbor.

In looking at the Religious Societies, meaningful connections can be seen between them and Spener's *collegia pietatis*. Both were voluntary associations that demanded loyalty to the established church from their membership. Moreover, both the *collegia pietatis* and the Anglican Religious Societies were primarily focused on mutually supporting one another's efforts to grow in piety. However, there were also important differences. The Religious Societies were more intentionally guided by rules that emphasized a disciplined practice of the means of grace as the key to the "holy and serious Life" the members had committed to strive after than were the *collegia pietatis*.[28] On the other hand, the *collegia pietatis* were more focused on "fraternal admonition and chastisement" as the most helpful path to the direct experience of the grace of God.

The Development of the Moravian *Banden* and Oxford Methodism

From the end of the 1670s through the 1720s, the role of small groups or conventicles for the promotion of piety increased in both German Pietism and the Church of England. For the purposes of the Wesleyan bands, the late 1720s marked another

---

[25] Ibid., 37 (emphasis original).

[26] Kisker, 153–154.

[27] See Wesley, "General Rules," in *Works* 9: 69–73.

[28] Citing Kidder's first rule: "All that entered into such a Society should resolve upon an holy and serious Life." Kidder, 13.

particularly important period in which the two different contexts of Continental Pietism and Anglicanism continued to develop in parallel ways. In Germany, a new form of small group organization was established, partially as the result of a revival at Herrnhut. These groups were focused on mutual confession of sins and were called *Banden*. In England, a small group of students at Oxford began to meet together in order to study and enter into a more disciplined practice of the Christian life.

Herrnhut: The Creation of the Moravian *Banden*

In the German context, in the summer of 1727, a revival occurred in Herrnhut related to the celebration of the feast of the Visitation of Mary.[29] One consequence of the revival was that it created the impetus to further organize community life at Herrnhut. Two key Moravian institutions developed as a result of the new focus on the role of community in Christian formation, the *Banden* (bands) and *Chor* (choir).

The *Banden* were created on July 9, 1727, and were divided by gender and marital status.[30] The first band consisted of married men, followed by a band of married women on February 9, 1728, one of single women on February 14, 1728, and the band of single men was formed last.[31] In the Moravian bands, "a strict form of mutual examination was practiced."[32] Because of the "mutual examination" that occurred in the *Banden*, they were "voluntary associations of a small group of persons."[33] Yet, despite their voluntary nature, the bands grew rapidly; there were seventy-seven bands in Herrnhut in 1732, eighty-five in 1733, and one hundred in 1734.[34] Part of the success of the bands seemed to

---

[29] The Feast of the Visitation of Mary at this time was celebrated on July 2; see Gottfried Schmidt, "Die Banden oder Gesellschaften im alten Herrnhut," *Zeitschrift für Brüdergeschichte 3* (1909): 145–146.

[30] Gottfried Schmidt, 146–147. Schmidt's "Die Banden oder Gesellschaften im alten Herrnhut" is a key source for the development of the Moravian *Banden*. For more on the beginnings of the Moravian *Banden* in 1727, see also Martin Schmidt, *John Wesley: A Theological Biography*, vol. 1., trans. Norman P. Goldhaw, 2 vols. (Nashville, TN: Abingdon, 1962), 1: 231–232; Arthur J. Freeman, *An Ecumenical Theology of the Heart: The Theology of Count Nicholas Ludwig von Zinzendorf* (Bethlehem, PA: Moravian Church in America, 1998), 259–260; A. J. Lewis, *Zinzendorf the Ecumenical Pioneer: A Study in the Moravian Contribution to Christian Mission and Unity* (Philadelphia: Westminster Press, 1962), 55–56 (Lewis argued that the bands started on July 19, not July 9); John R. Weinlick, *Count Zinzendorf* (Nashville, TN: Abingdon, 1959), 84; Gillian Lindt Gollin, *Moravians in Two Worlds: A Study of Changing Communities* (New York: Columbia University Press, 1967), 68; J. Taylor Hamilton and Kenneth G. Hamilton, *History of the Moravian Church: The Renewed Unitas Fratrum, 1722–1957* (Bethlehem, PA: Moravian Church in America, 1967), 32 (Hamilton argued that the *Banden* were first mentioned on February 8, 1727—before the revival that occurred in July of the same year); and Colin Podmore, *The Moravian Church in England, 1728–1760* (Oxford, UK: Clarendon Press, 1998), 31.

[31] Gottfried Schmidt, 148.

[32] Martin Schmidt, 1:232.

[33] Freeman, 260.

[34] Gottfried Schmidt, 149.

be due to the degree of intimacy and openness they facilitated. There was "nothing artificial or forced" in the *Banden*.[35] They "were marked by total frankness on the part both of the member describing the state of his soul and of his fellow members in their criticism of him. Thus they had something of the function of the confessional and anticipated to some degree modern 'group therapy.'"[36] The *Banden* could apparently also be unstable; when "no advantage appeared from these Bands, they were given up for a time and after a while renewed with a visible blessing."[37]

Count Nikolas Ludwig von Zinzendorf (1700–60) provided further insight into the rationale for the *Banden*:

> That we meet as bands with each other, that we confess one to the other the state of the heart and diverse imperfections, is not done in order to consult with our brothers and sisters because we could not get along without the counsel of a brother or sister. Rather is it done that one may see the rightness of the heart. By that we learn to trust one another; by that no brother or sister thinks of the other that things are going well with them if they are really going poorly.... That's why you talk to each other, why you unburden your hearts, so that you can constantly rely on each other.[38]

For Zinzendorf, the purpose of the *Banden* was not to become dependent on one another; it was to "see the rightness of the heart." Those who were involved in band meetings were transparent with one another so that they knew what was really going on in the depths of each other's lives. The Moravian bands were important, then, because they enabled the Moravians to avoid self-deception and to search their own hearts more fully. In the *Banden*, members held a mirror up to one another's lives, helping each person more clearly see the true state of their own life with God.

---

[35] Lewis, 55.

[36] Podmore, 31.

[37] Lewis, 56.

[38] The original quotation in German is *"Dass wir Bande mit einander halten, dass wir einer dem andern den Zustand seines Herzens und die mancherlei Mangelhaftigkeiten gestehen, das geschieht nicht, dass wir uns Rats bei den Geschwistern erholen müssten, dass wir nicht ohne den Rat eines Bruders oder Schwester zurecht kommen könnten: sondern damit man die Geradigkeit der Herzen sieht, damit wir einander vertrauen lernen, damit kein Bruder oder Schwester von dem andern denkt, das steht heute gut, wenns schlecht steht, dass sich keins einbilden darf, wie wohl dem Bruder, wie wohl der Schwester ist, wenn es ihnen weh ist. Darum sagt mans einander, darum schüttet man die Herzen gegen einander aus, damit man eine beständige Zuverlässigkeit von einander hat."* Zinzendorf, cited in Gottfried Schmidt, 154; translation in Freeman, 260.

In 1735, at what may have been the peak of the influence of the bands in Herrnhut, Christian David (1692–1751) summarized the purpose of the Moravian bands at this stage in their development:

> Initially there were among the brothers and sisters several who had a special trust in each other so that they began especially to form an association with the purpose (1) that they want to say to each other everything they have on their heart and mind; (2) that they want to remind and encourage each other concerning everything they can see or think of each other and yet always to encourage one another to the good in everything; (3) that they want to come together once every week, in the evening, to hold conference or bands with which they might get to know one another well from within and without; (4) that they wish to give each other the freedom for heart, life, and journey, to test and express everything, and so love one another as their own life, to keep watch, pray, struggle and fight for one another, and to bear, spare one another, and help make life easier which is otherwise difficult, and therefore have the community which is proper *Evangelio* [to the Gospel].[39]

The Moravian *Banden* did not continue for long without change or development. An initial adjustment was the appearance of classes. The classes were developed at a love-feast in 1731 when the bands for the married men were dissolved and divided into three groups, which effectively created a hierarchy of spiritual maturity. These new groups, which Moravian Bishop Arthur J. Freeman referred to as "small classes," replaced the bands that the married men had been in previously.[40] Freeman has argued that the appearance of these classes marked

---

[39] The original quotation in German is "*Es haben unter den Brüdern und Schwestern anfänglich einige, die ein sonderbares Vertrauen zusammen gehabt, sich angefangen besonders zu verbinden, und zwar zum 1) darauf, dass sie alles einander, was sie auf dem Hertzen und Gewissen haven, sagen wollen. Zum 2) dass sie über alles einander erinnern und ermahnen wollen, was sie von einander sehen, oder nur können dencken, und doch einander alles zu gute halten. Zum 3) dass sie alle Woche einmal und zwar Abends zusammen kommen wollen, Conferenz oder Banden zu halten, damit sie einander von innen und aussen recht mögen kennen lernen. Zum 4) Dass sie sich einander die Freyheit zum Hertzen, Leben und Wandel, alles zu prüfen und zu sagen, geben wollen, und einander sich so lieben, wie sein eigen Leben, für einander wachen, beten ringen und kämpfen, und einander tragen, verschonen, das Leben erleichtern helfen, was sonst schwer ist, und also am Evangelio recht Gemeinschaft haben.*" Christian David, "*Beschreibung und Zuverlässige Nachricht von Herrnhut in Ober-Lausitz, Wie es erbauet worden, und mit welcher Gestalt nach Lutheri Sinn und Meinung Eine recht Christliche Gemeine sich daselbst gesammelt und eingerichtet hat,*" in *Herrnhut im Herrnhut 18. Und 19. Jahrhundert: Drei Schriften von Christian David, Nikolas Ludwig von Zinzendorf und Heinrich Friedrich von Bruiningk*, 1 Teil (Hildesheim, DE: Georg Olms Verlag, 2000), 33–35; translation from Freeman, 260–261 (brackets as in Freeman).

[40] Freeman used the term "small classes" to distinguish these smaller groups from the "great classes," which were the larger groups that were divided based on age, gender, and marital status and were the immediate precursors for the Moravian choirs, 261.

the beginning of the end of the bands, as the classes "unfortunately...gradually took the place of the bands."[41] In fact, Zinzendorf himself noted that the bands were diminishing, writing, "Through that [the establishment of classes] the bands were destroyed....As soon as one distinguishes between souls, the bands stopped."[42] The *Banden* did not entirely disappear, however, as they played a key role in Moravian missionary strategy. Upon arriving in a new place, the Moravians seemed to instinctively organize bands.[43]

Aside from the bands, the *Chor* (choirs) were the other critical piece of Moravian communal organization. In *Moravians in Two Worlds: A Study of Changing Communities* (1967), Gillian Gollin argued that the bands were an "antecedent" to the choirs and not "synonymous with them."[44] The *Chor* arose in "response to a demand for greater spiritual fellowship....Through the provision of a common place of residence, the choirs were able to offer their members a much fuller and more extensive participation in religious activities than had been possible in the weekly or even biweekly meetings of the bands."[45] As the Moravian approach to Christian formation through community continued to develop, the *Chor* became obligatory, whereas the *Banden* had been voluntary.[46]

In *Serving Two Masters* (2000), Elisabeth W. Sommer further described the transition from the voluntary *Banden* to the division of the entire community into choirs. One of the keys to the development of the choir system was the extension of the initial division of the *Banden* by gender into a permanent living arrangement:

> This concept of fellowship along lines of age and sex was combined with a physical separation when a group of young men decided to leave houses...to live in one place for the sake of mutual edification....The number of Brothers attracted to this mutual living arrangement grew rapidly, and on May 7, 1739, all the Single Brothers in the *Gemeine*

[41] Ibid. In this account, the classes seem to be a bridge between the formation of the bands and the beginning of the choirs. Yet, the choirs were already present in some sense as the single men and single women each had separated themselves into separate living communities in 1728 and 1730 respectively. See Hamilton, 36; Craig D. Atwood, *Community of the Cross: Moravian Piety in Colonial Bethlehem* (University Park, PA: Pennsylvania State University Press, 2004), 173–174.

[42] Freeman, 262 (brackets original).

[43] Zinzendorf, according to Weinlick, "suggested the formation of small bands" during a three-week trip to the West Indies in late 1738; Weinlick, 146. Peter Böhler also famously started a band meeting at Fetter Lane in 1738.

[44] Gollin, 68. Although it is clear that the bands existed before the choirs, it is difficult to establish the beginning of the choirs. Gollin has argued that it is best to "trace its [the choirs] beginnings to the development of the bands in the later part of the seventeen-twenties, and to place the emergence of the choir system in the context of a gradual transformation of these bands over a period of at least ten years." Ibid.

[45] Ibid., 76.

[46] Ibid., 68.

at Herrnhut decided to build their own house and to work under one roof.... The Single Sisters Choir developed in a similar manner...by October 1740, they had purchased their own house where they could live as one.[47]

One way of understanding the development of Moravian communal practice, then, could be that it evolved in a way that tended to increase the bonds of community. The bands represented an initial effort to grow in holiness after the revival at Herrnhut in the summer of 1727. As the bands developed, people of the same gender and marital status began to live together, marking the beginning of the evolution of the choir system. During this period, the bands also began to be divided into classes, based on spiritual maturity. At Herrnhut, the experiment in communal living grew into a full-blown communal living arrangement as houses were built for people to live in based on gender, age, and marital status.

Of the various methods of Moravian organization, the bands were the closest forerunner of the Wesleyan bands, as the Wesleyan bands did not involve an attempt to live together in community. Yet, a connection can also be seen between Wesley's bands and the Moravian classes, as the Wesleyan bands did involve creating a sort of spiritual hierarchy for those who "wanted some means of closer union."[48] The second observation that can be made is that the logic of this structure may suggest why Peter Böhler began in England by starting bands, and not choirs. The bands could be seen as a first step in the efforts of Moravian missionaries to create pockets of Christian community in the mission field. This is further demonstrated in Bethlehem, Pennsylvania, for example, where the Moravians began with bands and eventually instituted the choir system found in Herrnhut.[49] As far as their influence on Wesley, the bands were the primary form of Christian communal practice that Wesley encountered in his initial contact with Peter Böhler and other Moravians.[50]

The Moravian *Banden* were a crucial forerunner of the early Methodist bands, which adopted their name. The Moravian band meeting was a voluntary small group that involved deep mutual accountability. They were also divided based on gender and marital status. The Methodist bands appropriated each of these characteristics from the Moravian *Banden*. The deep dependence of the Methodist

---

[47] Elisabeth W. Sommer, *Serving Two Masters: Moravian Brethren in Germany and North Carolina, 1727–1801* (Lexington, KY: University of Kentucky Press, 2000), 30.

[48] Wesley, "Plain Account," in *Works* 9: 266.

[49] Gollin, 74. This distinction does *not* correspond to the early Methodist structure of classes and bands. In the Methodist structure, the classes clearly expected a lesser degree of spiritual maturity than did the bands.

[50] Wesley described his trip to visit the Moravian settlement at Herrnhut in his *Journal*. See *Works* 18: 269ff.

bands on the Moravian bands is most clearly witnessed in looking at the place where Moravians and future Methodists came together, the Fetter Lane Society. However, before we can fully appreciate the significance of Fetter Lane, another development needs to be considered that was nearly simultaneous to the development of the Moravian *Banden*, and would also impact Fetter Lane and Wesley's conception of the band meeting—the initial development of Methodism at Oxford.

Oxford Methodism

While the Moravian *Banden* were continuing to gain momentum, a small group of students began meeting in Oxford in order to study together and commit to a disciplined practice of their faith. Later in his life, John Wesley would summarize the importance of this group: "The first rise of Methodism (so called) was in November 1729, when four of us met together at Oxford."[51] The "first rise of Methodism" began in the summer of 1729 when John Wesley returned from Epworth, where his father was the parish priest, and rejoined his brother Charles at Oxford. Richard P. Heitzenrater has described the beginnings of a corporate expression of John Wesley's earlier individual pursuit of holiness of heart and life:

> The two brothers and at least one friend... encouraged by each other's efforts, occasionally meeting together for study, prayer, and religious conversation, attending the Sacrament regularly, keeping track of their lives by daily notations in a diary, represent the earliest manifestations of what will become Oxford Methodism. The gatherings are not regular, not everyone attends every time, the daily routine is not set, the light recreation is still evident now and then, but the marks of the Wesleyan movement are present in the group.[52]

Heitzenrater further stressed the ambiguities and complexities of the "first rise of Methodism," as the group, when it began meeting again in November, continued to lack a formal structure or set meeting times. At this stage, the group "resembled an informal literary society more than anything else, consciously designed to promote learning and piety."[53] By 1730, a more regular pattern of meetings was developed and later in the year, the group intentionally began to expand their focus to include works of piety that were an expression of love of neighbor, such as visiting prisoners and the poor in Oxford.[54]

---

[51] Wesley, "Short History," 9: 430 (parentheses original).

[52] Richard P. Heitzenrater, "The Quest of the First Methodist: Oxford Methodism Reconsidered," in *Mirror and Memory: Reflections on Early Methodism* (Nashville, TN: Kingswood Books, 1989), 71.

[53] Ibid., 72.

[54] Heitzenrater noted that it was this move more than any other that caused their "notoriety" to increase. Ibid.

Unlike the German Moravians, the gradual coming together of a group of people concerned about holiness of heart and life at Oxford was not prompted by a prior revival. Rather, it was motivated by the desire of many of the members to find an assurance of their own salvation. Heitzenrater insisted that "it must be remembered that Wesley was deeply engaged in the search for 'a right state of soul.'"[55] As a result, Wesley was not primarily a pastor or guide of souls at this point. Rather, he was a fellow pilgrim seeking salvation. The Oxford Methodists, then, were "those who were striving for 'the one thing needful,' and to that end had a 'single intention' in life—'to please God' by improving 'in holiness, in the love of God and . . . neighbor.'"[56]

A key approach to the search for the "one thing needful" was a determination to avoid wasting time. In a letter to his mother Susanna (1669–1742), Wesley outlined the commitment of Robert Kirkham, one of the early Oxford Methodists, in a way that provides significant insight into the structure and motivation of the first Methodists:

> A little while ago Bob Kirkham took a fancy into his head that he would lose no more time, and waste no more money. In pursuance of which he first resolved to breakfast no longer on tea; next to drink no more ale in an evening, or however but enough to quench his thirst; then, to read Greek or Latin from prayers in the morning till noon, and from dinner till five at night. And how much may one imagine he executed of these resolutions? Why, he has left off tea, struck off his drinking acquaintance to a man, given the hours above specified to Greek Testament and Hugo Grotius, and spent the evenings either by himself or with my brother and me.[57]

Indeed, the Oxford Methodists were so disciplined in the use of their time and in their effort to practice their faith fully that Wesley recounted in a subsequent letter to his mother that they were accused of "being too strict . . . of laying burdens" on themselves "too heavy to be borne, and consequently too heavy to be of any use to us."[58]

Given the degree of self-discipline that characterized those who were part of Oxford Methodism, it is perhaps surprising that the boundaries of Oxford Methodism were difficult to pin down or precisely define. During this period, "there was no rite of initiation, no cause for exclusion. One's association was totally voluntary . . . the Methodists had no required regulations, no measurable

---

[55] Ibid., 76.

[56] Ibid., 77.

[57] Wesley, letter to Susanna Wesley, February 28, 1729/30, in *Works*, vols. 25–26, *Letters*, ed. Frank Baker (Oxford, UK: Clarendon Press, 1980), 25: 245–246.

[58] Wesley, letter to Susanna Wesley, June 11, 1731, in *Works* 25: 283.

parameters of membership, no single meeting place."[59] The main quality that those who were called Methodists had seems to have been "the desire to work out one's salvation and to engage in the pursuit of perfection."[60]

As Oxford Methodism became more recognized by those outside of the group itself, it began to gain a degree of cohesion and predictability in practice. The main activities of the Oxford Methodists can be categorized under three headings: scholarship, devotion, and social outreach.[61] For the purposes of a study of the forerunners of the Methodist band meeting, the Oxford Methodists' approach to devotion is of particular importance. Confession was a crucial part "of their group experience: not only did they compare diaries at some of their meetings as a means of confessing their own sins, but they did not hesitate to point out the faults of others."[62] The regular meetings that developed further illustrate the role of "religious talk," as even their study and discussion of particular books also involved "religious talk about their progress in holy living."[63] Thus, probing spiritual conversations were a key feature of the earliest developments of Methodism.

One way of understanding the relationship between the Oxford Methodists and the Religious Societies that preceded them would be to see the Religious Society that Samuel Wesley started at Epworth, in 1701, as a primary influence on the program of the Oxford Methodists. In his account of the Epworth Religious Society, Samuel Wesley summarized the intentions of the group: "First to pray to God; Secondly, to read the Holy Scriptures, and discourse upon Religious Matters for their mutual Edification; And Thirdly, to deliberate about the Edification of our neighbour, and the promoting it."[64] Samuel Wesley's intentions for the Religious Society at Epworth contained a more explicit endorsement of the importance of "discourse upon religious matters for mutual edification" than did either Woodward's or Kidder's versions of the rules of the Religious Societies. The Oxford Methodists, in their earnestness to work out their salvation, also emphasized the importance of probing spiritual conversation for "mutual edification." One of the chief differences was that their pursuit of holiness led them to meet more frequently than the customary weekly meeting of the Religious Societies.

Though the Oxford Methodists were influenced by the Religious Societies, they were not themselves a Religious Society. When Wesley mentioned to John Clayton in 1733 the possibility of formally creating a Religious Society

---

[59] Heitzenrater, "The Meditative Piety of the Oxford Methodists," in *Mirror and Memory*, 84.

[60] Ibid., 85.

[61] Heitzenrater provided this classification. See ibid., 85–98.

[62] Ibid., 89.

[63] Ibid., 88.

[64] Samuel Wesley, "An Account of the Religious Society begun in Epworth in the Isle of Axholm Linconshire, Feb:1, An: Dom: 1701-2," in W. O. B. Allen and Edmund McClure, *Two Hundred Years: The History of The Society for Promoting Christian Knowledge, 1698–1898* (London: Society for Promoting Christian Knowledge, 1898), 91.

at Oxford, Clayton disapproved of the idea, arguing that it would be "perhaps a snare for the consciences of those weak brethren that might choose to come among you."[65] Though we do not have Wesley's response to Clayton's objection, a Religious Society was not formally organized by the Methodists at Oxford. Therefore, it can be inferred from Clayton's response to Wesley's letter that Wesley ultimately decided against forming one in Oxford at that time.

The "first rise of Methodism" at Oxford, then, involved an informal adoption and intensification of many of the principles and structures of the Religious Societies, particularly as they were practiced by the one Samuel Wesley led at Epworth. As John Wesley and others resolved to do everything they could to sincerely pursue holiness, they instinctively turned to a more disciplined practice of prayer, as well as receiving the sacrament of Communion, reading the Bible, fasting, and serving the poor. The Oxford Methodists also frequently joined together to talk about their progress in the pursuit of holiness and to point out to one another areas where they believed someone was failing to make progress or continuing to sin. The fact that John Wesley was himself the main leader of the Oxford Methodists meant that the development of communal support and accountability that occurred in the late 1720s and early 1730s would influence the version of the band meeting that Wesley would develop a few years later. The Oxford Methodists can further be seen as a forerunner of the Wesleyan bands because they began to gather together in small groups in order to hold each other accountable for their individual pursuits of Christian perfection, an activity that would become distinctive of the Wesleyan bands.

The developments among the Oxford Methodists correspond to the changes to the communal structures developed by the Moravians at Herrnhut. As both groups sought to become more holy, they both began to enter into increasingly intense conversations about the states of their souls and any sins they had committed. There was also a degree of flexibility and change that was primarily motivated by the pursuit of holy living. One of the most important distinctions between the groups is that the Moravians gathered together *because they had experienced saving faith*, whereas the Oxford Methodists assembled *in order to seek salvation*.

Oxford Methodism Encounters Moravianism: The Development of the Fetter Lane Society

To this point, the focus has been on the parallel developments of communal support and accountability for the pursuit of holiness in two similar, yet distinct, traditions. These two traditions were not entirely separated from one

---

[65] John Clayton, letter to John Wesley, July [25], 1733, in *Works* 25: 352.

another, as Anthony Horneck, the founder of the first Religious Societies, was reared in the context of Continental Pietism. And yet, these traditions would be uniquely combined by John Wesley in a way that provided a key foundation for the Evangelical Revival that impacted eighteenth-century British Christianity itself. The beginnings of this synthesis are found in the initial contact that John Wesley had with Moravians on his trip as a missionary to Georgia, and in his more extensive interactions with Peter Böhler after his return to London in 1738. These events eventually led to the creation of the Fetter Lane Society and made possible Wesley's fusion of Moravian and Anglican piety.

John Wesley's Initial Encounters with the Moravians

Wesley's first entry in his manuscript journal on October 14, 1735, commemorated his boarding the *Simmonds*, the boat that would take him, Charles Wesley, Benjamin Ingham (1712–72), and Charles Delamotte (1714?–96) to Georgia. Toward the end of the first entry, Wesley described the purpose of his trip to Georgia: "The design that moved us all to leave our native country was not to avoid want…nor to gain riches and honour, which we trust he will ever enable us to look on as no other than dung and dross; but singly this—to save our souls, and to live wholly to the glory of God."[66] By October 21, Wesley reported that he and his companions began "to recover a little regularity" in their religious practice. Wesley portrayed their "common way of spending our time" as consisting of rising at four in the morning and praying privately for an hour, reading the Bible together for two hours, eating breakfast, public prayers, personal study, an hour-long meeting where they "met to give an account to one another of what we had done since our last meeting, and what we designed to do before our next," lunch, three hours of teaching or instructing others on board the ship, evening prayers, private prayer, communal reading, worship with the German Moravians, another hour-long meeting "to instruct and exhort one another," and finally going to sleep between nine and ten.[67] The trip to Georgia was apparently not viewed as an opportunity to relax the discipline that they had previously practiced in Oxford.

There were occasionally severe storms throughout the voyage to Georgia aboard the *Simmonds*. On November 23, a particularly severe storm woke Wesley in the middle of the night. He recorded in his manuscript journal that the storm "plainly showed me I was not fit, because not willing to die."[68] Wesley noticed not only his own fear during these storms, but also that the German Moravians, who were on board the *Simmonds* as well, seemed to have a peace during these

---

[66] Wesley, manuscript journal for October 14, 1735, in *Works* 18: 312.

[67] Wesley, manuscript journal for October 21, 1735, in *Works* 18: 314.

[68] Wesley, manuscript journal for November 23, 1735, in *Works* 18: 324.

moments that he lacked. During one worship service, Wesley wrote that "the sea broke over, covered the ship, and split the mainsail." Wesley noted the contrast between the Anglican and Moravian passengers: "Many of the English screamed out. The Germans looked up, and without intermission sang on."[69] In the published version of his *Journal*, which bears the marks of subsequent editing, Wesley added that when he asked one of the Moravians afterward if he was afraid to die, he responded, "I thank God, no."[70] Later, when Wesley met August Gottlieb Spangenberg (1704–92) in Georgia, Spangenberg directly asked Wesley whether he knew Jesus Christ and whether he had "the witness of the Spirit in your heart."[71] Wesley recorded that, "after my answering these, he gave me several directions, which may the good God who sent him enable me to follow."[72] It is significant that in Wesley's initial contact with the Moravians, he did not note their organization or their practices as a community. Rather, he was most impressed with the qualities that they possessed that he did not yet have: humility, meekness, and peace.[73] He was especially captivated by, and longed for, their assurance of salvation, even in the face of death.

As Wesley was introduced to the Moravians and began observing their way of life more closely, he continued organizing people together for a disciplined pursuit of holy living. In Savannah, he advised "the more serious among them to form themselves into a sort of little society, and to meet once or twice a week, in order to reprove, instruct, and exhort one another; second, to select out of these a smaller number for a more intimate union with each other."[74] The society that Wesley oversaw in Savannah "seemed to thrive throughout the remainder of Wesley's stay in the colony, and the attendance at public services continued to increase."[75] Wesley's efforts to instill ecclesiastical discipline in Georgia were interrupted when he infamously refused to serve Sophia Williamson Communion on August 7, 1737. As a result, charges were brought against Wesley by a grand jury in Savannah, leading him to determine that the time had come

[69] Wesley, manuscript journal for January 25, 1736, in *Works* 18: 345. In the published version of the *Journal*, Wesley added that the water "poured in between the decks, as if the great deep had already swallowed us up." Ibid., 18: 143.

[70] Wesley, *Journal* for January 25, 1736, in *Works* 18: 143.

[71] Wesley recorded his answer in the published *Journal*, but there was no explicit answer in the manuscript journal. The answer in the published *Journal* was "I do." However, he also further reflected: "I fear they were vain words." Wesley, *Journal* for February 7, 1736, in *Works* 18: 352; 146.

[72] Wesley, manuscript journal for February 8, 1736, in *Works* 18: 352.

[73] These are qualities that Wesley notes of the Moravians in his published account of his voyage to Georgia. Wesley, *Journal* for January 25, 1735, in *Works* 18: 142–143.

[74] Wesley, *Journal* for April 17, 1736, in *Works* 18: 157. This event marked what Wesley would later refer to as the "second rise of Methodism"; see Wesley, "Short History," in *Works* 9: 430. The search for a small number for "a more intimate union" may reflect Wesley's initial attempt to form something like a Moravian band.

[75] Richard P. Heitzenrater, *Wesley and the People Called Methodists* (Nashville, TN: Abingdon, 1995), 66.

for his return to England. When Wesley arrived in England, he met Peter Böhler, who was instrumental in Wesley's search for assurance in the months before his famous experience at Aldersgate Street on May 24, 1738.

The Fetter Lane Society

In Georgia, Wesley had been able to interact with Moravians in some detail, yet he continued to be distinguished from the Moravians by his role as an Anglican priest to the colonists in Georgia. Upon Wesley's return to London, this distinction would become less clear. In fact, the lines between Moravianism, Methodism, and the Church of England were sufficiently blurred that historians continue to contest many aspects surrounding the history of the Fetter Lane Society. Colin Podmore has recently claimed that John Wesley's perspective has dominated most accounts of the beginning and early years of the Fetter Lane Society.[76] Podmore has further argued that Wesley's account in his *Journal* of his own involvement in the Fetter Lane Society actually "exaggerated" his role and "underplayed the importance of the Moravian contribution."[77] Particular attention needs to be paid to the details of the formation and early development of the Fetter Lane Society in order to better understand the role it played in the creation of the early Methodist band meeting.

John Wesley's involvement in the Fetter Lane Society is beyond dispute. Wesley recorded in his *Journal* that, because of his brother Charles's ill health, he returned to London on May 1, 1738. Wesley discovered that his brother's health had physically improved, but that Charles was "strongly averse from what he called 'the new faith.'"[78] Wesley further recorded that "this evening our little society began, which afterwards met in Fetter Lane."[79] Thus, Wesley's *Journal* confirms Podmore's observation that Wesley was only present when the Fetter Lane Society was founded "by chance"; he was in London because of his brother's illness.[80] Podmore narrated the creation of the Fetter Lane Society as follows: "On the evening of 1 May Böhler invited a select group to gather at [James] Hutton's, and after discussion of the Moravian principles of fellowship, they agreed to form a band."[81] Podmore's conclusion was that this new society was essentially a Moravian band meeting created under the leadership of Peter Böhler.[82]

Because of the importance that historians would come to attribute to the Fetter Lane Society, much ink has been spilled about its origins. Was it a Church

---

[76] Podmore, 29.
[77] Ibid.
[78] Wesley, *Journal* for May 1, 1738, in *Works* 18: 236.
[79] Ibid.
[80] Podmore, 38.
[81] Ibid.
[82] Ibid., 40. For Wesley's full account, see his *Journal* for May 1, 1738, in *Works* 18: 235–237.

of England Religious Society? Or was it a Moravian society? The fact that none of the members, except Peter Böhler, were Moravians has been used as evidence that it was an Anglican Religious Society. On the other hand, the fact that membership was not confined to members of the Church of England (as was the case in the Religious Societies) and that the administration of the society was not placed under an Anglican priest have been offered as evidence that it was not an Anglican Religious Society.[83]

Frank Baker argued that Fetter Lane "has erroneously been called both the first Moravian and the first Methodist Society in England. In fact this Fetter Lane Society...was clearly for Anglicans only, fashioned after the pattern of the Religious Societies."[84] Though Baker was right to insist that the Anglicans who comprised the Fetter Lane Society seemed to have influenced its creation and development in ways that it would not have otherwise been affected had all of the members been Moravians, his account was nevertheless too simplistic. Baker's analysis also failed to account for the organization of the Fetter Lane Society into bands, which were patterned after the Moravian practice at Herrnhut and not the practice of the Anglican Religious Societies. Peter Böhler's presence and leadership also become incomprehensible in Baker's account.

According to Colin Podmore, the Fetter Lane Society "was in fact Moravian in foundation and character, even if initially Anglican in membership."[85] His analysis suggested that the early members of the Fetter Lane Society were Anglicans who converted to Moravianism. Podmore further argued that "Wesley may have influenced the rules' form, but their spirit was Böhler's."[86] This argument rests on two assumptions: (1) This new group marked a significant departure from the Anglican Religious Societies that Wesley and others were familiar with; and (2) the two rules that were initially agreed upon "describe a Herrnhut-style band."[87] These two rules were:

1. That they will meet together once a week, to confess their faults one to another, and pray for one another, that they may be healed.
2. That any others of whose Sincerity they are well assured, may if they desire it, meet with them for that Purpose.[88]

---

[83] For a summary of these arguments, see Podmore, 39.

[84] Frank Baker, "The People Called Methodists, 3. Polity," in *A History of the Methodist Church in Great Britain*, vol. 1, eds. Rupert Davies and Gordon Rupp (London: Epworth Press, 1965), 217 (henceforth Baker, "Polity").

[85] Podmore, 40.

[86] Ibid.

[87] Ibid.

[88] "Rules of the Fetter Lane Society" (R13.A19.2), quoted from Whitney M. Trousdale, "The Moravian Society, Fetter Lane, London," in *Proceedings of the Wesley Historical Society* 17 (1929): 30 (henceforth *PWHS*).

Scott Kisker's recent study of the Anglican Religious Societies provides grounds for mitigating Podmore's claim that the Fetter Lane Society was "Moravian in foundation and character." First, Kisker showed that Pietism had been an important influence on Anglicanism for nearly fifty years before the Moravians set foot on English soil. Kisker particularly pointed to the publication of Josiah Woodward's *Account of the Rise and Progress of the Religious Societies in the City of London* (1698) as making a major contribution "to the spread of the Religious Societies throughout England," as well as continuing to infuse Pietism into the Church of England.[89] Pietism, then, was already influencing the Church of England through the Religious Societies. Thus, the Religious Societies were a source of both Anglican and Pietist influence that was *not* Moravian.

Seeing the Anglican Religious Societies as a source of influence on Fetter Lane is even more plausible when John Wesley's perspective is included. Though Wesley's viewpoint should not dominate the discussion in ways that distort the picture, it would similarly distort the picture if Wesley were left out of it. Kisker saw Oxford Methodism as "perhaps the most prominent reinterpretation of the Religious Societies."[90] Kisker noted that the Religious Societies were key influences on both John and Charles Wesley because they were "the primary model of small piety groups known to the Wesley brothers."[91] Further, Wesley had become a member of the Society for the Promotion of Christian Knowledge in 1732, and he went to Georgia as a missionary under the Society for the Propagation of the Gospel in 1735. Wesley also read Horneck's *The Happy Ascetic* (1681) in 1733 and later read his *Exercise of Prayer* (1685).[92] Though the Moravians and Peter Böhler were leading influences in the period when the Fetter Lane Society was formed, the Religious Societies and the Church of England also shaped the Fetter Lane Society. Wesley did not check his Anglicanism at the door when he entered Fetter Lane.[93]

Including John Wesley's perspective is also crucial because accounts of the origins of the Fetter Lane Society are limited to the false option of either Church of England or Moravian influence if Wesley's presence is ignored. Wesley's own experiences in Oxford and Georgia are muted in the forced choice between the Church of England and Moravianism. At the point of Wesley's own involvement in Fetter Lane, he cannot be labeled simply as a proponent of either of these traditions. He had been influenced by both. When Wesley is kept in the picture,

---

[89] Kisker, 132.

[90] Ibid., 156.

[91] Ibid.

[92] Ibid., 157.

[93] This is further supported by the extent to which the Wesleys struggled to uphold Methodism's connection to the Church of England throughout their lives, despite John Wesley's discomfort with the presence of nominal Christianity within the membership of the Church of England.

the deeper significance of what was happening at Fetter Lane can be seen, a new synthesis of different approaches to holy living.

The circumstances surrounding the creation of Fetter Lane are further complicated when James Hutton's role is included. While John and Charles Wesley were in Georgia, James Hutton (1715–95) started a society that met in his own house. Hutton's society was "based loosely" on Oxford Methodism and intentionally sought to be a more radical version of the older Religious Societies.[94] Membership in Hutton's society, however, did overlap with the older societies, and the times of the meetings were set up so that people could attend both.[95] Hutton's society also seemed to serve as a periodic homecoming for members of the Oxford Methodists, who would often make contact with Hutton's society when in London.[96] When John Wesley returned to England in 1738, he introduced Hutton to Peter Böhler. On April 24, Böhler became convinced that he should attempt to form "those who had come under his influence into a band."[97] Though Hutton would ultimately switch his allegiance to the Moravians, suggesting that he did not bring any Anglican influence with him to Fetter Lane is an overstatement.

In *Reasonable Enthusiast: John Wesley and the Rise of Methodism* (2002), Henry D. Rack provided further evidence of the influence of Anglicanism on the Fetter Lane Society. Rack emphasized the disagreement between James Hutton and John Wesley that was the result of Hutton proposing a modified "leadership structure for the societies" in November 1738.[98] When Hutton suggested a more meaningful leadership role for himself, Wesley disagreed, arguing that as long as there was an Anglican priest in the society, there was no need for the level of lay leadership that Hutton was requesting. Wesley's emphasis on the importance of the leadership of a Church of England priest showed the prior influence of the Religious Societies.

Thus, although the creation of the Fetter Lane Society was influenced by Moravianism (contrary to Baker), Podmore's argument does not adequately recognize the extent to which Anglicanism also influenced the Fetter Lane Society. In this case, the most accurate assessment of the theological influences within the Fetter Lane Society was provided by one of the first interpreters of Fetter Lane, Martin Schmidt. According to Schmidt, "In spite of Böhler's powerful influence... the new society does not seem to have been organized after the pattern of Herrnhut in the strict sense, but was rather a compound of elements taken from

---

[94] Kisker, 160.

[95] Ibid.

[96] Ibid., 161.

[97] Ibid.

[98] Henry D. Rack, *Reasonable Enthusiast: John Wesley and the Rise of Methodism*, 3rd ed. (London: Epworth Press, 2002), 188.

the Religious Societies within the Church of England, and the Herrnhut model, and Wesley's own ideas and experiences."[99]

As Martin Schmidt's account suggested, the Fetter Lane Society was neither a Moravian band nor an Anglican Religious Society. Fetter Lane was impacted in crucial ways by both Moravian and Anglican communal piety, but it was neither of these. Rather, the Fetter Lane Society is best understood as the first intentional effort to merge the different approaches to the pursuit of holiness found in the Moravian *Banden* and the Anglican Religious Societies, including the modifications of the latter already introduced by John Wesley at Oxford and Georgia. This attempt to merge two different traditions meant that the identity of Fetter Lane was in tension. In fact, this tension ultimately proved to be more than the Society could bear, as Wesley and his followers would formally separate from Fetter Lane on July 20, 1740, after several months of disagreement over whether or not one seeking an assurance of the forgiveness of sins should practice the means of grace.[100] Wesley's insistence on the value of the means of grace in the search for the new birth was a major factor in his separation from the Fetter Lane Society.

Despite the controversy that split the Fetter Lane Society, the Fetter Lane bands were nevertheless direct predecessors for the early Methodist bands. In fact, the structure of the Fetter Lane bands was nearly identical to that of the bands for which Wesley would later provide leadership. After he left Fetter Lane, despite the conflict that led to his departure, Wesley continued to emphasize the importance of band meetings. Ultimately, Wesley did not separate from the Fetter Lane Society because he disagreed that members should meet in bands; rather, the separation occurred because of theological controversies such as "stillness" and the legitimate use of the means of grace.[101]

---

[99] Martin Schmidt, 1: 245.

[100] See Wesley, *Journal* for July 20, 1740, in *Works* 19: 162. Wesley also recorded in his manuscript diary on this date his attendance at the Fetter Lane Society, followed by "parted!" Wesley, manuscript diary for July 20, 1740, in *Works* 19: 427. In his 1741 sermon "The Means of Grace," Wesley defined the means of grace as "outward signs, words, or actions ordained of God, and appointed for this end—to be the *ordinary* channels whereby he might convey to men preventing, justifying, or sanctifying grace." *Works* 1: 381. Wesley's understanding of means of grace developed over time and came to include "instituted" and "prudential" means of grace. See, e.g., "Minutes of Several Conversations between the Reverend Mr. John and Charles Wesley, and Others," in *Works* 10: 855–858.

[101] "Stillness" is a term that referred to the argument made by Moravians such as Philip Henry Molther that prior to receiving justifying faith and the new birth, people should be still and wait. Molther's concern was that using the means of grace prior to justifying faith was a form of works righteousness. The proper use of the means of grace was a major source of tension between Wesley and Molther in the fall of 1739. Wesley's *Journal* during this period evidences his advocacy for a disciplined practice of the means of grace in the face of opposition to this commitment.

2

John Wesley's Structure and Theology of Discipleship

John Wesley believed that holiness is a fundamental part of the Christian life.[1] For Wesley, holiness was not a matter of indifference that was optional for an elite few. He also believed that holiness was best nurtured through a supportive and disciplined community. Wesley's dedication to creating and maintaining structures for communal Christian formation, then, came out of his conviction that holiness is necessarily social. This chapter examines Wesley's insistence on the necessity of holiness, as well as his claim that there is "no holiness but social holiness." Subsequently, the essential parts of Wesley's approach to social holiness are outlined, focusing particularly on the society, class, and band meetings. Wesley believed that people who consistently participated in these groups would in fact grow in their love of God and neighbor (i.e., become more holy). In creating the society, class, and band meetings, Wesley drew from both sources that he already knew and sources that were relatively new to him.

"Religion Itself": Holiness as Necessary for the Christian Life

Wesley's vision for Methodism was rooted in his conviction that holiness was necessary for the Christian life. Moreover, when Wesley talked about the importance of holiness, he was not talking only to Methodists, but to all who would be Christians. One of Wesley's most succinct endorsements of the importance

---

[1] The importance of holiness for Wesley's theology has been noted by previous scholars. For a few interpretations of Wesley's understanding of holiness, see Harald Lindström, *Wesley and Sanctification: A Study in the Doctrine of Salvation* (Nappanee, IN: Francis Asbury Press, 1980); Randy L. Maddox, *Responsible Grace*; Kenneth J. Collins, *The Theology of John Wesley*; and Ted A. Campbell, *Wesleyan Beliefs: Formal and Popular Expressions of the Core Beliefs of Wesleyan Communities* (Nashville, TN: Kingswood Books, 2010), esp. 229–233.

of holiness is found in "The Principles of a Methodist Farther Explained" (1746), where he contended that "holiness...is religion itself."[2] Wesley's insistence that holiness is the essence of Christianity is further seen in "Thoughts upon Methodism" (1786): "Methodism...is only plain scriptural religion, guarded by a few prudential regulations. The essence of it is holiness of heart and life."[3]

Wesley's emphasis on holiness and his insistence on its importance for the Christian life can be seen in numerous places in his writings. In the "Large Minutes," the answer given to the question "What may we reasonably believe to be God's design in raising up the preachers called 'Methodists'?" was: "To reform the nation, and in particular the Church, to spread scriptural holiness over the land."[4] Further, when the origins of Methodism were described in the "Large Minutes," holiness was featured prominently. In this account, Methodism began when it was revealed through study of Scripture that salvation was not possible "without holiness."[5] And even as the narrative mentioned shifts in their understanding, it reaffirmed that "still holiness was their point."[6] Thus, in the "Large Minutes," holiness is placed at the very center of early Methodism's self-understanding.

In preaching, Wesley frequently contrasted nominal and vital Christianity. In the sermon "The Almost Christian" (1741), for example, Wesley made a distinction between an "almost Christian" and an "altogether Christian." In this sermon, Wesley described an "altogether Christian" as a person who loves God, loves neighbor, and has faith that they are reconciled to God by the work of Christ.[7] Thus, Wesley's definition of a complete, or "altogether," Christian was essentially a combination of justifying faith and holiness.[8] Wesley concluded by exhorting his Anglican audience in Oxford: "May we all thus experience what it is to be not almost only, but altogether Christians! Being justified freely by his grace, through the redemption that is in Jesus, knowing we have peace with God through Jesus Christ, rejoicing in hope of the glory of God, and having the love of God shed abroad in our hearts by the Holy Ghost given unto us!"[9]

Another sermon where Wesley discussed the necessity of holiness, although from a slightly different perspective, was his 1785 sermon "Of the Church."

---

[2] Wesley, "The Principles of a Methodist Farther Explained," in *Works* 9: 227.

[3] Wesley, "Thoughts," in *Works* 9: 529.

[4] Wesley, "Minutes of Several Conversations between the Reverend Mr. John and Charles Wesley, and Others," in *Works* 10: 845.

[5] Ibid., 10: 875.

[6] Ibid.

[7] Wesley, "The Almost Christian," in *Works* 1: 137–139.

[8] For recent treatments of Wesley on justification and holiness, see Kenneth J. Collins, *The Theology of John Wesley*, 181–182. In particular, Collins argued that "Simply put, no true Christian holiness can precede justification, it must immediately follow it. Justification, properly speaking, ever occurs with regeneration; never one without the other." Ibid., 182; Randy L. Maddox, *Responsible Grace*, 150, 169–171. Maddox wrote that, for Wesley, "justification was inherently connected to the New Birth." Ibid., 150.

[9] Wesley, "The Almost Christian," in *Works* 1: 141.

When Wesley considered the holiness of the Church, he concluded that "the shortest and plainest" reason that can be given for why the church is referred to as "the holy catholic church" in the Apostles' Creed is that "the church is called 'holy' because it is holy; because every member thereof is holy, though in different degrees, as he that called them is holy."[10] In the sermon, Wesley insisted that the holiness that is a necessary property of the church requires holiness from those who are part of the church. Thus, "It follows that not only no common swearer, no Sabbath-breaker, no drunkard, no whoremonger, no thief, no liar, none that lives in any outward sin; but none that is under the power of anger or pride, no lover of the world—in a word, none that is dead to God—can be a member of his church."[11]

For Wesley, the least common denominator for Christian faith was holiness as expressed by Jesus in the greatest commandment: "You shall love the Lord your God with all your heart, and with all your soul, and with all your mind. This is the greatest and first commandment. And a second is like it: You shall love your neighbor as yourself."[12] For Wesley, Jesus' words were not advice for a select few; they were commandments for all who were created in the image of God. In fact, the crucial document that defined what was expected of every Methodist was "The Nature, Design, and General Rules of the United Societies" ("General Rules"). One way of understanding the "General Rules" is to see it as providing guidelines for helping people who had come to faith in Christ learn how to love God and neighbor through their lives. The second rule, "doing good...as they have opportunity doing good of every possible sort and as far as is possible to all men," was in harmony with the second part of the greatest commandment. The third rule, to "attend upon all the ordinances of God," was an instruction to cultivate the habits that would foster a love for God, the first part of the greatest commandment.[13] The "General Rules," then, were a practical guide to holiness.[14]

The logic of Wesley's understanding of holiness, or sanctification, led to the articulation of the doctrine of entire sanctification, or Christian perfection, which Wesley famously referred to as "the grand depositum which God has lodged with the people called Methodists; and for the sake of propagating this chiefly He appeared to have raised us up."[15] Wesley defined, discussed, and

---

[10] Wesley, "Of the Church," in *Works* 3: 55–56.

[11] Ibid., 56.

[12] Matthew 22:37–39 (NRSV).

[13] For the "General Rules," see Wesley, *Works* 9: 69–75.

[14] Wesley, in fact, referred to the "General Rules" in "A Plain Account of Christian Perfection" when he exhorted those who believed they had been entirely sanctified to "observe every rule of the Society, and the Bands, for conscience' sake." Wesley, *Works*, Jackson, 11: 433.

[15] Wesley, letter to Robert Carr Brackenbury, September 15, 1790, in *Letters* (Telford), 8: 238.

defended entire sanctification in letters, sermons, and treatises.[16] In the 1741 sermon "Christian Perfection," Wesley described "in what sense Christians are *not*, and…in what sense they *are*, perfect."[17] For Wesley, Christian perfection did not entail perfection of knowledge or freedom from mistakes, infirmities, and temptations.[18] Positively, Christian perfection brings freedom from outward sin, as well as freedom "from evil thoughts and evil tempers."[19] Toward the end of his 1777 treatise "A Plain Account of Christian Perfection," Wesley summarized his understanding of Christian perfection by considering it from several different angles:

> In one view, it is purity of intention, dedicating all the life to God. It is the giving God all our heart; it is one desire and design ruling all our tempers. It is the devoting, not a part, but all our soul, body, and substance to God. In another view, it is all the mind which was in Christ, enabling us to walk as Christ walked. It is the circumcision of the heart from all filthiness, all inward as well as outward pollution. It is a renewal of the heart in the whole image of God, the full likeness of Him that created it. In yet another, it is the loving God with all our heart, and our neighbour as ourselves. Now, take it in which of these views you please (for there is no material difference) and this is the whole and sole perfection…which I have believed and taught for these forty years, from the year 1725 to the year 1765.[20]

In his sermon "The Scripture Way of Salvation" (1765), Wesley described the four attributes of the faith by which Christians are sanctified or made holy. First, "it is a divine evidence and conviction…that God hath promised it in the Holy Scripture." Second, it is a faith that believes "that what God hath promised he is *able* to perform." Third, it is a faith that is convinced that God "is able and willing to do it *now*." And finally, the faith by which Christians are made perfect in love is a faith that God actually does this.[21]

Further, in the sermon "On Perfection" (1784), Wesley described "salvation from sin, from all sin" as "another description of perfection" that actually "expresses only the least, the lowest branch of it, only the negative part of the great salvation."[22] Wesley continued by chiding those who defended the

---

[16] In the treatise "A Plain Account of Christian Perfection As Believed and Taught by the Reverend Mr. John Wesley, From the Year 1725, to the Year 1777," Wesley insisted that his advocacy of Christian perfection had been consistent. In the treatise, he further defended and defined his understanding of Christian perfection. See Wesley, "A Plain Account of Christian Perfection," in *Works*, Jackson, 11: 366–446. In this essay, Wesley even referred to the "The Character of a Methodist" as "the first tract I ever wrote expressly on this subject." Ibid., 11: 370. This is significant because it is in "The Character of a Methodist" that Wesley conceded that the distinguishing marks of Methodism were "only the common, fundamental principles of Christianity." *Works* 9: 41.

[17] Wesley, "Christian Perfection," in *Works* 2: 100.

[18] Ibid., 2: 100–104.

[19] Ibid., 2: 105–120.

[20] Wesley, "A Plain Account of Christian Perfection," *Works*, Jackson, 11: 444.

[21] Wesley, "The Scripture Way of Salvation," in *Works* 2: 167–168 (emphasis original).

[22] Wesley, "On Perfection," in *Works* 3: 76.

necessity of sin in the Christian life: "In God's name, why are you so fond of sin? What good has it ever done you?...And why are you so violent against those that hope for deliverance from it!"[23] The persistence of holiness and Christian perfection in Wesley's theology has been referred to as "the single most consistent theme in Wesley's thought over the entire span of his ministry....He had been preaching the doctrine [of Christian perfection] in season and out."[24]

The doctrine of Christian perfection, therefore, "is not simply one among others for Wesley...the Methodist house is built of various structural elements...but the house itself is constituted by holiness...perfection is the goal of the Christian life."[25] For Wesley, Christian perfection should be seen as the norm for the Christian life because Wesley was convinced that "this is what God promises. Wesley...is convinced that at the conclusion of the life of grace, saints are the norm and the 'average Christian' is the exception."[26] The consistent emphasis that Wesley placed on the necessity of holiness for the Christian life led him to look for ways to support and promote the Christian's pursuit of holiness. Thus, a key question and concern for Wesley was how best to promote holiness.

"No Holiness but Social Holiness": The Role of Small Group Accountability in Wesleyan Methodism

Wesley's conviction that those who received the gifts of justifying faith and the new birth must grow in holiness led him to join people together to "watch over one another in love."[27] From the "first rise of Methodism" in Oxford in the late

---

[23] Ibid., 86.

[24] Albert C. Outler, "An Introductory Comment" to "On Perfection," in ibid., 70. Wesley explicitly made this argument in "A Plain Account of Christian Perfection" when he summarized the arguments of "The Character of a Methodist" and stated, "This is the very same doctrine which I believe and teach at this day; not adding one point, either to that inward or outward holiness which I maintained eight-and-thirty years ago." *Works*, Jackson, 11: 373. Randy Maddox noted Wesley's claim of consistency in "A Plain Account of Christian Perfection," arguing that "this claim must be taken with some reserve. There was indeed much more continuity in Wesley's teaching than his opponents allowed. However, there had also been more fluctuation of emphasis and nuancing of certain assertions than he was prone to admit overtly in the midst of controversy." Maddox, *Responsible Grace*, 180.

[25] Edgardo A. Colón-Emeric, *Wesley, Aquinas, and Christian Perfection: An Ecumenical Dialogue* (Waco, TX: Baylor University Press, 2009), 11.

[26] Ibid., 55. Colón-Emeric further argued that "The gift of holiness is not something given primarily for the benefit of the individual or the few but for the sake of the community so that no one will settle for a halfhearted pattern of Christian discipleship but will aspire to conformity with Christ. The perfect do not constitute a self-enclosed holy club; they are leaven; they are signs for the church and lights for the world." Ibid., 57.

[27] Wesley, "General Rules," in *Works* 9: 69.

1720s through the end of his life, John Wesley was convinced that holiness was necessarily social and best nurtured in an accountable Christian community.[28] Before turning to the specific aspects of the early Methodist structures for Christian communal formation, the theological rationale for these structures are considered from three different media and three different periods of Wesley's life.[29] The consistent conviction for Wesley was that holiness is social and most reliably formed through small group accountability structures. In each of the following passages, Wesley used stark language to insist upon the importance of communal formation for the Christian life.

The first passage comes from Wesley's preface to the 1739 edition of *Hymns and Sacred Poems*. In the preface, Wesley examined the "commendations...of an entire seclusion from men...in order to purify the soul."[30] Wesley argued that there was a chasm separating "the manner of building up souls in Christ taught by St. Paul, from that taught by the Mystics!...For the religion these authors would edify us in, is solitary religion."[31] This set the stage for Wesley's ringing endorsement of social holiness: "Directly opposite to this is the gospel of Christ. Solitary religion is not to be found there. 'Holy solitaries' is a phrase no more consistent with the gospel than holy adulterers. The gospel of Christ knows of no religion, but social; no holiness but social holiness."[32] Here we have what seems to be an intentionally strong and particularly bold statement from Wesley that not only argues for the importance of community for growth in holiness, but insists that there is no such thing as Christian holiness in isolation. In fact, for Wesley, attempting to become holy in isolation was as likely to be fruitful as attempting to become holy through adultery![33]

---

[28] Wesley, "Short History," in *Works* 9: 430.

[29] Ted A. Campbell argued that the variety of written communication available to scholars of John Wesley provides particular insight into Wesley's life; some of it was written for public consumption, and some of it was strictly private and personal. Campbell wrote, "Taken together, the letters, diaries, and *Journal* of John Wesley offer an unusually rich perspective on the private life of this eighteenth-century figure." Campbell, "John Wesley as diarist and correspondent," 130. The approach taken in this section seeks to take advantage of the variety of ways that Wesley communicated through writing by citing a "Preface" to a published work, a passage from Wesley's published *Journal*, and a private letter. One could also cite numerous references to class meetings, band meetings, and select society meetings from Wesley's private diaries as further support of the value Wesley placed on social holiness.

[30] Wesley, "Preface," *Hymns and Sacred Poems*, 1739, in *Works*, Jackson, 14: 319.

[31] Ibid., 321.

[32] Ibid.

[33] Colón-Emeric explicitly interacted with this quotation in *Wesley, Aquinas, and Christian Perfection*: "No one can grow in the happiness announced in the Beatitudes without the company of others. Without friends and enemies we are deprived of neighbors to love; how then can one attain that holiness without which it is impossible to see the Lord? For this reason Wesley famously states that: 'Holy solitaries' is a phrase no more consistent with the gospel than holy adulterers. The gospel of Christ knows of no religion, but social; no holiness but social holiness.'" Colón-Emeric,

Wesley objected to Christian practices that he felt isolated Christians from one another because he believed that people do not grow in love of God and neighbor by themselves. Here, Wesley was following an instinct that began with his involvement with the Oxford Methodists in 1729.[34]

Admittedly, this first example was from very early in Wesley's leadership of a discernible revival or movement. The question could fairly be asked: Did Wesley *continue* to believe that holiness was best nurtured in the context of communal Christian practice? The second and third examples of Wesley's insistence on the necessity of social holiness came after the benefit of more than two decades of experience as a leader of the Methodist revival. The second example is from an entry in Wesley's *Journal* on August 25, 1763:

> I was more convinced than ever that the preaching like an apostle, without joining together those that are awakened and training them up in the ways of God, is only begetting children for the murderer. How much preaching has there been for these twenty years all over Pembrokeshire! But no *regular societies*, no discipline, no order or connection. And the consequence is that nine in ten of the once awakened are now faster asleep than ever.[35]

When Wesley surveyed the fruits of the ministry of traveling evangelists such as George Whitefield in Pembrokeshire over a period of two decades, he lamented the lack of spiritual vitality that had resulted from such ministry.

Interestingly, Wesley did not seem to be bewildered by the state of the revival in Pembrokeshire. On the contrary, he offered a diagnosis that was simple, blunt, and confident. Those who were awakened were deader than they were previously because those who responded to the gospel were not joined together. With the benefit of more than twenty years of experience as one of the key leaders of the

131. One difficulty with Colón-Emeric's use of this quotation is that he equated it so closely with Wesley's series of sermons on the Sermon on the Mount, when the actual quote occurred in the 1739 "Preface" to Wesley's *Hymns and Sacred Poems*. The context of Wesley's quote is important because it occurred in the midst of Wesley's conflict with Moravians in the Fetter Lane Society who were advocating a more passive approach to the Christian life. Nevertheless, Colón-Emeric's interpretation of this quote, which occurred within the context of a discussion of the Beatitudes, is not at odds with the theological point that Wesley was making. Colón-Emeric wrote, "The Christianity that the Sermon on the Mount proclaims is a social reality. The holy tempers are exercised primarily though not exclusively in the context of love of neighbor; hence Wesley's great dislike of hermits and solitaries...a Christian without a mission is as worthless as salt that has lost its taste." Ibid., 130–131.

34 See chapter 1, "Oxford Methodism."

35 Wesley, *Journal* for August 25, 1763, in *Works* 21: 424 (emphasis original).

broader Methodist revival, Wesley was adamant that if there was "no discipline no order or connection" the result was predictable: Those who were awakened would become more lost than ever before. For Wesley, preaching the gospel without organizing Christians together into small groups would only bring Christians to life so that Satan could destroy them.[36]

The third example of Wesley's insistence on gathering people together for growth in holiness is found in another medium, personal correspondence, that occurred an additional twenty-five years after the previous quotation. In a letter to Edward Jackson on October 24, 1788, Wesley wrote:

> My Dear Brother—I commend you for denying tickets to all that have neglected meeting their classes, unless they seriously promise to meet them for the time to come. You cannot be too exact in this. You do well likewise to exhort all the believers that are in earnest or *would be* in earnest to meet in band. But the bands in every place need continual instruction; for they are continually flying in pieces.[37]

---

[36] Wesley recorded a similar instance of hard work among the preachers, where a lack of revival was connected to the absence of band meetings: "Both this evening and the next, I spoke exceeding plain to the members of the society. In no other place in Ireland has more pains been taken by the most able of our preachers. And to how little purpose! Bands they have none—four and forty persons in the society! The greater part of these heartless and cold, the audience in general dead as stones." *Journal* for April 20, 1769, in *Works* 22: 180. More than a decade later, Wesley recorded a similar conviction regarding the importance of classes and bands for vitality in Methodist societies: "Being informed that through the ill conduct of the preachers things were in much disorder in Colchester, I went down, hoping to 'strengthen the things which remained, that were ready to die.' I found that part of the class-leaders were dead and the rest had left the society; the bands were totally dissolved. Morning preaching was given up, and hardly any, except on Sunday, attended the evening preaching. This evening, however, we had a very large congregation, to whom I proclaimed 'the terrors of the Lord.' I then told them, I would immediately restore the morning preaching. And the next morning, I suppose an hundred attended. In the day-time, I visited as many as I possibly could in all quarters of the town. I then inquired who were proper and willing to meet in band. And who were fittest for leaders, either of bands or classes. The congregation this evening was larger than the last, and many again set their hands to the plough. O may the Lord confirm the fresh desires he has given, that they may no more look back!" *Journal* for January 14, 1782, in *Works* 23: 229. Finally, Wesley's *Journal* recorded an instance of revival because of the discipline of bands: "After preaching at the Foundery in the evening, I met the bands as usual. While a poor woman was speaking a few artless words out of the fullness of her heart, a fire kindled and ran as flame among the stubble, through the hearts of almost all that heard—so when God is pleased to work it matters not how weak or how mean the instrument!" *Journal* for January 30, 1761, in *Works* 21: 301.

[37] Wesley, letter to Edward Jackson, October 24, 1788, in *Letters* (Telford), 8: 98–99 (emphasis original).

Wesley's letter to Edward Jackson is one of many examples where Wesley wrote a personal letter exhorting the recipient to continue providing meticulous oversight of the classes and bands in the Methodist movement.[38] In this particular letter, Wesley pointed to the importance of meeting in bands for all who "are in earnest or *would* be in earnest." He also acknowledged that the bands were difficult to sustain, as they were "continually flying in pieces." Perhaps the most important thing to notice within the context of this letter, however, was that despite the fact that Wesley recognized the difficulty of sustaining the band meeting, he continued to work to encourage people throughout Wesleyan Methodism to use bands, and he struggled to keep them going. For someone who was so often content to use what worked, this suggests that Wesley himself had seen significant fruit from people meeting in bands. When they began to deteriorate, he did not simply move on to something new. Instead, he fought to preserve them.

The key reason for Wesley's continued advocacy of the band meeting was that he believed bands were essential for fostering growth in holiness and helping people to continue moving forward in their lives as Christians. Thus, the society, class, and band meeting (which are explored in the following sections of this chapter) and their continued use in Methodism throughout John Wesley's life demonstrate both the extent to which Wesley believed holiness was central to the Christian life and the reality that he believed holiness was most likely to be encouraged and strengthened through small group structures.

"Watching Over One Another in Love": The Society, Class, and Band Meeting

The society meeting, the class meeting, and the band meeting were the key structures that were intended to bring Wesley's vision for social holiness to life. One of the key documents where Wesley discussed the early Methodist structures of discipleship was "A Plain Account of the People Called Methodists" (1749). One difficulty with this document is that Wesley narrated the development of the various pieces of the Methodist structure as if the narrative described the historical development of these structures, as well as the way that these structures came to cohere in Methodism. In fact, "A Plain Account of the People Called Methodists"

---

[38] See also, e.g., Wesley, letter to John Mason, November 3, 1784, in *Letters* (Telford), 7: 247, where Wesley exhorted Mason to "Get as many as possible to meet in band. Be exact in every part of discipline, and give no ticket to any that does not meet his class weekly." Wesley also insisted that bands were essential to the vitality of societies in a letter to William Simpson. Wesley, letter to William Simpson, April 26, 1788, in *Letters* (Telford), 8: 57: "You should speak to every believer singly concerning meeting in band. There were always some in Yarm Circuit, though not many. No circuit ever did or ever will flourish unless there are bands in the large Societies."

did not provide an accurate chronology of the appearance of the various parts of the Methodist approach to Christian communal formation.[39] The inaccurate chronology also obscured the sources and influences of these structures. Nevertheless, the essay does provide insight into John Wesley's self-conscious presentation of the importance of the society, class, and band structures.

Parsing the chronological development of the various parts of the early Methodist structures for Christian communal formation with precision is difficult for a number of reasons. First, as mentioned, in John Wesley's own writing, the chronology was often inaccurate. When Wesley narrated the early developments of Methodism in an essay, he typically discussed the evolution of Methodism in a way that described its logical organization, rather than its chronological development. Thus, while documents such as "A Plain Account of the People Called Methodists" and "Thoughts upon Methodism" do provide helpful historical details about the beginnings of the societies, classes, and bands in early Methodism, these documents do not accurately describe the way these meetings actually came to be a part of early Methodism. Such writings also give the appearance that Wesley was always the key actor in the Methodist movement, often obscuring the sources and prior influences on which he depended. Nevertheless, in the development of the various pieces of the early Methodist structures of mutual support and accountability, Wesley drew both from sources he knew and sources that were relatively new to him in order to "spread scriptural holiness."

The Society Meeting

It is difficult to clearly differentiate the various Religious Societies that existed during the late 1730s, particularly the ones that John Wesley had some knowledge of or direct involvement in. The previous chapter showed that Wesley's development of the concept of a religious society as a gathering place for Methodists to "encourage each other in practical holiness" was an example of Wesley's drawing from sources that he was familiar with, namely the Anglican Religious Societies.[40]

---

[39] The most significant instance of inaccurate chronology for the purposes of this work occurred in Wesley's narration of the development of the class and band meetings. In "A Plain Account of the People Called Methodists," Wesley described the class meeting as preceding the band meeting. In this account, the bands arose as a result of people in classes wanting "some means of closer union," which was clearly not the case. See Wesley, "Plain Account," in *Works* 9: 266. The development of the band meeting is further discussed in the section "The Band Meeting" in this chapter.

[40] Quotation from Woodward, 121. See chapter 1, "Anthony Horneck and the Anglican Religious Societies." John Walsh also argued that "Some of the major techniques of the Revival...the consolidation of converts into small societies in which they could relate their spiritual experiences—these were features of the Welsh movement two or three years before they were adopted by Whitefield and Wesley in England." Walsh, "Origins of the Evangelical Revival," in *Essays in Modern English Church History: In Memory of Norman Sykes*, eds., G. V. Bennett and J. D. Walsh (New York: Oxford University Press, 1966), 134.

An account of Wesley's involvement with Religious Societies could begin at many places. For example, Wesley was present when the Fetter Lane Society was founded on May 1, 1738.[41] Nevertheless, the focus here is on the development of the society meeting as a *distinctly Wesleyan* piece of the early Methodist structures for discipleship. As the previous chapter noted, the questions of the identity (Moravian or Anglican?) and leadership (Peter Böhler, John Wesley, James Hutton, or Philipp Heinrich Molther?) of the Fetter Lane Society are contested.[42] Wesley was both a participant and, at least in some sense, a leader at Fetter Lane. However, Fetter Lane cannot ultimately be seen as distinctly Wesleyan as there were other key influences there, and Wesley's break from the group indicated that he was not ultimately able to persuade the membership of the Fetter Lane Society that his approach to Christian life and theology was correct.

And yet, Wesley was a person of some influence in the Fetter Lane Society. He formally broke with the Fetter Lane Society on July 20, 1740, by reading a statement that concluded: "I have borne with you long, hoping you would return. But as I find you more and more confirmed in the error of your ways, nothing now remains but that I should give you up to God. You that are of the same judgment, follow me."[43] Wesley's influence is further seen because eighteen or nineteen people left with him after he read his statement.[44] A few days later, he further recorded in his *Journal*: "Our little company met at the Foundery instead of Fetter Lane. About twenty-five of our brethren God hath given us already, all of whom think and speak the same thing; seven or eight and forty likewise of the fifty women that were in band desired to cast in their lot with us."[45]

The Foundery Society, then, was the first place where John and Charles Wesley were the key leaders, and as such, it can be seen to have been the first Wesleyan Methodist Society.[46] What happened at the Foundery Society? What were its key activities? What was it like to be involved in the life of this society?

---

[41] On Wesley's involvement in the founding of the Fetter Lane Society and other points of contact with Anglican Religious Societies, see chapter 1, esp. "Anthony Horneck and the Anglican Religious Societies," "Oxford Methodism," and "The Fetter Lane Society."

[42] See chapter 1, "The Fetter Lane Society."

[43] Wesley, *Journal* for July 20, 1740, in *Works* 19: 162. This occasion marked the end of a longer period of disagreement between Wesley and some of the advocates of stillness within the Fetter Lane Society. For a summary of this conflict, see Heitzenrater, *Wesley and the People Called Methodists*, 109–112.

[44] Wesley recorded the entirety of the paper he read in his *Journal*, with the following editorial comment: "I then, without saying anything more, withdrew, as did eighteen or nineteen of the society." *Works* 19: 162.

[45] Wesley, *Journal* for July 23, 1740, in *Works* 19: 163.

[46] Of course, there were previous places where the Wesleys were key leaders, such as among the Oxford Methodists and in their work as missionaries in Georgia. In this section, I focus on the Foundery Society because it is at this stage that the society, class, and band structure that would be distinctive of Wesleyan Methodism began to come together and when people were consciously

In "A Plain Account of the People Called Methodists," John Wesley described the beginning of the Foundery Society. The immediate events that led to the formation of the society, in this account, were John and his brother Charles Wesley preaching "in many parts of London" where they tried "to *convince* those who would hear what true Christianity was, and to *persuade* them to embrace it."[47] When people responded to the Wesleys' understanding of "true Christianity," they were "immediately... surrounded with difficulties."[48] People then began coming to Wesley "asking what they should do" because they were "distressed on every side, as everyone strove to weaken, and none to strengthen their hands in God."[49] John Wesley reported that he and his brother's advice was "Strengthen you one another. Talk together as often as you can. And pray earnestly with and for one another, that you may endure to the end and be saved."[50] Those who had been newly awakened, however, wanted the Wesleys to be more immediately involved. Wesley recorded the events that led to the creation of the first Wesleyan society as follows:

> They said, "But we want *you* likewise to talk with us often, to direct and quicken us in our way, to give us the advices which you well know we need, and to pray with us, as well as for us." I asked, Which of you desires this? Let me know your names and places of abode. They did so. But I soon found, they were too many for me to talk with severally so often as they wanted it. So I told them, "If you will all of you come together every Thursday, in the evening, I will gladly spend some time with you in prayer, and give you the best advice I can."
>
> Thus arose, without any previous design on either side, what was afterwards called a *Society*—a very innocent name, and very common in London for any number of people *associating* themselves together[51]

aligning themselves with the Wesleys in the face of conflict. An argument could also be made that the societies in Bristol came before and were thus the first distinctly Wesleyan societies. The difficulty with viewing the societies in Bristol as the first Wesleyan societies is that George Whitefield was the instigator of those societies and the primary authority until he invited Wesley to take over the leadership before his departure for Georgia. See Whitefield, letter to John Wesley, March 22, 1739, in *Works* 25: 611–612. For an argument that the Foundery was the first Methodist society, see T. McCullagh, "The First Methodist Society: The Date and Place of its Origin," in *PWHS* 3 (privately published, 1902): 166–172. More than thirty years later, Frederic Platt responded to the McCullagh article in "The First Methodist Society: The Date and Place of Its Origin," in *PWHS* 22 (privately published, 1939–1940): 155–164. John S. Simon pointed out that McCullagh had missed Wesley's *Journal* entry for December 24, 1739, in his argument. See Simon, *John Wesley and the Religious Societies*, 329.

[47] Wesley, "Plain Account," in *Works* 9: 254 (emphasis original).
[48] Ibid., 9: 255.
[49] Ibid., 9: 256.
[50] Ibid.
[51] Ibid (emphasis original). This account falls short of being an accurate historical account of the beginnings of the Foundery, particularly because the desire to come together seems to have spontaneously arisen, independent of any prior structure or organization.

In this passage, Wesley alluded to his dependence on the Anglican Religious Societies by noting that the term "Society" was "very common in London for any number of people *associating* themselves together." As Wesley's account of the first society continued, he described its goal—which "was obvious to everyone"—they "wanted to flee from the wrath to come."[52]

Another key source for the activities of the Foundery Society is John Wesley's *Journal*, which frequently mentioned events and occurrences at the Foundery. Wesley referred to a meeting at the Foundery in his *Journal* on July 23, 1740, which was three days after his formal separation from the Fetter Lane Society.[53] According to the editors of Wesley's *Journal*, Wesley "had occupied the Foundery since Nov. 11, 1739, when the separation [from the Fetter Lane Society], one stage of which is here noted, began to seem inevitable."[54] Thus, when Wesley formally separated from the Fetter Lane Society, a critical mass of people was already meeting at the Foundery Society, which was increased by those who left Fetter Lane with Wesley and joined the Foundery Society. Thus, even prior to the class meeting and the division of the societies into classes around 1743, the societies often fulfilled some of the functions of "watching over one another in love" that the classes and bands most clearly served after 1743.

In the explicit references to the Foundery Society in Wesley's *Journal*, the most frequent activity that Wesley mentioned was preaching.[55] His *Journal* also mentioned that prayer occurred in the context of these services, as well as the

---

[52] Ibid (emphasis original). One of the difficulties with Wesley's account of the "People Called Methodists" is that it was written as if it were a straightforward, chronological account of the beginnings of the Methodist movement. However, at a number of points, the chronology of "A Plain Account of the People Called Methodists" is inaccurate or misleading. E.g., in the passages that have just been cited, Wesley appeared to be discussing the events that led to the creation of the Foundery Society, which was established in London in late 1739. In this discussion, Wesley quoted directly from the "General Rules," which were not written until 1743. As the account continued, Wesley also presented the class meeting as a development of the need for increased discipline in the societies and the bands as coming into existence in order to meet the needs of members of classes who had been justified by faith and had "peace with God, through our Lord Jesus Christ" [quoting Romans 5:1] and "wanted some means of closer union." Ibid., 9: 266. However, Wesley himself first joined a band meeting in May, 1738. (See Wesley, *Journal* for May 1, 1738, in *Works* 18: 236. Part of this entry reads: "This evening our little society began, which afterwards met in Fetter Lane. Our fundamental rules were as follows ... 1. That we will meet together once a week to 'confess our faults one to another, and pray for one another that we may be healed.'") From the point of his own involvement in bands, Wesley consistently organized people involved in the Methodist movement into bands. From 1738 to February 1742, Methodists could join the society, with the bands being optional for the more serious members. The class meeting was not created until February 15, 1742. See Wesley, *Journal* for February 15, 1742, in *Works* 19: 251. See also the section on "The Class Meeting" in this chapter.

[53] Wesley, *Journal* for July 23, 1740, in *Works* 19: 163.

[54] *Works* 19: 163, fn. 38.

[55] See Wesley, *Journal*, 19: 196, 206; 20: 108, 487; 21: 135, 377, 403, 487; 22: 64, 303, 359; 23: 50.

reading of Scripture.[56] From Wesley's accounts, it appears that one of the key functions of the Foundery Society was corporate worship. At regular periods, the early Methodists would gather to read Scripture, hear a sermon, and pray. Singing hymns also became a predictable part of the worship service.

Beyond the activities of a worship service, there were several other activities that commonly occurred at the Foundery Society. One example was the watch-night. Wesley recorded one instance of a watch-night in his *Journal*, when a woman who intended to drown herself in a river heard singing as she walked by the Foundery when a watch-night was occurring. When the woman heard people singing, "she stopped and went in; she listened a while, and God spoke to her heart. She had no more desire to put an end to her life, but to die to sin and live to God."[57] Watch-nights were a common occurrence at the Foundery. Wesley summarized the first watch-night that was held in London on April 9, 1742, in his *Journal*:

> We had the first watch-night in London. We commonly choose for this solemn service the Friday night nearest the full moon, either before or after, that those of the congregation who live at a distance may have light to their several homes. The service begins at half an hour past eight and continues till a little after midnight. We have often found a peculiar blessing at these seasons. There is generally a deep awe upon the congregation, perhaps in some measure owing to the silence of the night; particularly in singing the hymn with which we commonly conclude:
>
> Hearken to the solemn voice!
>   The awful midnight cry!
> Waiting souls, rejoice, rejoice,
>   And feel the Bridegroom nigh.[58]

The activities that have been discussed so far within the context of the Foundery Society also occurred in the other Wesleyan Methodist societies. For example, when Wesley discussed the watch-night in "A Plain Account of the People Called Methodists," he specifically noted that the watch-night was continued "once a month...in Bristol, London, and Newcastle, as well as Kingswood."[59] The description that has been given thus far of the Foundery Society, then, was generally representative of a typical Wesleyan Methodist society.

---

[56] See Wesley, *Journal*, 19: 179; and diary, 19: 417.

[57] Wesley, *Journal* for September 28, 1747, in *Works* 20: 194.

[58] Wesley, *Journal* for April 9, 1742, in *Works* 19: 258–259. On the watch-night, see also Wesley, "Plain Account," in *Works* 9: 264–265.

[59] Ibid., 9: 264.

Another activity that was a common occurrence in Wesleyan Methodist societies was the love-feast, which was adopted from John Wesley's experience with the Moravians. Wesley recorded in his *Journal* on January 1, 1739, that "Mr. Hall, Kinchin, Ingham, Whitefield, Hutchings, and my brother Charles were present at our love-feast in Fetter Lane, with about sixty of our brethren."[60] The love-feast was a time when people shared their experiences of God. In one passage from his *Journal*, Wesley described the introduction of a love-feast to Methodists in Birstall, which was "the first of the kind which had been there."[61] Wesley recorded that "Many were surprised when I told them, 'The very design of a love-feast is a free and familiar conversation, in which every man, yea, and woman, has liberty to speak whatever may be to the glory of God.' "[62]

Evidently Wesley's explicit permission for women to speak was taken seriously, as he recorded that "Several then did speak, and not in vain: the flame ran from heart to heart. Especially while one was declaring with all simplicity the manner wherein God, during the morning sermon...had set her soul at full liberty."[63] The primary purpose of the love-feast, then, was glorifying God by giving testimony to how the Holy Spirit had been at work in one's life. At the love-feast Wesley wrote about in his *Journal* in 1761, the goals of glorifying God and giving testimony to the Spirit's work were evidently met. After the woman testified to her soul being set at "full liberty," Wesley wrote that "two men also spoke to the same effect, and two others who had found peace with God. We then joyfully poured out our souls before God and praised him for his marvellous works."[64]

The love-feast was another example of the way that Wesley saw community as key to fostering love of God and neighbor. Indeed, Wesley often spoke of the love-feast as a place where God's grace became contagious and spread from one person to another. This is illustrated by a passage from Wesley's *Journal* in February 1750 where Wesley recorded: "The honest simplicity with which several spoke, in declaring the manner of God's dealings with them, set the hearts of others on fire, and the flame spread more and more, till, having stayed near an hour longer than usual, we were constrained to part."[65]

Two other activities that were periodic occurrences of the Wesleyan Methodist societies were public fasts and Covenant Renewal Services. Public fast days

---

[60] Wesley, *Journal* for January 1, 1739, in *Works* 19:29; and diary for January 1, 1739, in *Works* 19: 369.

[61] Wesley, *Journal* for July 19, 1761, in *Works* 21: 336.

[62] Ibid.

[63] Ibid.

[64] Ibid.

[65] Wesley, *Journal* for February 18, 1750, in *Works* 20: 321. For more on the love-feast, see also Wesley, *Journal*, 19: 192; 21: 309, 344, 406; 23: 342–343; 24: 165, 190; and "Plain Account," in *Works* 9: 267–268.

were set by the Church of England and were observed by Methodists.[66] Wesley frequently recorded that attendance was particularly large in the Methodist societies when he preached at the public fast services, and he often expressed confidence that such a large and serious group of believers crying out to God would succeed in getting God's attention. A representative example is Wesley's *Journal* entry for February 6, 1756: "The Fast Day was a glorious day.... Every church in the city was more than full, and a solemn seriousness sat on every face. Surely God heareth that prayer, and there will yet be 'a lengthening of our tranquility.'"[67]

The Covenant Renewal Service involved a corporate commitment whereby people covenanted to serve God "with all our heart and with all our soul."[68] Wesley first mentioned the service in his *Journal* in 1747 when he recorded that on "Both this and the following days I strongly urged the wholly giving up ourselves to God and renewing in every point our covenant that the Lord should be our God."[69] In 1755, Wesley further encouraged Methodists to undertake this practice.[70] In "A Short History of the People Called Methodists" (1781), Wesley summarized the 1755 Covenant Renewal Service:

> I mentioned to our congregation in London a means of increasing serious religion, which had been frequently practised by our forefathers, the joining in a *covenant* to serve God with all our heart and with all our soul. I explained this for several mornings following, and on Friday many of us kept a fast unto the Lord, beseeching him to give us wisdom and strength, that we might "promise unto the Lord our God and keep it." On Monday at six in the evening we met for that purpose, at the French church in Spitalfields. After I had recited the tenor of the covenant proposed, in the words of that blessed man, Richard Alleine, all the people stood up, in token of assent, to the number of about eighteen hundred. Such a night I scarce ever knew before. Surely the fruit of it shall remain for ever.[71]

From an institutional perspective, the Wesleyan societies were the hub of early Methodism in particular localities. Methodists were divided into classes

---

[66] For references to public fasts that the Methodists observed, see Wesley, *Journal*, in *Works* 19: 180; 20: 23, 108; 21: 41, 135, 177–178, 247, 352; 23: 39, 117, 160, 193.

[67] Wesley, *Journal* for February 6, 1756, in *Works* 21: 41.

[68] Wesley, "Short History," in *Works* 9: 461.

[69] Wesley, *Journal* for December 25, 1747, in *Works* 20: 203.

[70] See Wesley, *Journal* for August 6, 1755, in *Works* 21: 23.

[71] Wesley, "Short History," in *Works* 9: 461. According to Frederick Hunter in an article in *PWHS*, "The Covenant Service was held on New Year's Day in 1748, and 1766, and each year from 1770 to 1778 except 1774... from 1782 onwards Wesley held it on the first Sunday in the year." See Hunter, "The Origins of Wesley's Covenant Service," in *PWHS* 22 (1939–40): 129.

and bands based on their membership in a particular society, and these meetings often met where the society met. A document that provides particularly
insightful information into the happenings of the Foundery Society is a letter
that Hannah Ball wrote to Patty Chapman describing activities related to the
Foundery Society in August 1776. The letter mentioned activities that occurred
at other Wesleyan Methodist societies, the West Street Chapel, in particular.
Because of the value of this letter for understanding the early Methodist societies, it is worth quoting at some length:

> The first night I was in London I went to a prayer meeting at west street
> chapil the next morning at six meet Molly Rockalls band ware I found
> one precious Soul intirily given up to god I felt my spirit united to her
> at the first interview they Rest was young in the ways of god. after that
> I had a Coach & went to the foundrey Mr Wesley preach'd from thees
> words "wherefore let him that thinketh he standeth; take heed lest he
> fall" the discourse was Very excellent & Very encouraging to me I Could
> only adore with silent adoration the god that brought me there after
> sarmont the Sacrament was gave to a great number of Communicants
> then I went to Mr parkinsons to dine after that to the foundrey again
> & had an opportunity of being present when Mr wesley meet the leders
> of the bands & Classes he allso baptis'd a woman I was glad to be pres-
> ent.... After that I hard him preach in Morefield to a Very great multi-
> tude the sun was Very hot & I was much futaged after that we Returned
> to the foundray ware was a genrall love-feast it was Very full & hot but
> a Refreshing season.... [Tuesday] was not able to Rise in the morning
> without doing my Self hurt so Rested untill after noon then went to
> the foundrey and hard Mr Wesley preach again & found it good to be
> there.... Thursday [heard] Mr Wesley again at the foundrey afterward
> meet in the bands and spoke my Experience went home with a glad
> heart I meet in one Class ware I was inabled to testify the goodness of
> god with out fear & found my Soul much blest a Friday there was a fast
> keep I went to the foundrey at nine & at one then the sacrament was
> gave.... Saturday morning I hard Mr. Mather from these words Blessed
> are the pure in heart for they shall See god. the discourse was food to my
> Soul. Sunday morning at six I meet Molly Rockall's band again.... Mr
> Wesley Read prayers & preach'd & gave the Sacrament after it was over
> pray'd Extempray & Mr Charles Wesley after him he was Very Excelent
> in prayer I was much pleased to see him. He looks a very gracious man.
> In the afternoon I had the privilege thro a friend to be a fue moments
> with Mr John Wesley alone which encouraged me much he ask how you
> did but did not say any thing about your not writing to him I had hear
> also an opportunity to meet with the Leders of bands & Classes his

brother Read prayers & he preach'd again after that meet the Sorcity & then tuck his leve giving the hymn book to Mr Mather to sing a fue Virces for him hear I Could but drop a tear being much affected....[72]

From Wesley's *Journal* and Hannah Ball's letter, the general contours of the early Methodist societies can be seen. The societies were a place where Methodists gathered together to worship God through prayer, reading Scripture, hearing a sermon, and singing hymns. The society was the particular layer of organization where multiple opportunities were provided for Methodists to gather together in order to encourage one another to continue growing in holiness. Watch-nights, love-feasts, public fasts, and Covenant Services were all oriented toward fostering love of God and neighbor. And all of these activities occurred within the context of community. As the Methodist movement grew and developed, in order to ensure that every Methodist was connected to others and that all were seeking to become more holy, the membership of each Methodist society was divided into class meetings.

The Class Meeting

Of the three key pieces of early Methodism's approach to discipleship through communal formation, the class meeting is the only one that was an original contribution of Methodism.[73] Scholars have described the basic function or purpose of the class meeting in various ways. David Lowes Watson, the most influential interpreter of the class meeting, has described the "essential purpose of the

---

[72] Hannah Ball, letter to Patty [Martha] Chapman, August 16, 1776, in Ball manuscript letter book, MAM, Ref: PLP 4/32.1.13 (spelling and punctuation as in the original; my transcription). Parts of this letter are quoted in *Works* 23: 25–26, fn. 12. The citation in *Works* referenced a published version of the letter from *The Methodist Recorder* (London, 1897), 1026.

[73] There are, however, several precedents for the name itself, as there were classes in the Moravian approach to communal formation, with which Wesley was familiar. See Wesley's description of Moravian life at Herrnhut in his *Journal* for August 11–14, 1738, in *Works* 18: 294–297, esp. 295. On the Presbyterian forerunners of the Methodist classes, see David Lowes Watson, "The Origins and Significance of the Early Methodist Class Meeting" (Ph.D. diss., Duke University, 1978), 143–145. Among the societies, classes, and bands, the class meeting has received the most focused scholarly attention. See Watson, Ph.D. diss.; and *The Early Methodist Class Meeting* (published version). See also William Walter Dean, "Disciplined Fellowship: The Rise and Decline of Cell Groups in British Methodism" (Ph.D. diss., University of Iowa, 1985); D. Michael Henderson, *A Model for Making Disciples: John Wesley's Class Meeting* (Nappanee, IN: Francis Asbury Press, 1997); and Goodhead, *A Crown and a Cross.* Two studies that focused primarily on the class meeting in American Methodism are David Francis Holsclaw, "The Demise of Disciplined Christian Fellowship: The Methodist Class Meeting in Nineteenth-Century America" (Ph.D. diss., University of California, Davis, 1979); and Philip F. Hardt, *The Soul of Methodism: The Class Meeting in Early New York City Methodism* (Lanham, MD: University Press of America, 2000). For a consideration of the relevance of Wesleyan communal formation for church renewal, see Howard A. Snyder, *The Radical Wesley and Patterns for Church Renewal* (Eugene, OR: Wipf and Stock, 1996).

class meeting" as "discipleship, the dynamic of the church's distinctive function in history."[74] The class meeting was developed as the result of a conversation about how to pay off the debt related to the building constructed for meetings of the societies in Bristol, called the New Room. Wesley summarized the meeting in his *Journal* on February 15, 1742:

> Many met together to consult on a proper method for discharging the public debt. And it was at length agreed (1) that every member of the society who was able should contribute a penny a week; (2) that the whole society should be divided into little companies or classes, about twelve in each class; and (3) that one person in each class should receive the weekly contribution of the rest and bring it in to the stewards weekly.[75]

In this entry, it is not entirely clear who articulated this approach to retiring the debt, or how it was agreed upon. What is clear, however, is that it was not John Wesley's creation. The only place where Wesley revealed the identity of the person responsible for the class system was in "Thoughts upon Methodism," which Wesley wrote more than forty years after the events themselves. Wesley's summary of the initial development of the class meeting revealed that it was Captain Foy who proposed the financial scheme for retiring the Bristol New Room debt.[76] Wesley's account of the origins of the class meeting and Foy's involvement provided a fairly concise summary of the class meeting's initial development:

> But when a large number of people was joined, the great difficulty was to keep them together. For they were continually scattering hither and thither, and we knew no way to help it. But God provided for this also, when we thought not of it. A year or two after Mr. Wesley met the chief of the society in Bristol, and inquired, "How shall we pay the debt upon the preaching-house?" Captain Foy stood up and said, "Let everyone in the society give a penny a week and it will easily be done." "But many of them," said one, "have not a penny to give." "True," said the captain, "then put ten or twelve of them to me. Let each of these give what they can weekly, and I will supply what is wanting." Many others made the same offer. So Mr. Wesley divided the societies among them; assigning a *Class* of about twelve persons to each of these, who were termed *Leaders*.[77]

According to Wesley's version of events, though he may not have been the author of the class meeting itself, he did give himself credit for being the one

---

[74] Watson, Ph.D. diss., 15.

[75] Wesley, *Journal* for February 15, 1742, in *Works* 19: 251.

[76] For speculation on the possible identity of Captain Foy, see J. H. Foster, "Bristol Notes," in *PWHS* 3 (1901): 64–65.

[77] Wesley, "Thoughts upon Methodism," in *Works* 9: 528 (emphasis original).

who recognized the usefulness of the class meeting for "watching over the souls of their brethren."[78] Thus, in "Thoughts upon Methodism," Wesley not only revealed Captain Foy's role in conceiving of classes, but he also staked his own claim to being the founder of the class meeting as a means of communal discipline within Methodism. Wesley continued:

> Not long after, one of these [a class leader] informed Mr. Wesley that calling on such an one in his house he found him quarrelling with his wife. Another was found in drink. It immediately struck into Mr. Wesley's mind, This is the very thing we wanted. The *leaders* are the persons who may not only receive the contributions, but also watch over the souls of their brethren. The society in London being informed of this, willingly followed the example of that in Bristol. As did every society from that time, whether in Europe or America. By this means it was easily found if any grew weary or faint, and help was speedily administered. And if any walked disorderly, they were quickly discovered, and either amended or dismissed.[79]

The class meeting, which was initially intended to be a means to retire a debt, evolved to become the key form of Christian communal formation in Wesleyan Methodism. The class meeting would come to be of such significance that it was viewed as fundamental to Methodist identity, becoming a basic requirement for membership in Methodism for decades. Ultimately, every Wesleyan Methodist society was divided into classes so that every member belonged to a weekly class meeting.[80]

The adoption of the class meeting throughout Methodism occurred quite quickly. Wesley recorded the initial development of the class meeting in his *Journal* on February 15, 1742. Just over a month later, on March 25, 1742, Wesley mentioned the beginning of class meetings in London:

> I appointed several earnest and sensible men to meet me, to whom I showed the great difficulty I had long found of knowing the people who desired to be under my care. After much discourse, they all agreed there could be no better way to come to a sure, thorough knowledge of each person, than to divide them into classes like those at Bristol, under the inspection of those in whom I could most confide. This was the origin of our classes at London,

---

[78] Ibid., 9: 529.

[79] Ibid., 9: 528–529 (emphasis original).

[80] Frank Baker noted that "the allocation of classes ignored differences of age and sex, and was based chiefly on topographical considerations." Baker, "Polity," 222. David Lowes Watson noted that classes "were divided…pragmatically, according to the topography of the society membership and the exigencies of available leadership." Watson, *The Early Methodist Class Meeting*, 94. William Walter Dean noted that "classes may have been theoretically composed of Methodists in the same geographical location." However, Dean argued that "the evidence suggests that many, perhaps most, were formed along lines of common interests." Dean, 274.

for which I can never sufficiently praise God; the unspeakable usefulness of the institution having ever since been more and more manifest.[81]

Seven years later, in "A Plain Account of the People Called Methodists," Wesley elaborated on the events that occurred in Bristol:

> 3. At length, while we were thinking of quite another thing, we struck upon a method for which we have cause to bless God ever since. I was talking with several of the society in Bristol concerning the means of paying the debts there, when one stood up and said, "Let every member of the society give a *penny* a week till all are paid." Another answered, "But many of them are poor, and cannot afford to do it." "Then," said he, "put eleven of the poorest with me, and if they can give anything, well. I will call on them weekly, and if they can give nothing, I will give for them as well as for myself. And each of you, call on eleven of your neighbours weekly; receive what they give, and make up what is wanting." It was done. In a while some of these informed me, they found such and such an one did not live as he ought. It struck me immediately. "This is the thing, the very thing we have wanted so long." I called together all the *Leaders* of the *Classes* (so we used to term them and their companies), and desired that each would make a particular inquiry into the behaviour of those whom he saw weekly. They did so. Many disorderly walkers were detected. Some turned from the evil of their ways. Some were put away from us. Many saw it with fear, and rejoiced unto God with reverence.
>
> 4. As soon as possible the same method was used in London and all other places. Evil men were detected, and reproved. They were borne with for a season. If they forsook their sins, we received them gladly; if they obstinately persisted therein, it was openly declared that they were not of us. The rest mourned and prayed for them, and yet rejoiced that, as far as in us lay, the scandal was rolled away from the Society.
>
> 5. It is the business of the Leader
>> (1) To see each person in his class once a week at the least; in order
>>   To inquire how their souls prosper;
>>   To advise, reprove, comfort, or exhort, as occasion may require.
>>   To receive what they are willing to give toward the relief of the poor.
>> (2) To meet the Minister and the stewards of the Society in order:
>>   To inform the minister of any that are sick, or of any that are disorderly and will not be reproved.
>>   To pay to the stewards what they have received of their several classes in the week preceding.[82]

---

[81] Wesley, *Journal* for March 25, 1742, in *Works* 19: 258.
[82] Wesley, "Plain Account," in *Works* 9: 260–261 (emphasis original).

Of particular interest in this passage is the description of the "business" of the class leader. The responsibilities of the class leader relating to her class were the same as they appeared in the "General Rules," which were published six years before "A Plain Account." However, the order of these responsibilities was different. In "A Plain Account," spiritual conversation about how each person's "soul prospers" was moved to the beginning and was followed by the class leader's role of offering advice, reproval, comfort, or exhortation as was needed based on each person's revelation of the state of their soul. The responsibility of receiving contributions toward the "relief of the poor" was moved to the end, whereas it was the first thing listed in the "General Rules." These changes are significant because the class meeting was originally created as a way to raise money. The reordering of the role of the class leader suggests that the leaders had come to be valued primarily for the role they played as spiritual directors, rather than as financial stewards, though both roles continued to be played by class leaders.

In Wesley's discussion of the class meeting, there are two themes that he typically highlighted: the maintenance of a basic standard of discipline and growth in holiness through Christian communal formation.[83] The immediate advantage of the class meeting was that the class system enabled Methodist discipline to be extended at a time when the Methodist movement was growing and becoming

---

[83] David Lowes Watson has further described the purpose of the class meeting to consist of "accountability for the basics of Christian discipleship—the means of grace and the works of obedience—without which no genuine progress could be made in the Christian life. It was precisely such an accountability which the class meeting sought to foster." Watson, *Early Methodist Class Meeting*, 122–123. Contrary to Watson's account, Andrew C. Thompson has recently argued that "the available evidence of the class meeting's purpose and significance, from Wesley and others, does not simply offer report after report of class members holding one another accountable for weekly faithful living. It rather consists of firsthand testimonies that the class was a practice where certain God-given goods were realized in the lives of class members through common aims and in the course of shared activity. They desired salvation, and for them the class became a preparatory forum for justification and a facilitative vehicle for sanctification." Andrew C. Thompson, "'To Stir Them up to Believe, Love, Obey'—Soteriological Dimensions of the Class Meeting in Early Methodism," *Methodist History* 48:3 (2010), 176–177. William Dean, in his Ph.D. dissertation, argued that Watson "did not miss the disciplinary purpose of the class meeting, but he over-emphasized the place of fellowship." Dean, 178. Instead, Dean argued that "the discipline of the class meeting set the stage for fellowship, initially in the class meeting, ultimately in the band meeting and the lovefeast." Ibid., 180. D. Michael Henderson considered the class meeting from an educational perspective and described it as focused primarily on "behavioral change." Henderson, 93. Andrew Goodhead has argued that the class meeting "created a distinct identity amongst the Methodist people ensuring the class was the crown of Methodism." Goodhead, 180. Goodhead's primary contribution to scholarship about the class meeting was that the class meeting was necessarily a "one-generational" group that could not have lasted beyond the first generation. Thus he argued that "Methodism could not escape Weber's routinization, Durkheim's totemism, or Troeltsch's mysticism/sect models. I use Troeltsch to show that the class meeting was a 'one-generational' model." Goodhead, 197. It is beyond the scope of this work to assess these claims, but at first glance, Goodhead's reductionist account of the class meeting seems suspect, as does the neatness with which the class meeting fits three different sociological models.

large enough that John Wesley could not guarantee quality control among the members of the Methodist movement by himself.[84] The new class system allowed for a form of discipline that Wesley valued but could not effectively institute in a Methodist movement that was rapidly changing and growing in the 1740s.[85] Wesley described the disciplinary function of the class meeting in a passage in his *Journal* from March 1747:

> I had been often told it was impossible for me to distinguish the precious from the vile, without the miraculous discernment of spirits. But I now saw, more clearly than ever, that this might be done and without much difficulty, supposing only two things: first, courage and steadiness in the examiner; secondly, common sense and common honesty in the leader of each class. I visit, for instance, the class in the Close, of which Robert Peacock is leader. I ask, "Does this and this person in your class live in drunkenness or any outward sin? Does he go to church, and use the other means of grace? Does he meet you as often as he has opportunity?" Now if Robert Peacock has common sense, he *can* answer these questions truly, and if he has common honesty, he will. And if not, some other in the class has both, and can and will answer for him. Where is the difficulty then of finding out if there be any disorderly walker in this class? And, consequently, if any other? The question is not concerning the heart, but the life. And the general tenor of this I do not say cannot be *known*, but cannot be *hid*, without a miracle.[86]

---

[84] The way that this discipline was visibly expressed was through class tickets that were issued quarterly. The use of tickets to "fence" the society actually preceded the advent of the class meeting. Wesley first mentioned the use of tickets in order to avoid the continued presence of "disorderly walkers" in the "United Society" at a meeting of the bands in Bristol in February 1742. See Wesley, *Journal* for February 24, 1742, in *Works* 19: 183–184. Rupert E. Davies, in his "introduction" to vol. 9 of *Works* suggested that this point was debatable, pointing to an article in *PWHS*. See *Works* 9: 12; and John H. Verney, "Early Wesleyan Class Tickets: Comments and Catalogue," in *PWHS* 31 (1957): 2–9, 15, 34–38, 70–73. David Lowes Watson summarized the use of class tickets in *Early Methodist Class Meeting*, appendix H, 208.

[85] As previously mentioned, William Walter Dean made a distinction between "class discipline and band fellowship" arguing that David Lowes Watson overemphasized the place of fellowship in classes. Dean, 178. I believe that Dean made too much of this distinction, and that the class meeting was both a place of discipline and fellowship. Or, to put it differently, the class meeting was a place where certain outward rules were expected to be kept, but these rules were intended to usher the members of the class closer to the presence of the living God. Dean's categories downplayed one of the key functions of the class leader, which was inquiring how the soul of each person in their class "prospers" every week. See Wesley, "General Rules," in *Works* 9: 70. This question was not focused solely on outward rules, but was rather focused on the state of the person's relationship to God.

[86] Wesley, *Journal* for March 8, 1747, in *Works* 20: 162–163 (emphasis original).

In other words, Wesley believed that the class meeting was helpful because it provided a straightforward way of ensuring that Methodists were not living in open sin and that they were practicing the means of grace.

The purpose of the class meeting, however, was not only to ensure that Methodists were not hypocrites. In "A Plain Account of the People Called Methodists," Wesley placed the primary emphasis elsewhere:

> It can scarce be conceived what advantages have been reaped from this little prudential regulation. Many now happily experienced that Christian fellowship of which they had not so much as an idea before. They began to "bear one another's burdens," and "naturally" to "care for each other." As they had daily a more intimate acquaintance with, so they had a more endeared affection for each other. And "speaking the truth in love, they grew up into him in all things which is the head, even Christ; from whom the whole body, fitly joined together, and compacted by that which every joint supplied, according to the effectual working in the measure of every part, increased unto the edifying itself in love."[87]

In this passage, Wesley highlighted the benefits that came from Christian fellowship, bearing each other's burdens and speaking the truth in love. And, according to Wesley, as Methodists experienced deeper fellowship, they "had a more endeared affection for each other." Further, as they learned to speak candidly to one another in class, Wesley found that they also grew in their relationship with Christ. Thus, the class meeting served to help Methodists grow in their love of God and neighbor, one of Wesley's favorite definitions of holiness. Wesley valued the class meeting, then, not only because it provided a form of discipline for ensuring that Methodists lived the kind of lives that the "General Rules" called for, but also because the class meeting helped every Methodist learn to love God and neighbor more. However, the key communal support structure that Wesley believed was most helpful for growth in holiness was not the class meeting, but the band meeting.

The Band Meeting

Unlike the class meeting, but similar to the society meeting, the early Methodist band meeting was derived from sources with which Wesley was previously familiar.[88] The band meeting was the crucial piece of John Wesley's approach to "social

---

[87] Wesley, "Plain Account," in *Works* 9: 262.

[88] Wesley's discussion of the band meeting typically obscured these prior influences. One notable exception was in Wesley's exchange with Thomas Church. In "The Principles of a Methodist Farther Explained," Wesley addressed a question that Church put to him in his response to Wesley's "An Answer to the Rev. Mr. Church's *Remarks*." Wesley quoted Church, "In a note at the bottom of p. 8 you observe, 'The Band Society in London began May 1, some time before I set out for Germany.'

holiness." The key document for the early Methodist band meeting is Wesley's "Rules of the Band Societies," which outlined the rules that governed the practice of band meetings.[89]

In the "Rules of the Band Societies," Wesley described the basic guidelines, or rules, of the Wesleyan bands. The band rules were organized in three sections: The first outlined the purpose and goals of band meetings. The second contained eleven questions that were asked of prospective band members before they were admitted to a band. Finally, the third described the structure or focus of the weekly band meeting itself.

The band rules began by describing the purpose of the bands: "The design of our meeting is to obey that command of God, 'Confess your faults one to another, and pray one for another that ye may be healed.'"[90] In order to accomplish this purpose, those who were in a band would meet once a week, attend the weekly meeting on time, and begin with "singing or prayer." After the beginning of the meeting, the basic format of the rest of the meeting was "To speak, each of us in order, freely and plainly the true state of our souls, with the faults we have committed in thought, word, or deed, and the temptations we have felt since our last meeting." After every person had revealed the "true state" of their soul, the meeting ended with a prayer "suited to the state of each person present." The final guide or "intention" of the weekly meeting was a bit redundant and reinforced the fourth. It read, "To desire some person among us to speak *his* own state first, and then to ask the rest in order as many and as searching questions as may be concerning their state, sins, and temptations."[91]

For both theological and practical reasons, there were several prerequisites for joining a band meeting. The second section of the "Rules of the Band Societies" described these prerequisites. In order to join a band, one first had to answer eleven questions that related to the person's present spiritual state and their willingness to enter into the frank, blunt, and piercing conversation that was the essence of the band meeting. The questions relating to the person's spiritual state pointed to the need for members of bands to have "the forgiveness of sins,"

Would you insinuate here that you did not set it up in imitation of the Moravians?" Wesley's response acknowledged the impact of the Moravians on the bands that started in May 1738, but he deflected attention away from the Moravians to a mistake in Church's earlier reply: "Sir, I will tell you the naked truth. You had remarked thus: 'You took the trouble of a journey to Germany to them, and were so much in love with their methods that at *your return* hither you set up their Bands among your disciples.' This was an entire mistake. For that Society was set up, not only before I *returned*, but before I *set out*. And I designed that note to *insinuate* this to *you*, without telling your mistake to all the world." Wesley, *Works* 9: 169.

[89] For the entire text of the "Rules of the Bands," see appendix C. See also Wesley, "Rules of the Bands," in *Works* 9: 77–78.

[90] Ibid.

[91] Ibid. "His" is italicized in the original to indicate that it can be substituted for "her" as needed, see *Works* 9: 77, n. 2.

"peace with God," and "the witness of God's Spirit" with their spirit that they were "a child of God."[92] Prospective members were also asked if "the love of God" was "shed abroad" in their heart and if any sin either "inward or outward" had control over their life.[93] The final six questions examined the person's willingness to be candid with the members of the group, as well as their willingness to receive honest criticism from the members of the group. A representative question was "Do you desire to be told of all your faults, and that plain and home?"[94]

Finally, the third section of the "Rules of the Band Societies" described the basic format of the weekly band meeting itself, which was oriented around five questions that were to be asked at every meeting:

1. What known sins have you committed since our last meeting?
2. What temptations have you met with?
3. How was you delivered?
4. What have you thought, said, or done, of which you doubt whether it be sin or not?
5. Have you nothing you desire to keep secret?[95]

The early Methodist band meeting, then, was focused on a piercing conversation about where each member was spiritually.[96] As the citation of James 5:16 suggests, the primary activity of the band meeting was the confession of specific sins to the group.

The key source where Wesley expanded on his own understanding of the role that the band meeting played in Wesleyan Methodism is "A Plain Account of the People Called Methodists." Again, though Wesley's chronology of the development of the society meeting, the class meeting, and the band meeting was inaccurate, "A Plain Account" does give insight into how he saw these pieces fitting together after the various parts of the structure were all in place. In the beginning of his account of the rise of the band meeting, Wesley described how the bands complemented the class meetings and continued to play a vital role in the Methodist structures for communal Christian formation:

> By the blessing of God upon their endeavors to help one another, many found the pearl of great price. Being justified by faith, they had "peace

[92] Ibid.

[93] Ibid.

[94] Ibid.

[95] The fifth question was removed in 1779 or 1780. See *Works* 9: 78, fn. 12. The fifth question was also omitted in the Jackson edition of *Works*. See *Works*, Jackson, 8: 273.

[96] This is one place where the history of confession and penance is of particular significance, as this list of questions resembles the practice of private confession. The standard history on the development of the theology and practice of penance is Bernhard Poschmann, *Penance and the Anointing of the Sick*, trans. Francis Courtney (New York: Herder and Herder, 1964).

with God, through our Lord Jesus Christ." These felt a more tender affection than before to those who were partakers of like precious faith; and hence arose such a confidence in each other that they poured out their souls into each other's bosom. Indeed they had great need so to do; for the war was not over, as they had supposed. But they had still to wrestle both with flesh and blood, and with principalities and powers; so that temptations were on every side; and often temptations of such a kind as they knew not how to speak in a class, in which persons of every sort, young and old, men and women, met together.

These therefore wanted some means of closer union: they wanted to pour out of their hearts without reserve, particularly with regard to the sin which did still "easily beset" them, and the temptations which were most apt to prevail over them. And they were the more desirous of this when they observed, it was the express advice of an inspired writer, "Confess your faults one to another, and pray one for another, that ye may be healed."[97]

On the one hand, this passage suggests that many people did in fact receive the gift of justification in the context of participation in a class meeting, as they found "the pearl of great price"—justification by faith.[98] Wesley believed that sharing a common faith allowed for an increased confidence in one another. However, the increase in confidence led to a desire for closer union than they could have in the context of the class meeting, where all of the members had not experienced justification. After the advent of the class meeting, the band meeting was at least as valuable, as involvement in the class meeting seemed to have given many Methodists a taste of the possibilities of "social holiness" that caused them to want to delve deeper. According to Wesley, the band meeting helped people go farther in their journey toward holiness of heart and life:

Great and many are the advantages which have ever since flowed from this closer union of the believers with each other. They prayed for one another, that they might be healed of the faults they had confessed— and it was so. The chains were broken, the bands were burst in sunder, and sin had no more dominion over them. Many were delivered from the temptations out of which till then they found no way to escape. They were built up in our most holy faith. They rejoiced in the Lord more abundantly. They were strengthened in love, and more effectually provoked to abound in every good work.[99]

---

[97] Wesley, "Plain Account," in *Works* 9: 266–267.

[98] This is further supported by the research of Thomas R. Albin. See Albin, "'Inwardly Persuaded': Religion of the Heart in Early British Methodism," in *"Heart Religion" in the Methodist Tradition and Related Movements*, ed., Richard B. Steele (Lanham, MD: Scarecrow Press, 2001), 45.

[99] Wesley, "Plain Account," in *Works* 9: 266–268.

The previously cited accounts of the band meeting reveal a few more details that have not yet been made explicit. The bands were divided based on gender and marital status, so that married men were in one group, married women in another, single men in another, and single women in another. As Wesley states in "A Plain Account of the People Called Methodists," these groups were intended to provide a place where people could "pour out of their hearts without reserve." In other words, the division based on gender represented a pastoral awareness that the "besetting sins" of women and men, and married and single people were not only different, but they were also things that men and women were likely to be uncomfortable talking about together.

Wesley's description of the bands also revealed that they were intended to be smaller than class meetings. One of the key reasons that the bands needed to be smaller than the classes was because the bands required more intimacy and vulnerability than did the classes. The band meeting involved confession of all known sins that each member had committed since the last meeting. Each member would also reveal any ways that they had been tempted over the past week and how they were "delivered" from the temptation. Further, band meetings involved conversation about what members had "thought, said, or done, of which you doubt whether it be sin or not?" And finally, every member was directly asked if they were hiding anything, if there was anything they "desired to keep secret." Of the three structures of the Methodist "method," the band meeting was the one where the most candid, direct, and searching conversations occurred related to the particularities of how people were falling short of the holiness that they were called to enter into as Christians.

Two further groups came out of the band meeting: penitent bands and select societies. Wesley described the function of both in "A Plain Account of the People Called Methodists." Wesley noted that "while most of these who were thus intimately joined together [in bands] went on daily from faith to faith, some fell from the faith."[100] When "the exhortations and prayers used among the believers did no longer profit these," Wesley separated them from the rest of the bands because "they wanted advice and instructions suited to their case."[101] Wesley described the meetings for penitents, where "all the hymns, exhortations, and prayers are adapted to their circumstances; being wholly suited to those who *did* see God, but have now lost the light of his countenance; and who mourn after him, and refuse to be comforted till they know he has healed all their backsliding."[102] Wesley described the goal of the penitent bands as follows: "By applying both the threats and promises of God to these real (not nominal) *penitents*, and by crying to God in their behalf, we endeavoured to bring them back to the great

[100] Ibid., 268.
[101] Ibid., 269.
[102] Ibid (emphasis original).

Shepherd and Bishop of their souls."[103] According to Wesley, these gatherings of penitents were often a particular blessing, as many of the penitents "soon recovered the ground they had lost. Yea, they rose higher than before; being more watchful than ever, and more meek and lowly, as well as stronger in the faith that worketh by love."[104] In fact, the penitent bands were sometimes so successful that they were the means by which people came to experience entire sanctification: "They now outran the greater part of their brethren, continually walking in the light of God, and having fellowship with the Father, and with his Son, Jesus Christ."[105]

In Wesley's theological account of the Methodist approach to communal Christian formation, then, the penitent bands were a place where people were particularly aware of their dependence on God's grace and where such dependence made them more receptive to receiving a renewed outpouring of sanctifying grace. In Wesley's narration in "A Plain Account of the People Called Methodists," it was the penitent bands that led to the select societies:

> I saw it might be useful to give some advices to all those who thus continued in the light of God's countenance, which the rest of their brethren did not want, and probably could not receive. So I desired a small number of such as appeared to be in this state to spend an hour with me every Monday morning. My design was, not only to direct them now to *press after perfection*; to exercise their every grace, and improve every talent they had received; and to incite them to love one another more, and to watch more carefully over each other; but also to have a *select company* to whom I might unbosom myself on all occasions, without reserve, and whom I could propose to all their brethren as a pattern of love, of holiness, and of all good works.[106]

As the contours of the early Methodist approach to Christian formation through community came into focus, the goals of the society, class, and band meetings were not radically different; they each functioned to usher the person into a deeper relationship with others and with God. From this angle of vision, the select society was the pinnacle of early Methodism, the place where Methodists

---

[103] Ibid (emphasis original). Wesley continued with comments that both disparaged the Roman Catholic practice of penance and acknowledged the early church's practice of communal penance: "not by any of the fopperies of the Roman Church, although in some measure countenanced by antiquity. In prescribing hair-shirts and bodily austerities we durst not follow even the ancient Church; although we had unawares, both in dividing οι πιστοι, the believers, from the rest of the society, and in separating the *penitents* from them, and appointing a peculiar service for them." Ibid.

[104] Ibid.

[105] Ibid. For more on the penitent bands, see Albin, "'Inwardly Persuaded,'" 51–52.

[106] Wesley, "Plain Account," in *Works* 9: 269–270 (emphasis original).

were incited to love one another even more and to press after perfection even more intentionally.

The level of holiness that was manifest by those in select societies meant that "they had no need of being encumbered with many rules, having the best rule of all in their hearts."[107] In contrast to the "General Rules" and the "Rules of the Band Societies," because of the degree to which the love of God had been shed abroad in the hearts of those in the select societies, they were governed by freedom more than by regulation.[108]

The particularities of both the class meeting and the band meeting can be better understood by comparing and contrasting them with each other.[109] Attendance at a weekly class meeting was required for every person who wanted to continue to be a member of the Methodist movement. The band meeting was never required at any level of Methodism. Classes and bands both met weekly. A class could have men and women and married and single persons in the same class, though they were not always co-ed. Bands were divided based on gender and marital status.[110] The class meeting typically had around twelve members, though they were frequently larger.[111] The band meeting typically had five to

[107] Ibid., 270.

[108] Wesley described the three rules that guided the select societies: "First, let nothing spoken in this society be spoken again.... Secondly, every member agrees to submit to his minister in all indifferent things. Thirdly, every member will bring once a week all he can spare toward a common stock." Ibid.

[109] Dean compared the class and band meeting in Dean, 157. Specifically, Dean argued that "It was the band meeting, therefore, that was the true fellowship meeting in Methodism's cell group system. The class provided the necessary preparation for that fellowship through discipline and instruction." Similarly, David Lowes Watson contended that "the format of the class meeting was not intentionally conducive to an intensive group experience. Rather than the fostering of interpersonal relationships, which was quite specifically the dynamic of the bands and select societies, the class meeting was at once more pragmatic and more task-oriented. It was first and foremost...an instrument of planned behavioral change." David Lowes Watson, *Early Methodist Class Meeting*, 132. Here, Watson echoed Henderson's view of the class meeting as oriented toward behavioral change. See Henderson, 93–112. Thomas R. Albin, on the other hand, understood the various pieces of the Methodist structure to have been organized "in accordance with their distinctive understanding of divine grace, so that different groups were organized to meet the needs of people at different points in their spiritual life." Albin, "'Inwardly Persuaded,'" 39. In particular, Albin argued that "the structure created by the Wesleys for members who had experienced *justifying* grace and the new birth was the band meeting." Ibid.

[110] Wesley, "Plain Account," in *Works* 9: 267.

[111] Dean's examination of class books in the second half of the eighteenth century showed that the range of class size was from five up to sixty or seventy members, but "the vast majority...fell in the twelve to twenty range. The 'average' size for a class is one of those elusive figures that would be suspect even if we had the basic statistics. The average size of the classes whose records I have found, using the highest point of membership in each class, was about twenty." Dean, 276. Heitzenrater similarly argued that Wesleyan societies were "divided into classes...neighborhood subdivisions of about twelve persons, each having an assigned leader." Heitzenrater, *Wesley and the People Called Methodists*, 118.

seven members, though they were occasionally slightly larger.[112] As is suggested by the "General Rules," the basic activity of the class meeting was a response to the question, "How does your soul prosper?" A person's answer to this question was often followed by a suitable response from the class leader. On the other hand, according to the "Rules of the Band Societies," the principle activity of the band meeting was confession of specific sins. According to the "General Rules," the only condition required of someone who wanted to be admitted into a Methodist society was "a desire to flee from the wrath to come, to be saved from their sins."[113] In other words, there was no doctrinal or experiential litmus test for entry into a class meeting. According to the "Rules of the Band Societies," on the other hand, the ability to testify to an experience of justifying faith and new birth were preconditions of admission into the band meeting, as well as a willingness to submit to piercing spiritual conversation about one's own faults.

Despite their differences, Wesley continued to believe that both the class meeting and the band meeting were of value to Methodism. In his summary of his teaching on entire sanctification in "A Plain Account of Christian Perfection," Wesley quoted from "Farther Thoughts on Christian Perfection":

> If you would avoid schism, observe every rule of the Society, and of the Bands, for conscience' sake. Never omit meeting your Class or Band; never absent yourself from any public meeting. These are the very sinews of our Society; and whatever weakens, or tends to weaken, our regard for these, or our exactness in attending them, strikes at the very root of our community. As one saith, "That part of our economy, the private weekly meetings for prayer, examination, and particular exhortation, has been the greatest means of deepening and confirming every blessing that was received by the word preached, and of diffusing it to others, who could not attend the public ministry; whereas, without this religious connexion and intercourse, the most ardent attempts, by mere preaching, have proved of no lasting use."[114]

One way of describing the development of Wesley's approach to communal Christian formation would be to describe the society, class, and band meetings (as well as the penitent bands and the select societies) as providing a path for

---

[112] Heitzenrater described the bands as "small groups of five to ten persons who voluntarily banded together for intense spiritual nurture and support." Heitzenrater, *Wesley and the People Called Methodists*, 104. Dean averaged the band lists that were reprinted in *City Road Chapel, London and its Associations* from 1742 to 1745 and found that the average size was six people per band meeting. Dean, 162. For the list of the members see, George J. Stevenson, *City Road Chapel, London and its Associations: Historical, Biographical, and Memorial* (London: George J. Stevenson, ca. 1872), 28–38.

[113] Wesley, "General Rules," in *Works* 9: 70.

[114] Wesley, "A Plain Account of Christian Perfection," in *Works*, Jackson, 11: 433.

ongoing growth in holiness. Each group was generally designed to enable people to become more holy at various stages in the Christian life.

When Wesley narrated the development of the societies, classes, and bands in "A Plain Account of the People Called Methodists," he did not focus narrowly on one particular part of the Way of Salvation. Rather, he focused on the ways that the various structures helped people to "work out their salvation."[115] Thus, when Wesley described the only criterion for admission to a society as "a desire to flee from the wrath to come, and to be saved from their sins" he also insisted that "wherever this desire is fixed in the soul, it will be shown by its fruits."[116] The "fruit" that Wesley expected to see was identified in the "General Rules."[117] At one level, the class meeting provided a means for correcting or removing those who "gave way to the sins which had long easily beset them."[118] At another level, and perhaps more significantly, the class meeting was found to help people experience a "more endeared affection for each other" and grow in love of Christ.[119] As Methodists became accustomed to this level of communal practice, and as they grew in their love for God and neighbor, many did in fact find "the pearl of great price. Being justified by faith."[120] As these people experienced justifying faith, they came to feel the need for more communal support, not less. They "wanted some means of closer union" so that they could "pour out of their hearts without reserve."[121] In Wesley's account, as newborn Methodists wanted to become more holy, they realized that in order to do so, they needed to talk candidly about the sin in their own lives. When they did, Wesley testified that the chains of sin "were broken, the bands were burst in sunder, and sin had no more dominion over them."[122] And yet, the journey was not over even at this point, as penitent bands and select societies were formed for those who returned to sin or who had experienced such an infusion of God's sanctifying grace that they were "continually walking in the light of God."[123]

Though the society, class, and band meetings were all oriented toward growth in holiness in some sense, the band meeting was unique because it could be taken for granted that all the members of the band had experienced

---

[115] Wesley, "Plain Account," in *Works* 9: 256.

[116] Ibid., 257.

[117] I have previously argued that the "General Rules" themselves can be seen as a guide for growth in holiness. See the discussion of the "General Rules" in the section " 'Religion Itself': Holiness as Necessary for the Christian Life" in this chapter.

[118] Wesley, "Plain Account," in *Works* 9: 260.

[119] Ibid., 262.

[120] Ibid., 266.

[121] Ibid.

[122] Ibid., 268.

[123] Ibid., 269.

the new birth and were ready to pursue holiness "in earnest." As such, Wesley continued to value the band meeting because it represented the key piece of the Methodist "method" that related to Methodism's hope to be used by God to "spread scriptural holiness." Put differently, when compared to the society meeting and class meeting, the band meeting was particularly focused on growth in holiness, whereas the society meeting and class meeting were more oriented toward bringing someone to the point of receiving justifying faith and the accompanying new birth.

3

The Bands as a Key to the Distinctive Wesleyan Synthesis of Anglican and Moravian Piety

The place where Wesley's synthesis of Anglican and Pietistic piety was most visible was in his version of the band meeting.[1] The Anglican emphasis on the importance of a disciplined practice of the means of grace is a visible influence on the Wesleyan band meeting. Yet, the Moravian emphasis on the importance of a direct encounter by the individual with the Holy Spirit that led to assurance is also a visible influence on Wesley's conception of the band meeting. Thus, the distinct theological contribution of the Wesleyan bands was the conjunction of the Moravian emphasis on justification by faith and assurance with the Anglican emphasis on growth in holiness through disciplined spiritual practices.

Wesley's synthesis of Moravian and Anglican piety brought him into conflict with leaders of the Church of England and the Moravians at Herrnhut and Fetter Lane. His insistence on the necessity of a direct experience of God's justifying grace and subsequent assurance of one's forgiveness led to conflicts with Anglicans. Conversely, his persistent advocacy of the importance of the practice of the means of grace prior to justification and the new birth led to confrontation with the Moravians in the Fetter Lane Society. For Wesley, the logic of the Way of Salvation meant that Methodists who experienced the gift of justifying faith and the new birth should have sought out the "advantages" that came from a "closer union of the believers with each other."[2] As a result, the fact

---

[1] Previous scholars have noted the "conjunctive" nature of Wesley's theology, the way in which he attempted to hold together various concepts that were in tension. However, Wesley's conjunction of Anglican and Moravian piety in the Wesleyan band meeting has not been adequately recognized. On Wesley as a conjunctive theologian, see Albert C. Outler, "John Wesley as Theologian—Then and Now," in *The Wesleyan Theological Heritage*, eds., Thomas C. Oden and Leicester R. Longden (Grand Rapids, MI: Zondervan, 1991), 55–74; Albert C. Outler, *Theology in the Wesleyan Spirit* (Nashville, TN: Discipleship Resources, 1975), 71; and Collins, *The Theology of John Wesley*, 4–5.

[2] Wesley, "Plain Account," in *Works* 9: 268. In this passage, Wesley described the advantages of the band meeting for those who had been justified by faith.

that involvement in a band meeting was not the norm for Methodists who had experienced the new birth suggests that Methodism fell short of John Wesley's vision for it.

Anglican Piety in the Wesleyan Band Meetings

The impact of Anglican piety, particularly as seen through the Religious Societies, on Wesley's version of the band meeting is especially seen in the period between Wesley's initial involvement in the Fetter Lane bands and his creation of the "Rules of the Band Societies." Not long after his initial involvement with the Fetter Lane Society and his experience of assurance on May 24, 1738, Wesley traveled to Germany, with the purpose of visiting the Moravians at Herrnhut.[3] After his immersion in the communal approach to the Christian life as practiced at Herrnhut, Wesley processed this experience upon his return to England. The fact that Wesley did not endorse everything he experienced at Herrnhut can be seen in his correspondence with James Hutton regarding changes that Hutton and others proposed to the band meeting format in his absence. In a letter to John Wesley on November 23, 1738, Hutton described the consideration of selecting monitors, a form of oversight that Wesley had encountered at Herrnhut, and the role that they would play in the Fetter Lane bands:

> Out of the rest of the lots will be chosen two persons monitors, whose business will be to tell everyone what faults are observed in him, concealing his informer. And no defence of himself to be allowed, only put to his own heart, no farther notice being taken of anything unless the person persist in his misbehaviour. These are to meet with the leaders of the bands.[4]

Wesley did not approve of this Moravian practice, noting in his response to Hutton that he had "thought much...of the monitors" and had concluded that the "design is not right...for several reasons."[5] The final reason that Wesley gave for objecting to the use of monitors reflected the influence of the Anglican Religious Societies on Wesley's conception of the band meeting. Wesley wrote: "A general monitor commissioned by God to reprove every one of his brethren you

---

[3] Wesley initially noted this "determination" in his *Journal* for June 7, 1738, in *Works* 18: 254. Leaving England in the middle of June, Wesley traveled throughout Germany until his return to England on September 16, 1738. Though Wesley spent most of his energy recounting his interactions with the Moravians at Herrnhut, he also recorded his visit to Lutheran Pietists, particularly at Halle. See Wesley, *Journal*, in *Works* 18: 255–297; 19: 5–12.

[4] James Hutton, letter to John Wesley, November 23, 1738, in *Works* 25: 586.

[5] Wesley, letter to James Hutton, November 26, 1738, in *Works* 25: 591.

have, so long as you have any priest or deacon among you."[6] In other words, monitors were not needed because the Fetter Lane bands already contained ordained priests from the Church of England, whose God-given authority made monitors redundant.

Wesley's dependence on the Anglican Religious Societies was especially visible at this point, because Religious Societies were led by Anglican priests.[7] Wesley argued for the need to recognize the authority of the Church of England in the Fetter Lane bands more explicitly and at further length in a letter he wrote to Hutton the next day:

> As to the monitors, I have one more doubt. I believe bishops, priests, and deacons to be of divine appointment (though I think our brethren in Germany do not). Therefore I am tender of the first approach towards 'pastors appointed by the congregation.' And if we should begin with appointed fixed persons to execute *pro officio*, I doubt it would not end there.... My brother, suffer me to speak a little more. If as a fool, then as a fool bear with me. I believe you don't think I am (whatever I was) bigoted either to the ancient church or the Church of England. But have a care of bending the bow too much the other way. The national church to which we belong may doubtless claim some, though not an implicit, obedience from us.[8]

Thus, one of Wesley's initial points of conflict with the Fetter Lane Society was related to preserving some place for a proper recognition of the authority of the Church of England therein.[9]

A particular aspect of Anglican piety that was expressed in the Religious Societies was the belief that progress in the Christian life came as the result of a consistent practice of the means of grace.[10] This conviction is seen in the structure of the Religious Societies themselves, whose rules focused on a disciplined practice of the means of grace. Similarly, the Wesleyan bands sought to provide structure and rules for the ongoing pursuit of holiness. The "Rules of the Band Societies" evidence a commitment to an earnest pursuit of holiness. The value placed on discipline and structure is seen in the stipulation that members of the

---

[6] Ibid., 592.

[7] Richard Kidder's version of the rules for Religious Societies, e.g., stipulated that members of a Religious Society "chuse a Minister of the Church of England to direct them." Kidder, 13.

[8] Wesley, letter to James Hutton, November 27, 1738, in *Works* 25: 592–593.

[9] Henry D. Rack further outlined the disagreement between Wesley and Hutton in *Reasonable Enthusiast*, 188.

[10] John Spurr expressed this aspect of Anglican piety: "One can say that the Anglicans preferred a constant striving to an instantaneous and—as they saw it—presumptuous assurance of personal salvation." John Spurr, "The Church, the societies and the moral revolution of 1688," 138.

bands meet weekly, arriving "punctually at the hour appointed."[11] Though the meeting was primarily focused on speaking "freely and plainly the true state of our souls," a commitment to a disciplined practice of the means of grace is further seen in the instruction to begin the meeting with "singing or prayer," and end in prayer.[12]

Further, Wesley seemed to have valued the band meeting, which was a weekly meeting focused on confession of sin, because he saw the bands themselves as a means of grace. Wesley recorded several experiences in band meetings where the bands seemed to facilitate an encounter with God. In his *Journal*, Wesley wrote about one encounter with God at a meeting of the bands at the Foundery in 1759: "In the evening, we had another kind of congregation at the Foundery, by whom I was much comforted, but much more in meeting the bands, when all our hearts were melted down by the power of God."[13] Nearly two years later, Wesley recorded a similar experience, again among the bands at the Foundery: "While a poor woman was speaking a few artless words out of the fullness of her heart, a fire kindled and ran as flame among the stubble, through the hearts of almost all that heard—so when God is pleased to work it matters not how weak or how mean the instrument!"[14] Thus, experience showed Wesley that when Methodists came together in bands, people's hearts tended to "catch fire" or be "melted" by God's transforming presence. Moreover, Wesley was sufficiently convinced of the value of the band meeting as a means of grace that he specifically cited the bands as a "prudential" means of grace for Methodists.[15] In fact, his discussion of the prudential means of grace in the "Large Minutes" asserted that the society, class, and band structure was God's particular gift to Methodism.[16]

And yet, the place where the influence of Anglican piety on the Wesleyan band meeting may be seen most clearly is in Wesley's addition of the "Directions given to the Band Societies" to the "Rules of the Band Societies" in 1744, six years after the "Rules of the Band Societies" were originally written, but only one year after the "General Rules" were first published. When Wesley revisited the "Rules of

---

[11] Wesley, "Rules of the Bands," in *Works* 9: 77.

[12] Ibid.

[13] Wesley, *Journal* for March 28, 1759, in *Works* 21: 181.

[14] Ibid., January 30, 1761, 21: 301. This also provides an example of the ways popular Methodist experiences often transcended conventional class boundaries.

[15] In the "Large Minutes" under the prudential means of grace for Methodists, two questions are asked: "Do you never miss any meeting of the society? Neither your class or band?" Wesley, *Works* 10: 857.

[16] Ibid. Wesley listed the prudential means of grace for Methodists in general (see previous note), as well as the prudential means of grace for Methodist preachers and assistants. Under both, the importance of the Methodist structures for communal formation was underscored. For example, under preachers, the minutes stated, "As Preachers. Do you meet every society weekly? Also the leaders? And bands, if any?" Ibid.

the Band Societies," he wanted to make sure that the practice of the means of grace was seen as a key component of Methodism from any level of its organization. As a result, the "Directions" for the bands were essentially a condensed version of the "General Rules," following the same structure and basic content of the three rules of the "General Rules," but with a subset of rules under each of those three that more explicitly spelled out what each of the original rules meant.[17] Members of the band societies were reminded to "carefully abstain from doing evil," to "zealously...maintain good works," and to "constantly...attend on all the ordinances of God."[18] The addition of the "Directions given to the Band Societies" to the "Rules," then, represented the impact of the Anglican Religious Societies on the bands themselves, as Wesley's affirmation of the importance of a disciplined practice of the means of grace led him to append a form of the "General Rules" to the band "Rules."

The final way that Anglican piety influenced Wesley's conception of the band meeting is seen in a letter he wrote to his brother Charles on April 21, 1741. In the letter, John outlined the reasons that he "dares in no wise join with the Moravians."[19] According to Wesley, the Moravians were "by no means zealous of good works, or at least only to their own people."[20] Here Wesley highlighted the key affirmation that became the second rule in the "General Rules," where Methodists were exhorted to do good, "by being in every kind merciful after their power, as they have opportunity doing good of every possible sort and as far as is possible to all men."[21] The zeal for good works that John Wesley felt the Moravians lacked was a typical value of Anglican Religious Societies. For example, in Woodward's version

---

[17] In the "Directions given to the Band Societies," e.g., the first rule is "Carefully to abstain from doing evil." Under this, several things that are to be avoided are listed, such as "neither to *buy nor sell* anything at all on the Lord's Day"; "Not to *mention the fault of any behind his back*, and to stop those short that do"; and "To use no *needless self-indulgence*, such as taking snuff or tobacco, unless prescribed by a physician." See John Wesley, "Directions given to the Band Societies," in *Works* 9: 79. David Lowes Watson noted the connection between the "Directions given to the Band Societies" and the "General Rules." Watson wrote, "The early *Rules of the Band Societies* were supplemented in December 1744 with a series of *Directions*...which took the *General Rules* of the societies and gave them a very particular focus. Band members were to abstain from evil *carefully*, to maintain good works *zealously*, and to attend on all the ordinances of the church *constantly*." Watson, *Early Methodist Class Meeting*, 117 (emphasis original). In my view, Watson made too much of this distinction. For example, the second "General Rule" stated, "It is expected of all who continue in these societies that they should continue to evidence their desire of salvation...by doing good, by being in *every kind* merciful after their power, as they have opportunity doing good of *every possible sort* and *as far as is possible* to all men." Wesley, "General Rules," in *Works* 9: 72 (emphasis mine). It would be difficult to sustain the argument that this is a less "zealous" commitment to good works than is found in the "Directions given to the Band Societies."

[18] Wesley, "Directions given to the Band Societies," in *Works* 9: 79.

[19] Wesley, letter to Charles Wesley, April 21, 1741, in *Works* 26: 56.

[20] Ibid.

[21] Wesley, "General Rules," in *Works* 9: 72.

of the rules of the Religious Societies, members were to "contribute at every *Weekly Meeting*, what he thinks fit towards a *Publick Stock* for Pious and Charitable Uses."[22]

The final critique that Wesley made in his letter to Charles was that the Moravians "make inward religion swallow up outward in general."[23] By 1741, John Wesley felt that Moravian spiritual practice overemphasized the immediate experience of God's grace through their understanding of assurance at the expense of the importance of relying on a disciplined practice of the means of grace.

Pietistic Piety in the Wesleyan Band Meetings

Although the impact of Anglican piety was evident in the early Methodist band meetings, there were also significant signs of the influence of Pietistic piety. Wesley's conception of the band meeting was influenced by his involvement in the creation and development of the Fetter Lane Society bands, his experience of communal formation among the Moravians at Herrnhut in 1738, and his own emphasis on the importance of the witness of the Spirit, particularly as a prerequisite for involvement in his version of the band meeting. The Fetter Lane Society was the key context for Wesley's development of his own version of the band meeting. As previously discussed, Wesley was present when the Fetter Lane Society began, and he was also involved in the bands at Fetter Lane.[24] The deep influence of the Fetter Lane Society on Wesley's conception of the bands can be seen in a comparison of the beginning of the Fetter Lane Rules with Wesley's "Rules of the Band Societies." The minutes of the Fetter Lane Society preserved the Fetter Lane Rules, which noted the rationale and basic structure of the society: "In obedience to the Command of God by St. James (5:16) and by the Advice of Peter Boehler: (a It was agreed . . . . 1. That they will meet together once a week, to confess their faults one to another, and pray for one another, that they may be healed."[25] John Wesley's version, "The Rules of the Band Societies," stated the

---

[22] Woodward, 122 (emphasis original).

[23] Wesley, letter to Charles Wesley, April 21, 1741, in *Works* 26: 56–57.

[24] The influence of Pietism on the Fetter Lane Society has also already been traced. In fact, conversations regarding the instantaneous nature of the gift of justifying faith with Peter Böhler that took place prior to the formation of the Fetter Lane Society were also significant for Wesley's conception of the band meeting. See Wesley, *Journal* for April 22, 1738, in *Works* 18: 233–234.

[25] "The Rules and Orders of a Religious Society meeting at Present in a Room in Fetter Lane," in *PWHS* 17 :30. The original is at the Archives of the United Brethren in Herrnhut, Germany, ref: R13. A19.2. This rule, according to Wesley's *Journal*, was the guiding rule of the bands at Herrnhut. See Wesley, *Journal* for August 11–14, 1738, in *Works* 18: 292. For a complete text of "The Rules and Orders of a Religious Society meeting at Present in a Room in Fetter Lane" and "The account of the Fetter Lane Society" as found in D. Benham's *Memoirs of James Hutton*, 29ff., see appendixes A and B in this volume.

rationale of the band as follows: "The design of our meeting is to obey that command of God, 'Confess your faults one to another, and pray one for another that ye may be healed.'"[26]

The place where the impact of Moravian piety may have been most visible in the "Rules of the Band Societies" was in the list of questions asked of each person who sought admission to a band, particularly the first four:

1. Have you the forgiveness of your sins?
2. Have you peace with God, through our Lord Jesus Christ?
3. Have you the witness of God's Spirit with your spirit that you are a child of God?
4. Is the love of God shed abroad in your heart?[27]

Because of his Anglican upbringing, Wesley did not see the necessity of a new birth experience until his first encounters with the Moravians. As a result, he would not have asked these questions of his friends at Oxford, nor would he have been able to affirmatively answer them for himself at that point. However, because of the influence of the Moravians, Wesley came to see a direct experience of God's justifying grace and the witness of the Spirit as prerequisites for the growth in holiness on which the Wesleyan bands focused.[28]

Wesley's approach to the pursuit of holiness, then, was strongly influenced by the crisis that was brought on by meeting Moravians who had a strong assurance of the forgiveness of their sins and their status as God's children.[29] Because of these interactions, Wesley came to insist on the importance of the new birth

[26] Wesley, "Rules of the Bands," in *Works* 9: 77. A closer comparison of the entirety of the "Rules of the Bands" with the "Rules and Orders of a Religious Society meeting at Present in a Room in Fetter Lane" shows that the first section in the "Rules of the Band Societies," which consisted of six "intentions," was nearly identical to the Fetter Lane "Rules." However, in Wesley's version, the second section, which contained eleven questions to be asked before someone was "admitted amongst us" are all unique to Wesley's "Rules," with the exception of the final question: "Is it your desire and design to be on this and all other occasions entirely open, so as to speak everything that is in your heart, without exception, without disguise, and without reserve?" This question contained parts of question nineteen in the Fetter Lane "Rules." Finally, the Fetter Lane "Rules" did not contain a list of questions to be asked at every meeting, while the final section of Wesley's band "Rules" contained five such questions. There were also numerous rules in the Fetter Lane "Rules" that have thirty or thirty-three parts, depending on which version. The rules that were unique to the Fetter Lane documents were primarily practical details related to how the bands were divided, how often they should meet, discipline of current members, and admission of new members.

[27] Wesley, "Rules of the Bands," in *Works* 9: 77.

[28] See Richard P. Heitzenrater, "Great Expectations: Aldersgate and the Evidences of Genuine Christianity," in *Mirror and Memory*, 147.

[29] Heitzenrater has narrated the impact of the Moravians on Wesley's theological and spiritual development in "Great Expectations," 106–149. This essay was also published in Randy L. Maddox, ed., *Aldersgate Reconsidered* (Nashville, TN: Kingswood Books, 1990), 49–91.

and the good news that God's children can know and feel that their sins were forgiven.[30] Prior to Wesley's involvement in the Fetter Lane Society, neither the Religious Societies nor the Oxford Methodists required prospective members to testify to an experience of the new birth. Wesley's inclusion of questions that asked about the forgiveness of sins, "peace with God," and the witness of the Spirit in the "Rules of the Band Societies," therefore, represents a crucial point where Wesley was influenced by Moravian theology and practice.

Not long after his initial involvement with the Fetter Lane Society, and his experience of assurance at Aldersgate Street on May 24, 1738, John Wesley visited the Moravians at Herrnhut. One of the repeated emphases of Wesley's conversations at Herrnhut was related to the Moravian understanding of justification by faith. Toward the beginning of the trip to Germany, Wesley recorded Count Zinzendorf's summary of justification, which included an emphasis on the instantaneous nature of justification: "The moment a man flies to Christ he is justified."[31] Many of Wesley's subsequent conversations at Herrnhut reinforced the experience of receiving the gift of justification immediately upon renouncing the sufficiency of their own efforts and turning in faith to Christ as their only hope for salvation. In a sermon by Christian David that Wesley recorded in his *Journal*, David preached, "This then do, if you will lay a right foundation. Go straight to Christ with all your ungodliness. Tell him, Thou, whose eyes are as a flame of fire searching my heart, seest that I am ungodly. I plead nothing else.... Therefore bring me to him that justifieth the ungodly."[32] Wesley also recorded the account he received from a student at Herrnhut, Albinus Theodorus Feder:

> I (said he) for three years fought against sin with all my might, by fasting and prayer and all the other means of grace. But notwithstanding all my endeavours I gained no ground; sin still prevailed over me; till at last, not knowing what to do farther, I was on the very brink of despair. Then it was that having no other refuge left I fled to my Saviour as one lost and undone, and that had no hope but in his power and free mercy. In that moment I found my heart at rest, in good hope that my sins were forgiven.[33]

[30] Charles Wesley gave voice to this in a hymn he wrote after his conversion: "O how shall I the goodness tell, / Father, which thou to me hast showed? / That I, a child of wrath and hell, / I should be called a child of God! / Should know, should feel my sins forgiven, / Blest with this antepast of heaven!" Hymn #29, in *Works* vol. 7, *A Collection of Hymns for the use of the People called Methodists*, eds. Franz Hildebrandt and Oliver A. Beckerlegge (Nashville, TN: Abingdon, 1983), 116.

[31] Count Zinzendorf, quoted by Wesley, *Journal* for July 12, 1738, in *Works* 18: 261.

[32] Christian David, quoted by Wesley, *Journal* for August 10, 1738, in *Works* 18: 272.

[33] Albinus Theodorus Feder, quoted by Wesley, *Journal* for August 11, 1738, in *Works* 18: 284.

Feder's testimony evidences one of the crucial convictions of the Moravian understanding of justifying faith: It is a free gift that is given entirely through the merits of Christ and cannot be earned or coerced by human works. Though Wesley would come to disagree with the Moravian tendency to view the practice of the means of grace as a potential hindrance to the reception of justifying faith and assurance, Wesley agreed with the Moravian insistence on "salvation by faith alone."[34] In fact, as early as April 22, 1738, Wesley concluded that the Moravian view of justification by faith was in harmony with the doctrine of the Church of England. Wesley wrote, "I had now no objection to what he [Böhler] said of the nature of faith, viz., that it is (to use the words of our Church), 'A sure trust and confidence which a man hath in God, that through the merits of Christ *his* sins are forgiven, and *he* reconciled to the favour of God.' "[35]

Wesley's continued insistence on the importance of the experience of justification by faith and assurance for the band meeting can also be seen, albeit indirectly, in the "Directions given to the Band Societies." It is significant that Wesley did not revise the "Rules of the Band Societies" themselves in order to explicitly include the practice of the means of grace. Instead, he simply added a new document. Thus, questions like "Have you the witness of God's Spirit with your spirit that you are a child of God?" continued to be prerequisites for involvement in the band meeting and reinforced the importance of the assurance of one's adoption as a child of God prior to growth in holiness.[36]

The Moravian insistence on the necessity of salvation by faith and the new birth for growth in the Christian life is also evident in Wesley's version of the band meeting. The first four questions that were to be asked of potential band members particularly reflected this emphasis. In order to be admitted into a Wesleyan band meeting, a prospective member had to be able to affirmatively answer the question "Have you peace with God through our Lord Jesus Christ?"[37] This question, and others like it, asked about the person's present relationship with God. As such, Wesley's "Rules of the Bands" preserved the Moravian conviction that an experience of forgiveness and assurance of God's love was necessary for growth in holiness.

The Moravian influence on Wesley's conception of the band meeting is further seen in his writing about the band meeting in various letters. In two letters to James Hutton and the Fetter Lane Society in 1739, Wesley described the

---

[34] Wesley, *Journal* for March 6, 1738, in *Works* 18: 228. Heitzenrater argued in "Great Expectations" that this emphasis, along with the importance of the witness of the Spirit, were the "two ideas from 1738 [that] continued to find a central place in Wesley's theology even though he modified their explanation." Heitzenrater, "Great Expectations," 147.

[35] Wesley, *Journal* for April 22, 1738, in *Works* 18: 233–234 (parenthesis original, brackets mine).

[36] Wesley, "Rules of the Bands," in *Works* 9: 77.

[37] Ibid.

contexts in which early Methodists experienced forgiveness of their sins and the new birth. In the first letter, Wesley recorded several examples of field preaching, when he "offered Jesus Christ, as our wisdom and righteousness, sanctification, and redemption."[38] Wesley then recorded preaching in a society where "there was great power, and many were convinced of sin."[39] Not only were many "convinced of sin," but many people also experienced the new birth in Methodist societies. Wesley recorded one particular instance of a woman who, during a sermon Wesley preached at Newgate, "was seized with such pangs as I never saw before. And in a quarter of an hour she had a new song in her mouth, a thanksgiving unto our God."[40] Thus, the "Rules of the Band Societies," Wesley's *Journal*, and his personal correspondence each provide evidence of the impact of Moravian piety on the Wesleyan band meeting.

The "Rules of the Band Societies" as the Key Synthesis of Anglican and Pietistic Piety

The band meeting is of particular significance for the study of the eighteenth-century Evangelical Revival because Wesley's version of the band meeting represents a unique blend of Anglican and Pietistic piety. The key place where this synthesis occurred is in the "Rules of the Band Societies," which Wesley wrote while he was involved in the Fetter Lane Society. With the "Rules of the Band Societies," Wesley created a small group structure with clear guidelines and rules that served to focus the group on the primary task of speaking "freely and plainly the true state of our souls, with the faults we have committed in thought, word, or deed, and the temptations we have felt since our last meeting."[41] At first glance, this practice may appear to be entirely dependent on the Moravian *Banden*. However, the details of the "first rise of Methodism" at Oxford and Wesley's voyage to Georgia show that John Wesley and others were already engaged in this sort of deep introspection and communal confession of sin before their initial encounters with the Moravians. Wesley's insistence on the importance of Christian communal formation for progress in the Christian

[38] Wesley, letter to James Hutton and the Fetter Lane Society, April 16, 1739, in *Works* 25: 632–633.

[39] Ibid., 25: 632.

[40] Wesley, letter to James Hutton and the Fetter Lane Society, April 30, 1739, in *Works* 25: 640. The context of this letter is interesting, as Wesley recorded feeling "led, I know not how, to speak strongly and explicitly of predestination, and then to pray that if I spake not the truth of God he would stay his hand, and work no more among us; if this was his truth, he would 'not delay to confirm it by signs following.'" It was after this that Wesley recorded the experience just cited. Ibid., 25: 639–640.

[41] Wesley, "Rules of the Bands," in *Works* 9: 77.

life, then, actually predated his first encounters with the German Moravians on board the *Simmonds* on his way to Georgia. However, the "Rules of the Band Societies" adds an emphasis on a prior experience of justification and assurance to the disciplined pursuit of holiness found in the Anglican Religious Societies and Oxford Methodism.

If the "Rules of the Band Societies" are of particular importance for Wesley's understanding of the band meeting, then any study of the Wesleyan bands must wrestle with the problem of the actual date that the "Rules" were published. Despite the fact that the published version of the band rules cited that they were "Drawn up Dec. 25, 1738," this date has been disputed.[42] Colin Podmore has argued that the published date of the "Rules of the Band Societies" was "clearly a mistake for 1739."[43] If the date printed in the various published editions of the "Rules of the Bands" was incorrect, this would point to a significant oversight in the work of the editors of the *Bicentennial Edition of the Works of John Wesley*. The introductory comments to the "General Rules" and the "Rules of the Bands" do not question that the "Rules of the Bands" were written in 1738. In fact, the introductory section begins: "Wesley drew up his *Rules of the Band Societies* ... in December 1738, before the emergence of the distinctively Methodist societies in Bristol and London."[44] This comment highlighted the significance of properly dating the "Rules." The primary issue at stake is how quickly Wesley began seeing himself as the key leader of particular band meetings and how long the Moravians continued to exert primary influence over his thinking about the organization and conduct of bands. The year 1739 was a key period in which John Wesley began to assert his authority and leadership in the emerging revival. When he formed bands in Bristol in April of 1739, for example, was he simply using the rules that had been in use at the Fetter Lane Society, or had he anticipated his increasing leadership role and already created a set of rules that particularly bore his own seal of approval?

There are several reasons to question the accuracy of the published date of the "Rules of the Bands."[45] First, Wesley did not begin organizing a society separate from Fetter Lane until the end of 1739. On December 24, 1739, Wesley's *Journal* recorded that, "After spending part of the night at Fetter

---

[42] Ibid.

[43] See Podmore, 66, fn. 211. In this context, Podmore argued that the band "Rules" could not have been written on Christmas of 1738 because there was no need for them then, as Wesley was not preparing for separation and autonomy from Fetter Lane at that time.

[44] Rupert E. Davies, ed., *Works* 9: 67. Frank Baker, who was the textual editor for vol. 9 of the *Bicentennial Edition of the Works of John Wesley*, also argued that the band "Rules" were drawn up in December 1738. See Baker, "Polity," 1: 219.

[45] This paragraph is dependent on e-mail correspondence with Colin Podmore, January 12, 2011. When I e-mailed Podmore requesting clarification on his comment at 66, fn. 211, asserting that the date of the band "Rules" was "clearly a mistake," he listed these three reasons as evidence against the feasibility of 1738 being the correct date for the "Rules of the Band Societies."

Lane, I went to a smaller company, where also we exhorted one another."[46] Second, the "General Rules" begin with the following statement: "In the latter end of the year 1739 eight or ten persons came to me in London who appeared to be deeply convinced of sin, and earnestly groaning for redemption.... This was the rise of the United Society, first at London, and then in other places."[47] If Wesley began organizing bands that were under his direct leadership in 1738, it seems that the "General Rules" would mention the earlier date, rather than 1739.[48] Third, it was at the beginning of 1740 that Wesley purchased the Foundery, which would have made the need for distinctive rules more obvious. Related to this, Wesley did not formally separate from the Fetter Lane Society until July 20, 1740.[49]

On the other hand, though the precise date of December 25, 1738, cannot be demonstrated to be correct, there is evidence that Christmas 1738 is *more accurate* than Christmas 1739. There are at least four reasons that make it plausible that the publication date of the "Rules of the Band Societies" is accurate. First, after visiting Herrnhut in the summer of 1738 and experiencing Moravian communal practice firsthand, Wesley made arguments that critiqued Moravian practice and suggested ways in which it should be altered. The place where this is most clearly seen was in Wesley's disagreement with James Hutton about the use of monitors in the Fetter Lane Society.[50] Wesley appeared to have lost the argument about the value of monitors as he wrote to Hutton: "The case of the monitors is past; so let it rest. Only I cannot approve of that circumstance...the forbidding the person reproved to answer."[51] Thus, it is plausible that Wesley's disagreements with Hutton provided further impetus for Wesley to begin thinking about his own approach to band meeting rules. In fact, when the "Rules of the Band Societies" are read in this light, it is striking that many of the questions focus on the willingness of the prospective member to receive open criticism from every member of the band. One question, for example, asks, "Do you desire that every one of us should tell you from time

[46] Wesley, *Journal* for December 24, 1739, in *Works* 19: 131.

[47] Wesley, "General Rules," in *Works* 9: 69.

[48] This argument is the least persuasive of the three, in my view, as Podmore seemed to equate the "General Rules" with the "Rules of the Band Societies" in a way that does not necessarily follow. My understanding is that the "General Rules" were created for all who were members of early Methodism, while the "Rules of the Band Societies" were created specifically for those who were members of the voluntary band meetings. In my judgment, this weakens the force of this part of Podmore's argument, because the "General Rules" were a new source in their own right and would not logically need to show dependence on the rules for band meetings. Further, in point of fact, Wesley was organizing bands well before the end of 1739.

[49] See Wesley, *Journal* for July 20, 1740, in *Works* 19: 162.

[50] Wesley's correspondence with Hutton was discussed in the section "Anglican Piety in the Wesleyan Band Meetings" in this chapter.

[51] Wesley, letter to James Hutton, December 1, 1738, in *Works* 25: 595.

to time whatsoever is in *his* heart concerning you?"[52] When the context of the dispute with Hutton about monitors is kept in view, this question could be seen as an intentional corrective, ensuring that monitors would not be permitted in Wesley's version of the bands.[53]

The second argument in favor of the published date of the "Rules of the Band Societies" comes from John Wesley's diary. On January 4, 1739, Wesley's diary contained two suggestive entries: At 10:15 a.m., Wesley wrote, "Writ for our Society." And at 11:00 p.m., Wesley wrote, "Writ our orders."[54] It is possible that "our orders" referred to the new version of the "Rules of the Band Societies."[55] The correct date of the "Rules" cannot be conclusively proved based on this evidence. However, it does provide data that support the possibility that "our orders" refers to Wesley's version of the band "Rules."

The third argument in favor of the published date of the "Rules of the Band Societies" is that the date of the "Rules" was never corrected during (or after) Wesley's lifetime. Although it is certainly possible that the date that appeared in the printed edition of the "Rules of the Band Societies" was incorrect, this possibility seems to be mitigated by the fact that Wesley did not correct the date in his own lifetime. According to the editors of the *Bicentennial Edition*, eighteen English editions of the "Rules of the Band Societies" have been identified. Among the listed variants, the printed date of the rules is not one of them.[56] If the date was incorrect, it seems odd that Wesley would not have noticed the inaccuracy and corrected it during his lifetime, or at least that someone else would have challenged the published date.

The final argument in favor of 1738 as the proper date for the "Rules of the Band Societies" is based on the fact that Wesley was involved as the leader and organizer of bands well before December 25, 1739. On March 22, 1739, George Whitefield wrote to Wesley, asking him to come to Bristol to continue the work

---

[52] Wesley, "Rules of the Bands," in *Works* 9: 78. "His" is italicized in the original to indicate that it can be substituted for "her" as needed. See *Works* 9: 77, fn. 2.

[53] This context may further clarify the final original question of the five questions that were to be asked at each meeting, "Have you nothing you desire to keep secret?" This question was dropped from editions of the "Rules of the Band Societies" starting around 1780. See *Works* 9: 78, fn. 12. This question may have been added as a direct response to the element of secrecy that Wesley seemed to think Hutton and others were adding to the monitor system, where the source of the reproof was not divulged and the person was not given an opportunity to respond.

[54] Wesley, diary for January 4, 1739, in *Works* 19: 369.

[55] Heitzenrater, *Wesley and the People Called Methodists*, 90. Ultimately, Heitzenrater seemed uncertain of the proper date of the "Rules," as he wrote, "The 'Rules of the Band Societies' which Wesley later dated 25 December 1738 (actually 1739?) was a revised version of the Fetter Lane Society rules." Ibid. (parenthetical question original). Dean expressed similar ambiguity: "This emphasis on openness and intimate confrontation was to become even clearer when, only six months later, John Wesley (probably) drew up the "Rules for the Band-Societies" [*sic*]. Dean, 125 (again, parenthesis original).

[56] For the list of variants, see Wesley, *Works* 9: 550–551.

Whitefield had been doing. In writing to Wesley, Whitefield urged him to bring his organizational gifts to shore up and strengthen those who had been converted under Whitefield's preaching. Whitefield wrote, "Many are ripe for bands. I leave that entirely to you—I am but a novice; you are acquainted with the great things of God."[57] Wesley eventually responded positively to George Whitefield's call, arriving in Bristol on March 31, 1739.[58] By April 4, 1739 Wesley was organizing bands, as his *Journal* recorded:

> In the evening three women agreed to meet together weekly, with the same intention as those at London, viz., "To confess their faults one to another and pray one for another, that they may be healed." At eight, four young men agreed to meet in pursuance of the same design.[59]

This passage indicates not only that John Wesley was organizing bands in Bristol by the beginning of April, 1739, but that he saw this as consistent with the previous precedent of the groups that were already meeting weekly in London. It is plausible that Wesley anticipated forming both of these groups and created a list of rules in order to help structure the life of the groups in a way that was consistent with his deepest convictions.

A document entitled "A Method of Confession, drawn up by Mr. Whitefield, for the Use of the Women belonging to the Religious Societies—Taken from the Original, under Mr. Whitefield's own Hand," is very similar to the "Rules of the Bands."[60] James 5:16 is cited as the rationale for the groups, and the first six questions are the same, with some minor differences in wording. The second section of "A Method of Confession" contains four questions that are not in the "Rules of the Bands" (2, 7, 8, and 9). It also omits the eighth question and changes the order of several of the other questions. The fourth section of "A Method of Confession" adds a question: "What comforts or communications have you had from God, since our last meeting?" and does not include the final

---

[57] George Whitefield, letter to Wesley, March 22, 1739, in *Works* 25: 612.

[58] Wesley, *Journal* for March 31, 1739, in *Works* 19: 46.

[59] Ibid., 47.

[60] Just before this book went to press, Randy Maddox made me aware of this document, which was published in *Gentleman's Magazine* in May 1739. The entire "A Method of Confession" is transcribed from the 1739 publication as appendix E. The full document and the correspondence in which "A Method" is situated will be published in Randy L. Maddox, "John Wesley's Earliest Published Defense of the Emerging Revival in Bristol," forthcoming in *Wesley and Methodist Studies* (2014). "A Method of Confession" deserves careful reading and further analysis. I have not been able to deal with this source adequately in this book because of the timeline for publication. It raises significant questions about Wesley's and/or Whitefield's relationship with women, particularly when considering them pressing women with questions about the proper object of love, such as "Whom do you love just now, better than any other person in the world?" as well as, "How do you feel yourself, when he comes, when he stays, when he goes away?"

question in the "Rules of the Bands," which was: "Have you nothing you desire to keep secret?" What is most intriguing about "A Method of Confession," however, is the addition of an entire section of ten questions that are focused on the proper object of love and whether the women "take more pleasure in anybody than in God?"[61]

Given the entry in Wesley's *Journal* from April 4, 1739, there is reason to suspect that "A Method of Confession" may have been created by Wesley and not Whitefield, as he appears to have been the one who started the bands in Bristol during this time.[62] As far as the date of the "Rules of the Bands," the publication of "A Method of Confession" provides tangible evidence that some form of the "Rules of the Bands" was in use prior to the date Podmore proposes.[63] Thus, there is strong evidence that the printed date of the "Rules of the Bands" is correct, or at least more accurate than a posited date that is an entire year later.

Regarding the "Rules of the Band Societies," what is of primary importance is the way that the document evidences the synthesis of Anglican and Moravian piety. The Wesleyan band meeting represented both an organizational, as well as a theological, synthesis of Moravian and Anglican piety. In his version of the band meeting, Wesley combined the Anglican understanding of the importance of a disciplined practice of the means of grace with the Moravian understanding of the need for the "living faith" that resulted from people receiving an assurance of the forgiveness of their sins and their new status as children of God.[64] The synthesis of a disciplined practice of the means of grace in order to directly experience God's "preventing, justifying and sanctifying grace" became the hallmark of Methodism and was vital to its subsequent growth.[65] As Wesley's conception of the means of grace developed after his separation from the Fetter

---

[61] Here, questions about gender dynamics in early Methodism are particularly at the forefront and should be central to further discussions of gender analysis in early Methodism.

[62] There is admittedly no way to demonstrate this. And the fact that the title attributes "A Method of Confession" to Whitefield, even saying that it was derived from the original "under Mr. Whitefield's own Hand" further complicates who the original author was. In an e-mail to the author on March 12, 2013, Randy Maddox hypothesized that the document is by Wesley, not Whitefield.

[63] In a forthcoming article, where Randy Maddox highlights "A Method of Confession," he evaluated an earlier version of the argument I have just made, concluding that "this document seals Watson's case, demonstrating that a list similar to that later printed by Wesley was in use among Methodists in early 1739." See Maddox, "John Wesley's Earliest Published Defense of the Emerging Revival in Bristol," forthcoming in *Wesley and Methodist Studies* (2014), 14.

[64] The quotation is from a conversation with Peter Böhler that Wesley recorded in his *Journal*: "I met Peter Böhler again, who now amazed me more and more, by the account he gave of the fruits of living faith—the holiness and happiness which he affirmed to attend it." Wesley, *Journal* for March 23, 1738, in *Works* 18: 232.

[65] Wesley articulated this synthesis in the sermon "The Means of Grace." Wesley defined means of grace as "outward signs, words, or actions ordained of God, and appointed for this end—to be the *ordinary* channels whereby he might convey to men preventing, justifying, or sanctifying grace." Wesley, "The Means of Grace," in *Works* 1: 381.

Lane Society, his view of grace and the means of grace broadened to include the band meeting itself as a "prudential" means of grace for Methodists.[66] The role of the band meeting in Wesley's development of this synthesis has not yet been appreciated.

Wesley continued to insist on both parts of this synthesis through the structures of Methodism and through his preaching and teaching. Moreover, Wesley further believed that the ability of Methodism to hold together both the importance of the consistent practice of the means of grace and the value of a Spirit-given assurance of one's status as a child of God was key to Methodism's vitality. As late as 1786, Wesley continued to insist that Methodist discipline was essential for Methodism's vitality.[67] For Wesley, the bands were essential to Methodist discipline not only because they aided the "flourishing" of individual Methodist's pursuit of holiness, but also because the bands seemed to contribute to the vitality of Methodist societies.[68]

Within the structures of communal formation, the band meeting was the first place where Wesley brought a disciplined practice of the means of grace together with an emphasis on the witness of the Spirit. The significance of this conjunction in the Wesleyan approach to communal formation developed along with his theology. This synthesis would later be expressed in the class meeting as well. The classes brought a disciplined practice of the means of grace together with the discussion of the state of the souls of the members of the classes in a way that allowed for broader participation and aided in the initial search for justification by faith and peace with God. The synthesis of Moravian and Anglican piety that was initially expressed in the band meeting was eventually broadened by Wesley so that people who were "seeking the power of godliness" could join together in their search for the witness of the Spirit and assurance of their status as children of God.[69]

Conflict with Anglicans and Moravians because of the Wesleyan Synthesis

Wesley's combination of Anglican and Moravian piety in the band meeting created tension in his relationship with both leaders within the Church of England and the Moravians because he insisted on the value of parts of the other tradition. Thus, one of the key reasons for Wesley's conflict with the Moravians

[66] Wesley's inclusion of the band meeting as a prudential means of grace in the 1763 Minutes has already been cited. See *Works* 10: 857.

[67] Wesley, "Thoughts upon Methodism," in *Works* 9: 527.

[68] See Wesley, letter to William Simpson, April 26, 1788, in *Letters* (Telford), 8: 57.

[69] The phrase "power of godliness" occurs in Wesley, "General Rules," in *Works* 9: 69, when Wesley discussed the "rise of the United Society" at the beginning of the document.

was because Wesley persistently emphasized the importance of practicing the means of grace prior to the experience of justification by faith and the new birth. Similarly, Wesley's conflict with some Anglicans was because of his arguing for the significance of justification by faith and the importance of assurance for subsequent growth in holiness.

John Wesley's relationship with Anglicanism was complex. At times, Wesley made what appeared to be ironclad commitments to the Church of England. At other times, he suggested that concrete expressions of Anglicanism were little more than a form of pseudo-Christianity that made people immune to the transformation that came with fully receiving the grace of God. In his 1746 essay "The Principles of a Methodist Farther Explained," Wesley sounded both of these notes. On the one hand, when his standing as a member and minister in the Church of England was challenged, he responded with what seemed to be deep loyalty:

> Nothing can prove that I am no *member* of the Church till I either am *excommunicated* or *renounce* her communion, and no longer join in her doctrine, and in the breaking of bread, and in prayer. Nor can anything prove I am no *minister* of the Church, till I either am *deposed* from my ministry or *voluntarily renounce* her, and wholly cease to teach her doctrines, use her offices, and obey her rubrics for conscience' sake.[70]

But on the other hand, when he subsequently discussed England's status as a "Christian country," he seemed to believe that the necessary qualities of such a country were rarely found among the English populace:

> Where are the Christians from whom we may properly term England a "Christian country"? The men who have the mind which was in Christ, and who walk, as he also walked? Whose inmost soul is renewed after the image of God, and who are outwardly holy, as he who hath called them is holy? There are doubtless a few such to be found. To deny this would be *want of candour*. But how few! How thinly scattered up and down! And as for a Christian, visible church, or a body of Christians, visibly united together, where is this to be seen?[71]

In this quotation, Wesley criticized the state of Christianity in England on two grounds: First, he argued that few English had experienced inward renewal of their souls, which seemed to be a reference to the importance of justification and the new birth. Second, even fewer were subsequently growing in holiness.

[70] Wesley, "The Principles of a Methodist Farther Explained," in *Works* 9: 195 (emphasis original).
[71] Ibid., 9: 225 (emphasis original).

Yet, Wesley felt that holiness was essential to the Christian life and that growth in holiness was most likely to occur within the context of Christian community. Wesley's passion for communal Christian formation in order to support growth in holiness would not itself have immediately prompted resistance among Anglicans. After all, the desire to promote holiness through communal practice was the essence of the Anglican Religious Societies. It was Wesley's insistence on the importance of the prior experience of justifying faith for growth in holiness and his insistence that holiness was an essential attribute of Christian identity, not an optional appendage, that prompted opposition from some Anglicans.

The particular part of the synthesis found in the Wesleyan band meeting that caused tension in Wesley's relationship with some Anglicans, then, was the importance of justification by faith and the value of the witness of the Spirit. When Wesley became convinced of the Moravian understanding of justification, he began preaching the necessity of justification and the new birth to his friends and in Anglican churches. His insistence on its importance often led to conflicts in both contexts.

Elizabeth Hutton, for example, was appalled at John Wesley's insistence immediately after Aldersgate that he had not been a Christian until May 24, 1738. Hutton wrote to John's brother Samuel Wesley Jr. of her conversation with John. She recorded her response to John: "If you was not a christian ever since I knew you, you was a great hypocrite, for you made us all believe you was one."[72] In responding to Hutton's letter, Samuel Wesley Jr. was on Hutton's side, not his brother's. Samuel concluded his letter to Hutton: "I heartily pray God to stop the progress of this lunacy."[73]

When John Wesley preached on the importance of justifying faith and the new birth from Anglican pulpits, his message often was not positively received, and he was frequently told he would not be invited back. It was common in the years immediately following his experience at Aldersgate Street, that after preaching in an Anglican church, Wesley would record something like the following in his *Journal*: "I am content to preach here no more," indicating that at the end of the service, it was made clear to him he would not be invited back.[74] Charles Wesley recorded similar experiences in his manuscript journal. On November 12, 1738, for example, Charles recorded: "Mr Piers refused me his pulpit, through fear of man, pretending tenderness to his flock."[75]

---

[72] Elizabeth Hutton, letter to Samuel Wesley, Jr., June 6, 1738, in *Original Letters, by John Wesley, and His Friends, Illustrative of His Early History, with other Curious Papers, Communicated by the Late Rev. S. Badcock* (Birmingham, UK: Thomas Pearson, 1791), 69, cited in Richard P. Heitzenrater, *The Elusive Mr. Wesley*, 2nd ed. (Nashville, TN: Abingdon Press, 2003), 262.

[73] Samuel Wesley, Jr., letter to Elizabeth Hutton, June 17, 1738, in *Original Letters, by John Wesley*, 75.

[74] Wesley, *Journal*, February 4, 1739, in *Works* 19: 34. See also ibid., 13, 16, and 28.

[75] Charles Wesley, *The Manuscript Journal of the Reverend Charles Wesley, M.A.*, 2 vols., S. T. Kimbrough Jr. and Kenneth G. C. Newport, eds. (Nashville, TN: Kingswood Books, 2008), 1: 152.

The negative response by some Anglicans to Methodist preaching and practice is also seen in the discussion of Methodism's relationship to the Church
of England in the 1744 Minutes. In the Minutes, the Church of England was
affirmed as "the congregation of English *believers*, in which the *pure word* of God
preached, and the sacraments duly administered."[76] And when the question was
asked, "Do we separate from the Church?" the answer was: "We conceive not: we
hold communion therewith, for conscience' sake, by constantly attending both
the Word preached and the Sacraments administered therein."[77] The background
tension between the Methodists and some leaders of the Church of England was
seen in the further question, "Do you not entail a schism of the Church? I.e., Is it
not probable that your hearers after your death will be scattered into all sects and
parties? Or that they will form themselves into a distinct sect?"[78] This question was
answered in four parts:

(1) We are persuaded, the body of our hearers will even after our death remain in
the Church, unless they be thrust out.
(2) We believe notwithstanding either that they will be thrust out, or that they will
leaven the whole Church.
(3) We do, and will do, all we can, to prevent those consequences which are supposed likely to happen after our death.
(4) But we cannot with a good conscience neglect the present opportunity of saving souls while we live, for fear of consequences which may possibly or probably
happen, after we are dead.[79]

Initially, this seems to be evidence of clear loyalty to Anglicanism. However, the
caveat "unless they be thrust out" turned the focus back to Anglicanism and
whether it would be loyal to its members who were called Methodists. Thus, as
Wesley considered the relationship of Methodism to Anglicanism in 1744, he saw
two likely scenarios. One possibility was that the Church of England would formally reject the Methodists. The other possibility was that Methodism would inject
a power into the Church of England that would cause it to rise, the way yeast works
in dough. Wesley hoped that Methodism would help Anglicans come to experience
the new birth and grow in holiness through the Methodist approach to communal
Christian formation.[80] Further, in the final part of the answer, one can appreciate

---

[76] Wesley, "The Doctrinal Minutes, 1749, Conversation the First, Wednesday, June 27 [1744]," in
Works 10: 784 (italics original).
[77] Ibid.
[78] Ibid., 785.
[79] Ibid.
[80] The two possibilities of Methodism either transforming the Church of England or the Church of
England "thrusting out" the Methodists are in contrast to Colin Williams and David Lowes Watson's
suggestion that Wesley primarily envisioned a third option, that of Methodism as an *ecclesiola in*

why the Methodist insistence that souls needed to be saved within the membership of the Church of England would have been offensive to many Anglican leaders and members of Anglican parishes.

Ultimately, Wesley's relationship to Anglicanism cannot be adequately understood if his emphasis on justification by faith, assurance, and holiness is overlooked. In fact, Wesley often emphasized these themes with particular force when speaking to primarily Anglican audiences. When he preached at the University Church of St. Mary in Oxford in 1744, Wesley called on his audience to "confess that we have never yet seen a Christian country upon earth."[81] In case anyone thought Oxford was excluded from the previous statement, Wesley explicitly asked, "Is this city a *Christian* city? Is Christianity, *scriptural* Christianity, found here?"[82] The implication in what followed was that Oxford did not meet Wesley's standard of a Christian city. Wesley even addressed another way that people might potentially let themselves off the hook. Some who heard Wesley may have assumed his "high" standards for Christianity would apply only to those who were preparing to be ordained in the Church of England. In order to make sure his audience understood that he was talking about *all* Christians, he said, "Let it not be said that I speak here as if all under your care were intended to be clergymen. Not so; I only speak as if they were all intended to be Christians."[83] Wesley reinforced the eternal significance of what he thought was at stake in the final paragraph of the sermon, "Lord, save, or we perish!"[84] Wesley was so deeply convinced that "scriptural Christianity" was intimately connected with being "filled with the Holy Ghost" and ongoing growth in holiness that he was unwilling to compromise on its necessity, even at great cost to his relationship with some in his native church.[85]

The synthesis found in the Wesleyan bands not only led to tensions in Wesley's relationship with several Anglicans, his attempt to hold Anglican and Moravian emphases together also led to strains in his relationship with many Moravians.

---

ecclesia. Colin Williams, *John Wesley's Theology Today: A Study of The Wesleyan Tradition in the Light of Current Theological Dialogue* (Nashville, TN: Abingdon Press, 1960), 152–153; Watson, Ph.D. diss., 5–6; Watson, *Early Methodist Class Meeting*, 127, 175. Frank Baker's discussion of Methodism as an *ecclesiola in ecclesia* had a different emphasis. Baker's use of the term highlighted the degree of separation that was already occurring within the Church of England (i.e., the Methodists were becoming a recognizable church within the Church of England). See Baker, *John Wesley and the Church of England* (London: Epworth Press, 1970), 106, 116–117. Collins, on the other hand, argued for a form of mutual dependence that carried a different connotation than the idea of an *ecclesiola in ecclesia*; Collins, 253. Finally, Methodist historian David Hempton viewed Methodism vis à vis the Church of England as a "clever parasite" that took what it needed from the environment provided by the Church of England and "then established an independent existence by embracing the enthusiasm and populism that Anglicanism generally despised." Hempton, *Methodism: Empire of the Spirit*, 19.

[81] Wesley, "Scriptural Christianity," in *Works* 1: 173.
[82] Ibid., 174 (emphasis original).
[83] Ibid., 176.
[84] Ibid., 180. See Matt. 8:25.
[85] Ibid., 179.

In fact, one of the key themes of the first four extracts of Wesley's *Journal* was his relationship with the Moravians and the disagreements that led to his separation from the Fetter Lane Society. The preface to the second extract focused on his relationship with Moravians and the advent of the dispute about stillness and the practice of the means of grace. Assigning a rather grandiose role to himself in the fight against Moravian stillness, which arose in September 1739, Wesley wrote, "I think therefore it is my bounden duty to clear the Moravians from this aspersion. And the more because I am perhaps the only person now in England that both *can* and *will* do it."[86]

The preface to the second extract of John Wesley's *Journal* also highlighted one of the key areas of disagreement between John Wesley and the Moravians: the role of the means of grace prior to the new birth. Wesley clung to the Anglican insistence on the importance of the means of grace for the Christian life, even prior to receiving the gift of the new birth. When Wesley left the Fetter Lane Society, he recorded reading a paper that charged some of the Moravians with teaching:

> 2. That a man ought not to use those *ordinances* of God which our Church terms "means of grace," before he has such a faith as excludes all doubt and fear, and implies a new, a clean heart.
>
> 3. You have often affirmed that "to search the Scriptures," *to pray*, or *to communicate*, before we have this faith, is *to seek salvation by works*, and that till these works are laid aside no man can receive faith.[87]

It is significant that Wesley's reason for his separation from Fetter Lane was precisely because of the repudiation of the value of the means of grace prior to receiving justifying faith. In other words, a major reason—if not the major reason—for Wesley's separation from the Moravians at the Fetter Lane Society was because he could not concede the importance of a disciplined practice of the means of grace *at every stage* of the Christian life. From this vantage point, it is not surprising that the "General Rules," which were written a few years after Wesley's separation from the Fetter Lane Society, contained an explicit endorsement of the importance of "attending upon all the ordinances of God" for those who are earnest in their desire "to flee from the wrath to come, to be saved from their sins."[88]

---

[86] Wesley, *Journal*, preface to *Journal* 2, September 29, 1740, in *Works* 18: 220 (emphasis original). Ironically, this preface was dated after Wesley had formally separated from Fetter Lane after declaring, "I have warned you hereof again and again, and besought you to turn back to the law and the testimony. I have borne with you long, hoping you would return. But as I find you more and more confirmed in the error of your ways, nothing now remains but that I should give you up to God." *Journal* for July 20, 1740, in *Works* 19: 162.

[87] Ibid. (emphasis original).

[88] Wesley, "General Rules," in *Works* 9: 70–73.

Wesley's synthesis of Anglican and Moravian piety in the bands led to conflicts with many of the people who were closest to him and had been most important in his spiritual development. Nearly a year after his bitter separation from the Fetter Lane Society, for example, Wesley recorded in his *Journal* after an encounter with Peter Böhler, "I marvel how I refrain from joining these men. I scarce ever see any of them but my heart burns within me. I long to be with them. And yet I am kept from them."[89] Despite the strains that Wesley's synthesis of Anglican and Moravian piety placed on his relationship with both groups, Wesley was determined to keep what he saw as the best insights of both.

The Band Meeting as the Ideal Location for the Pursuit of Holiness of Heart and Life in Early Methodism

On Wesley's understanding, a person who did not love God and neighbor was simply not really a Christian. Wesley made this case as clearly, and bluntly, as he could on two occasions when he preached at the University Church of St. Mary in Oxford, which would have been one of the most visible platforms Wesley could have expected to have within Anglicanism.[90] In "The Almost Christian," Wesley preached that the love of God and neighbor is "the right and true Christian faith" that involves "a sure trust and confidence...that by the merits of Christ his sins *are* forgiven, and he reconciled to the favour of God."[91] In a move that was typical of Wesley, he then directly asked his audience if they were altogether Christians. First, he asked, "Are not many of you conscious that you never came thus far? That you have not been even 'almost a Christian'? That you have not come up to the standard of heathen honesty? At least, not to the form of Christian godliness."[92]

If, as is seen in the sermon "The Almost Christian," the essence of "altogether" or real Christianity for Wesley was love of God and neighbor brought to life by living faith, the question that Wesley sought to answer with the band meeting was: How is growth in holiness best nurtured? As has been argued, the band meeting was the main place in Wesley's method that planned for growth in holiness. On Wesley's account, the society meeting was "a company of men 'having the form, and seeking the power of godliness,' united in order to pray together, to receive the word of exhortation, and to watch over one another in love, that they may help each other to work out their salvation."[93] In other words, justification

---

[89] Wesley, *Journal* for April 6, 1741, in *Works* 19: 190.

[90] These two sermons were "The Almost Christian" (1741) and "Scriptural Christianity" (1744). See *Works* 1: 131–141, 159–180.

[91] Wesley, "The Almost Christian," in *Works* 1: 137–139 (emphasis original).

[92] Ibid., 140.

[93] Wesley, "General Rules," in *Works* 9: 69.

and the witness of the Spirit were not expected or required for participation at the level of either the society meeting or the class meeting. The design of the class meeting was to "more easily discern whether they are indeed working out their own salvation."[94] Thus, the class leader met with their class every week to receive contributions toward the relief of the poor, to "inquire how their souls prosper," and to give guidance and direction to each member of their class.[95] Again, the class meeting did not require a prior experience of justifying faith or assurance in order to participate in it. In fact, one scholar has argued that "Almost half of the early British Methodists came to saving faith *after* they had completed their time on trial and entered full membership in the class meeting."[96]

The level of organization that did presuppose a prior experience of justifying faith was the band meeting. Because an experience of the forgiveness of sins, faith in Christ, and assurance of one's salvation were all required for entry into a band meeting, the band meeting was the basic structure that was ideally suited toward nurturing growth in holiness.[97] The prerequisite of a direct experience of God's grace was particularly important because it meant that the band meeting provided a location where members had already experienced the new birth and assurance and, as a result, could turn direct attention to the pursuit of holiness itself.

The importance of holiness in Wesley's theology and the focus of the band meeting on growth in holiness help to explain Wesley's continued insistence on the value of the band meeting even after the advent of the class meeting and its success throughout Wesleyan Methodism. Later in life, Wesley continued to reiterate the ongoing importance of the bands for Methodism's mission and vitality. In 1785, less than a decade before his death, Wesley exhorted Jonathan Coussins to "encourage all believers to meet in bands and to observe the Band rules exactly."[98] Later the same year, Wesley wrote to Thomas Wride, urging him, "In every place where there is a sufficient number of believers do all you can to prevail upon them to meet in band."[99] One of the reasons that Wesley continued to implore his traveling preachers to preserve existing bands and to start new ones was because the band meeting was the engine of holiness in Methodism. If bands were removed, there would no longer be a structure that primarily focused on growth in holiness. Again, fewer than three years before his death, Wesley implored William Simpson to "speak to every believer singly concerning meeting in band. . . . No circuit ever did or ever will flourish unless there are bands in the large Societies."[100] With the perspective of nearly fifty years after his experience

---

[94] Ibid.

[95] Ibid., 70.

[96] Albin, "Inwardly Persuaded," 45 (emphasis original).

[97] See Wesley, "Rules of the Bands," in *Works* 9: 77.

[98] Wesley, letter to Jonathan Coussins, February 25, 1785, in *Letters* (Telford), 7: 259.

[99] Wesley, letter to Thomas Wride, November 17, 1785, in *Letters* (Telford), 7: 301.

[100] Wesley, letter to William Simpson, April 26, 1788, in *Letters* (Telford), 8: 57.

of assurance at Aldersgate Street, then, John Wesley continued to see the band meeting as essential to the "flourishing" of Methodist societies.

Contrary to some recent discussions of the class meeting, when Wesley talked about the "sinews" of the Methodist societies, he was actually referring to *both* the class meeting and the band meeting.[101] Both classes and bands were key sources of strength for Methodism because, from Wesley's perspective, they facilitated different but nevertheless essential steps in the Christian life. The classes nurtured the new birth and assurance, while the bands facilitated growth in holiness.

It is important to recognize that Wesley saw both the class and band meetings as the "sinews" or source of strength for early Methodism, then, because limiting the source of strength to the class meeting would restrict the scope of early Methodism's goal—"spreading scriptural holiness"—in a way that distorts early Methodist theology and practice. Citing only the class meeting as the "sinews" of Methodism seems to imply that the class meeting was more important for early Methodist piety than the band meeting was. In one sense, this assessment is correct, as the class meeting did become a mandatory requirement for membership in Methodism and, as we will see, Wesley recognized the decline of the band meeting in his own lifetime. And yet, as the full citation from "A Plain Account of Christian Perfection," where Wesley endorsed both the class and bands as "the very sinews of our Society," and the previously cited letters written by Wesley both demonstrate, Wesley insisted that the presence and active functioning of band meetings were indispensable for Methodism's ongoing strength.

One reason the class meeting has been seen as more significant than the band meeting in early Methodist practice is because the class meeting was a requirement for membership in early Methodism and the band meeting was not. However, the fact that the band meeting was not required for every Methodist primarily reflects the early Methodist conviction that a desire for salvation was necessary for entrance into a Methodist society, and not an experience of conversion itself, more than it reflects Wesley's value of the band meeting, which presupposed a conversion experience. A related reason that the class meeting was required and the band meeting was not was due to pastoral considerations. The class meeting provided necessary accountability for people who wanted to "flee from the wrath to come."[102] It could be reasonably required, then, because the class only required that each member talk about the general state of their soul. On the other hand, the band meeting could not be required because not

---

[101] The relevant quotation is "Never omit meeting your Class or Band; never absent yourself from any public meeting. These are the very sinews of our Society." Wesley, "A Plain Account of Christian Perfection," in *Works*, Jackson, 11: 433.

[102] Wesley, "General Rules," in *Works* 9: 69.

every Methodist had experienced justification and the new birth, and so did not meet the requirements for involvement in a band meeting. Though Wesley did not explicitly state this, a related pastoral concern was likely that requiring people to enter into groups where they confessed their sins to one another would have been imprudent. Thus, while the logic of the Wesleyan Way of Salvation strongly suggested that every Methodist who had experienced the assurance of the forgiveness of their sins would benefit from being in a band meeting, the structure of the band meeting meant that it was a discipline that would be most likely to be effective if it was entered into voluntarily.

Despite Wesley's continued advocacy of the value of the band meeting, it did experience significant decline during his lifetime. In the letter previously quoted that Wesley wrote to Edward Jackson in 1781, for example, Wesley noted that the bands "will again fly in pieces if you do not attend to them continually."[103] Nearly two years later, Wesley wrote to Joseph Taylor that "the children will require much attention; and the bands too, or they will moulder away."[104] Similarly, in Wesley's letter to William Simpson in 1788, Wesley alluded to the difficulty of sustaining the bands in a reference to one particular circuit: "There were always some [bands] in Yarm Circuit, though not many."[105] These letters demonstrate that while Wesley sensed that the future of the band meeting was precarious, he was determined to do everything he could to strengthen its standing within Methodism.

One of the primary ways a history of the early Methodist band meeting impacts the history of early Methodism is that the bands highlight Wesley's emphasis on holiness and his struggle to keep Methodism committed to ongoing growth in holiness above all potential distractions. Thus, Wesley argued for the importance of the band meeting to the end of his life because he recognized that the decline of the band meeting implied a basic failure in Methodism's mission to "spread scriptural holiness." In other words, if the early Methodist message involved preaching "salvation by faith, preceded by repentance, and followed by holiness," then the people who experienced "salvation by faith" should actually become more holy, even to the exclusion of sin.[106] And as it has been previously argued, Wesley was convinced that holiness was best nurtured in the context of Christian community. Theology and practice were so integrated in Wesley's understanding that they were dependent on one another. And so Wesley wrote in 1786, "I am not afraid that the people called Methodists should ever cease to exist in Europe or America. But I am afraid lest they should exist as a dead sect, having the form of religion without the power. And this undoubtedly will be the case unless they hold fast both the doctrine, spirit, and discipline with which

[103] Wesley, letter to Edward Jackson, January 6, 1781, in *Letters* (Telford), 7: 47.

[104] Wesley, letter to Joseph Taylor, September 9, 1782, in *Letters* (Telford), 7: 139.

[105] Wesley, letter to William Simpson, April 26, 1788, in *Letters* (Telford), 8: 57.

[106] Wesley, "Thoughts upon Methodism," in *Works* 9: 528.

they first set out."[107] Doctrine gave purpose to Methodist discipline, and discipline brought Methodist doctrine to life in individual Christians.

In 1786, Wesley continued to insist that the "essence" of Methodism was "holiness of heart and life."[108] However, he also insisted that Methodism's value was deeply connected to the essentials of Methodism's doctrine, spirit, and discipline. Wesley wrote, "If even the circumstantial parts are despised, the essentials will soon be lost. And if ever the essential parts should evaporate, what remains will be dung and dross."[109] Thus, the early Methodist band meeting should be seen as an "essential" part of Methodism's attempt to foster holiness of heart and life.

The early signs of the death of the band meeting, then, were one of the key reasons that John Wesley felt that Methodism was failing toward the end of his life. Wesley's general frustration with the state of Methodism is seen in his sermon "On God's Vineyard" (1787):

> Why will ye still bring forth wild grapes? What excuse can ye make? Hath God been wanting on *his* part? Have you not been warned over and over? Have ye not been fed with the sincere milk of the word? Hath not the whole word of God been delivered to you, and without any mixture of error? Were not the fundamental doctrines both of free, full, present justification delivered to you, as well as sanctification, both gradual and instantaneous? Was not every branch both of inward and outward holiness clearly opened and earnestly applied? And that by preachers of every kind, young and old, learned and unlearned?[110]

As Wesley removed one excuse after another for Methodism's bearing "wild grapes," he turned to Methodism's insistence on the importance of communal Christian formation for growth in holiness. "Was not another cause of it [bearing wild grapes] your despising that excellent help, union with a Christian society? Have you not read, 'How can one be warm alone?' And, 'Woe be unto him that is alone when he falleth'?"[111] The "despising of Christian society," then, was an indication of indifference toward holiness. And because the band meeting was focused on holiness, its decline pointed to the failure of the Methodist mission to "spread scriptural holiness." If John Wesley's vision for Methodism were actualized, the norm of Methodist experience would have been that people would be awakened to their need for salvation by hearing the gospel preached in the fields

---

[107] Ibid., 527.

[108] Ibid., 529.

[109] Ibid.

[110] Wesley, "On God's Vineyard," in *Works* 3: 516 (emphasis original).

[111] Ibid., 517.

or in the context of society meetings. They would then repent of their sins and seek to "flee from the wrath to come" by joining a society and committing to participate in a weekly class meeting, where they would continue to seek justification by faith in Christ and the assurance of their acceptance as God's children. For those who received the gift of forgiveness and new birth, they would then continue to join together to watch over one another in love, particularly as they pursued holiness of heart and life in the context of the band meeting. And yet, well before Wesley's death, it had become clear that Methodists who were in band meetings were the exception, when they should have been the norm.

4

Early Popular Methodist Experience of the Band Meeting

The Band was of great service to me.

—Sarah Barber*

Wesley's conception of the band meeting and the role that this particular form of communal formation played in his theology of discipleship are crucial for an adequate account of Wesley's understanding of the Christian life. And yet, the significance of the band meeting for early Methodism is contingent on its appropriation within popular Methodist practice. If the various parts of the early Methodist "method" were preparing people for growth in holiness, which Wesley believed was most likely to happen within the bands, those who experienced justification, the new birth, and assurance should have sought the "closer union" that the bands were intended to provide.[1] The remainder of this work focuses on the popular reception of the band meeting and the ways that actual band meetings functioned in eighteenth-century British Methodism.

Popular Methodist primary source materials from the eighteenth to early nineteenth centuries reveal that the band meeting, with a few notable exceptions, did largely function according to Wesley's understanding when it was present and active. Despite significant evidence that attests to the existence of bands well into the nineteenth century, they do not appear to have been the norm for Methodists who experienced justification and the new birth. The most important deviation from Wesley's conception of the band meeting, then, is that the band meeting was not normative for early Methodists from 1738 to 1801.

---

* Epigraph is from Sarah Barber's account of her spiritual experience in the Early Methodist Volume (EMV). Sarah Barber, letter to Charles Wesley, May 1740, EMV 7.

[1] Wesley, "Plain Account," in *Works* 9: 266.

The Bands before the Advent of the Class
Meeting (ca. 1738–1742)

The Lord did bless me greatly in that ordinance.
—Henry Thornton**

From John Wesley's involvement in the Fetter Lane Society to the advent of the class meeting, the band meeting was the primary location of Christian communal formation within early Methodism. The key source materials that provide the historian access to the popular Methodist experience of bands from 1738 through 1742, the initial period of Wesley's development and leadership of bands, are manuscript letters and diaries. A particularly valuable collection of letters is the Early Methodist Volume, which is housed at the Methodist Archives in the special collections of the John Rylands University Library at the University of Manchester in England.[2] The Early Methodist Volume contains fourteen documents that are dated from 1738 through 1742 and contain at least one reference to a band meeting.[3] Another particularly valuable source,

---

** Epigraph is from Henry Thornton, letter to Charles Wesley, November 26, 1741, MAM, Ref: MAM DDCW 8/9, 17.

[2] Until relatively recently, the EMV has been largely overlooked by Methodist historians. Recent publications that have worked with the EMV include D. Bruce Hindmarsh, *The Evangelical Conversion Narrative*, esp. chapter 4, "White-Hot Piety: The Early Methodist Laypeople"; Phyllis Mack, *Heart Religion in the British Enlightenment*; and Andrew Goodhead, *A Crown and a Cross*. Hindmarsh provided a particularly helpful summary of the contents of the EMV: "A little-known scrapbook at the John Rylands Library, Manchester, contains 151 items, most of which are letters to Charles Wesley. The provenance of the collection in its present form is not known, but the manuscripts date from 1738 up to a few weeks before Charles Wesley's death in 1788. The archive includes forty-one conversion narratives, forty accounts of pious deaths, and nine reports of deathbed conversions.... There are also ten accounts of illness or suffering, two third-person memoirs, and a few letters reporting what evangelicals often called remarkable or alarming providences.... The balance of the collection consists of correspondence related largely to controversial issues in early Methodism such as the apocalyptic frenzy inspired by Thomas Maxfield and George Bell in 1762–3 and the schism that followed" (130).

[3] The EMV contains references to bands beyond this period as well. The documents from the EMV that contain band references for this period are: EMV 1, Margerit Austin, letter to Charles Wesley, May 19, 1740; EMV 2, Elizabeth Hinson, letter to Charles Wesley, May 25, 1740; EMV 7, Sarah Barber, letter to Charles Wesley, May 1740; EMV 17, Joseph Carter, letter to Charles Wesley, November 1741; EMV 18, Samuel Webb, letter to Charles Wesley, November 20, 1741; EMV 16, Thomas Cooper, letter to Charles Wesley, 1741; EMV 20, William Barber, letter to Charles Wesley, 1741; EMV 86, Hannah Hancock, letter to Charles Wesley, April 1742; EMV 53, Elizabeth Downes, letter to Charles Wesley, April 13, 1742; EMV 87, Elizabeth Halfpenny, letter to Charles Wesley, May 1742; EMV 126, Elizabeth Sais, letter to Charles Wesley, May 1742; EMV 136, Joan Webb, letter to Charles Wesley, May 1742; EMV 128, Mary Thomas, letter to Charles Wesley, May 24, 1742; and EMV 129, Naomi Thomas, letter to Charles Wesley, June 1742. EMV 13, Mary Ramsay, letter to Charles Wesley, June 4, 1740, does not contain an explicit reference to a band meeting, but mentions finding "much comfort in meeting at Sister Robinson's," which, based on other letters, is likely a reference to a band meeting led by Sister Robinson.

which has been consulted even less, is William Seward's manuscript diary from September 6–October 15, 1740.[4] This unpublished manuscript diary contains multiple references to band meetings and a description of how to organize and conduct a band meeting. Other significant sources are cited in this section, including primary source material published in the *Arminian Magazine* and the *Proceedings of the Wesley Theological Society*.

For the sake of facilitating comparisons between 1738–1742 and 1743–1765, this section and the next are divided based on parallel themes that emerge from the primary source materials. First, the organization and practices of band meetings are considered based on these sources. Second, popular references to bands in the earliest period show that the band meeting was a place where Methodists searched for justifying and sanctifying faith and assurance. Another theme of the material from 1738–1742 is that the band meeting was a place where searching and blunt conversation occurred. Finally, the discussion of participation in bands by lay Methodists, especially among those who were in London, shows the impact of the tensions in the Fetter Lane Society, particularly relating to Moravians who advised against the use of the means of grace prior to receiving justifying faith.

The Organization and Conduct of Band Meetings

The key source that provides information about the organization and conduct of the band meeting in the period prior to the arrival of the class meeting that is from a perspective other than John Wesley's is William Seward's manuscript diary for September 6 to October 15, 1740. Seward's diary covers the weeks of his life before his death as a result of head injuries received at the hands of an anti-Methodist mob at Hay on October 22, 1740.[5] In his diary, Seward frequently mentioned recommending the band meeting to people he met throughout his traveling and preaching.[6] In the period before Seward's falling out with the Wesleys, his diary contains a detailed description of how to organize and conduct a band meeting, as well as multiple references to his own advocacy of the importance of band meetings to those to whom he preached.[7]

On September 8, 1740, Seward wrote in his diary that after preaching at Cardiff on the fifth chapter of the Gospel of Matthew, he "advised them to meet

---

[4] The Seward manuscript diary has not been published and is housed at Chetham's Library in Manchester, England, Ref: A.2.116.

[5] Wesley references Seward's death in his *Journal*. See *Journal* for October 27, 1740, in *Works* 19: 172. See also ibid., note 75.

[6] This volume is of further historical interest because in the period of time that the volume covers, Seward became a bitter opponent of the Wesleys, with particular focus on confrontations with Charles Wesley.

[7] For a full excerpt of the section on the organization and conduct of a band meeting, see appendix E.

in Bands—to Confess their faults to one another & to pray for each other yt they may be heald."[8] Similarly, on September 19, Seward recorded that he

> Rose Early & Spoke above an hour from the wagon I Spoke from last night—upon Xtiany Confess their faults one to another & praying one for another that they may be healed—Recommend Bands unto them private & publick & Love feasts as mentiond before at the Gloster Societies.[9]

Seward's advocacy of the importance of band meetings was informed by his own participation in bands. On September 23, he recorded going "to my Dear Br. Wesleys Lodgings where both in Bands & private we exercised much in Prayer & Blessed be God there was Unity."[10]

The most extended discussion in Seward's diary of bands is an entry written on September 17, where Seward recorded not only his typical exhortation to meet in band, but further recorded the instructions he gave his audience on how to form and conduct an individual band meeting, as well as the "general Band" and love-feasts. This unpublished account provides a particularly illuminating account of the early practice of band meetings. As such, it is worth quoting at some length:

> We Exhorted them to Meet in Band, publick & private 5 or 6 in a Band & to have their Love feasts—According to the Example of the churches of Xt. at London & Bristol the order I was Enabled to leave ym. was to this purpose—none to be of the Band but Such who know their Sins are forgiven or are Earnestly Seeking forgiveness private Bands to Meet at Some of the Brethrens houses for one hour in a Week—to Confess their Faults one to another to pray one for the other that they may be healed—the Leader of the Band to begin with Singing & Extempore prayer then to Confess her own faults & Temptations & also declare wt—Communications she has had from above—then examines every one Singley—& Conclude wth. Extempore prayer wherein every one is desired to Exercise their Gifts & Talents—& to pray as their own & Brethrens States—Require—& no One to be of ye Band who is not willing & desirous to have their Hearts Search'd to ye bottom—& freely to be told of all their faults—that So Sin may not be Sufferd upon them.[11]

---

[8] Seward, diary for September 8, 1740.

[9] Ibid., September 19, 1740, 98–99.

[10] Ibid., September 23, 1740, 147.

[11] Ibid., September 17, 1740, 59–61.

Seward's account of the proper conduct of a band meeting is very similar to John Wesley's "Rules of the Band Societies." Seward's account framed the purpose of the band meeting by quoting James 5:16, just as Wesley's "Rules" did. Seward's organization of the weekly meeting is also similar to Wesley's. Seward suggested that each meeting should begin and end with prayer.[12] The key activity was also the same in both accounts, the confession of one's faults and temptations.[13] Finally, Seward, like Wesley, restricted participation in band meetings to people who were willing to "have their Hearts Search'd to ye bottom—& freely to be told of all their faults."[14]

Seward's account, however, was not entirely in line with Wesley's "Rules." Written nearly two years after the "Rules of the Band Societies," Seward's account reflected the impact of lay Methodism on the early development of the Wesleyan bands. A key difference is that Seward mentioned a band leader, while Wesley's "Rules" did not. Interestingly, Seward also consistently used feminine pronouns to describe the leader, who confessed "her own faults" and declared the "Communications she has had from above."[15] As will be seen in the next section, there were many more female bands in the Foundery Society than male bands. Wesley's "Rules," however, did not describe the role of a leader of the bands, and give the impression that the bands did not have a leader. Instead of mentioning a leader, Wesley's "Rules" described the chief activity of the band meeting as consisting of the members "speaking, each of us in order, freely and plainly the true state of our souls, with the faults we have committed in thought, word, or deed, and the temptations we have felt since our last meeting."[16] Seward's account, then, points to a significant difference between Wesley's conception and early Methodist practice. The presence of leaders in the bands is further attested to in other sources. In fact, John Wesley must have known that bands had leaders. William Oxlee, in a letter to Wesley, described a meeting with "ye Leaders of ye bans" without describing to Wesley what band leaders were, which suggests that Oxlee assumed Wesley had prior knowledge of their existence.[17] In this instance, it is likely that Seward more accurately described the Methodist practice of meeting in bands from 1738 through 1742 than did the "Rules of the Band Societies."

Another prominent theme in the primary source references to the conduct of band meetings from 1738 through 1742 was the directness of the conversations,

---

[12] Ibid., 60.

[13] Wesley, "Rules of the Bands," in *Works* 9: 77; and Seward, diary for September 17, 1740, 60.

[14] Seward, diary for September 17, 1740, 61.

[15] Ibid., 60.

[16] Wesley, "Rules of the Bands," in *Works* 9: 77.

[17] William Oxlee, letter to John Wesley, April 13, 1739, MAM, Ref: MA 1977/610/106. In the section discussing 1743 through 1765, we will further see that Wesley himself referred to band leaders in private correspondence.

which were often searching and blunt, that occurred in band meetings. When Sarah Barber asked to be allowed to join Sister Robinson's band meeting, for instance, Robinson bluntly denied her admission because she "had no faith."[18]

Although John Wesley intended for the band meeting to be a place where people's hearts were searched "to the bottom," the blunt statements made in band meetings, particularly as recorded in the accounts in the Early Methodist Volume, seem to have occasionally been perceived by the recipient as harmful to their search for peace with God.[19] In Margerit Austin's search for justification, a comment by a member of her band made her doubt her motives and even whether she had actually received the gift of faith. Austin described a sermon that Charles Wesley preached. After the sermon, Austin wrote:

> I Saw I was free and that Christ had Paid the Debt So I Came away with great Joy: and att night your text was who hath believed our report or to whom is the arm of the Lord revealed then I had Such Joy that I Could Scarce forbear Speaking: I Came to you the next Day being Saturday and told you: and you told me I was Justified att wapping: I fownd your prayers very helpful that morning.[20]

At this point in her account, then, it appeared that Austin had just had a major breakthrough in her journey to become an "altogether Christian." Indeed, she seemed to have been converted to Christian faith. However, she went on to write that the next day she attended her band meeting and "one of my Sisters in Band told me that my Coming to you was Self and that did me much harm for then I thought all that I Did or all ye Joy I had was Self."[21]

There are no further details about this particular band meeting, but one wonders whether the "Sister" who rebuked Austin did so out of entirely pure motives. Regardless, in this instance, the blunt conversation was initially harmful, though not fatal, to Austin's Christian journey, as it stalled her progress, though she did subsequently have an experience where she heard the voice of the Lord tell her that her sins were forgiven. Interestingly, Austin seemed to need the direct experience of assurance in order to trump the doubt brought on by the piercing conversation in the band meeting.

Sarah Barber's account gives further insight into the dynamics that could make the close relationships that the bands tried to foster ambivalent. Barber revealed that after her conversion experience, "I was going to Speak of it but Satan Stopt my mouth because there was Several Sisters had received the Same

[18] Sarah Barber, EMV 7.
[19] Quotation is citing Wesley, "Rules of the Bands," in *Works* 9: 78.
[20] Margerit Austin, letter to Charles Wesley, May 19, 1740, EMV 1.
[21] Ibid.

gift....I was going to Speak but was Stopt for thought if I Spoke it Would only Seem as if I wanted to be Like them in So much that I did not Speak."[22] Barber's account suggested that the closer community that the bands tried to foster could lead to an unhelpful self-consciousness, which in Austin's case was increased by a band member telling her that she was selfish.

And yet, the searching conversations that occurred in bands were often experienced as helpful. Elizabeth Sais recalled an encounter in a band meeting when Charles Wesley himself questioned her spiritual state. Sais experienced this conversation as painful, but ultimately necessary and helpful to her spiritual state. Her account is worth quoting extensively because it shows the connection of Charles Wesley's correction to her subsequent experience of God's presence:

> You met our Private Band, when you ask'd me if I was not troubled with Self and Pride, which Struck me as Dead, for I knew not what to Answer And when I came under the word, I found it to be Quick and Powerfull and Sharper than any Two Edg'd Sword, Piercing, even to the Divinding Asunder of Joints and Marrow and Discerner of the Thoughts and Intents of the heart, for I was So Sensibly cut by it as my Body might be by a Sword, and would often wish to withdraw my Self from Such Searching. Thus I went on Mourning for the Loss of my Saviour as one that Mourneth for his only Son, I was as Noahs Dove, and could find no rest, till I was again taken into the Ark, The Name of a Saviour was as Ointment Pourd forth, I hungerd and Thirstd for my Lord. and every Place Seemd Melancholy by Reason of his Absence, I could not lift my heart to God, for he Seem'd as Though he was not Pacified with me, I had no Power to Pray to God, but to the Son, It was he to whom I Sued for Pardon, that he might reconcile me again to his offended Father, which he did One Night I was at Prayer. For before I had Ended my Prayer to Christ, that he might reconcile me to his Father I could not only cry my Lord, but my Lord and my God. And in the Night, time, I had Such a view of the Presence of God, that humbled me to the Dust, I became in his Sight as a Dead Dog, I Saw, that I was in his Sight less than Nothing and Vanity; and as a beast of the Field. During my Seeing the Vision The Words that came to my Mind were those, I will make all my Goodness Pass before thee Behold there is a Place by me, and Thou Shalt Stand upon a Rock; And it Shall come to Pass, while my Glory Passeth by, that I will Put thee in a Clift of the Rock, and will cover thee with My Hand when I Pass by; And I will take away mine Hand, and thou Shalt See my Back Parts: but my Face Shall not be Seen. So Gracious a Sight it was, that I know

---

[22] Sarah Barber, EMV 7.

not how to forget it, "Rejoice O Heavens, and ye that Dwell therein, Shout with Joy ye Worms of the Earth, for the Lord Omnipotent's Condescension in Thus Humbling himself to behold a Sinful Worm, even Dust and Ashes, And favouring me with Such Amazing Love and Condescension. After this, the Lord was Pleasd to uncover my heart more and more, and So all Evil Tempers did beset me Sore, but the Lord gave me Strength as my Day was, I have gone through Close Trials, which always work'd together for my good.[23]

Sais's account contained a vivid description of her experience in a way that addressed Charles Wesley's concern that she was "troubled with Self and Pride." In her account, the experience was painful, but necessary for deeper growth.

Another source that provides insight into the role of searching conversation in the early Methodist experience of the band meeting is Henry Thornton's account of his spiritual experience. Thornton's account is preserved in a forty-one page manuscript addressed to "the Reverend Charles Wesley."[24] Thornton's account is unique because of the role that his social standing played in his involvement in the bands. Thornton's affluence was, according to John Wesley, potentially a hindrance to his ability to participate in a band. In fact, this was the primary concern that Thornton recalled Wesley raising about his entry into one of these groups:

When your Br (Mr. John Wesley) came to Town he asked me if I wo'd go into Band. but, says he, I suppose our Br. Thornton is too much a Gentleman to be in Band with poor people? (or to that effect) I was, at those words, much confounded, and wished I had been a Beggar rather than a Gentleman. I answer'd I was not such a Gentleman, but yt. I wo'd go into Bands.[25]

Thornton was subsequently received into "Br. Hodges's Band," which apparently did not give Thornton any special treatment, as he recalled that "Br. Hodges...gave me always good, Comfortable & seasonable—exhortations, and used to Sound me to ye bottom. I did not like it at first, but I tho't he did it for my Good, therefore I submitted to it, and ye Lord did Bless—me greatly

---

[23] Elizabeth Sais, letter to Charles Wesley, May 1742, EMV 126.

[24] Henry Thornton, letter to Charles Wesley, November 26, 1741, MAM. The date is listed in the calendar for the collection as November 6, 1741; however, at the end of the document, the date is November 26, 1741. The "2" is slightly obscured by other writing on the same line, and its absence in the calendar is likely a simple oversight.

[25] Ibid., 16–17 (in the margin, this part of the account is dated June 1740).

in yt Ordinance."[26] Wesley's initial concern seems to have been legitimate, as Thornton acknowledged that he did "not like" being "sounded to the bottom." Yet, Thornton ultimately testified that the searching conversations that occurred in the context of the band meeting were beneficial to his spiritual growth.

Thornton's account provides a concrete example of the ways in which the bands could moderate or transcend class differences among eighteenth-century Methodists. One explanation for Thornton's strong desire to be "a Beggar rather than a Gentleman" if that is what it took to be in a band meeting, even though it meant that he was "sounded to the bottom" by people beneath his social standing, was because the band meeting provided a new kind of social intimacy as industrialization began to transform English society. The band meeting, then, was a key piece of the "riot of association in the age of associations," providing community at a time when previous forms of community were being disrupted or lost.[27] Band meetings such as Thornton's also connected people who would have otherwise been separated by class boundaries.[28]

Thornton concluded his account by reflecting on his overall experience of the bands:

> As to my being in Band: I have great reason to bless God, that I was admitted,—for I do not remember, that I ever—parted without a Blessing. being always—desirous to open my whole Heart & speak plainly, for fear I should hide any—thing in my Heart. I always desire any—of ye Band wo'd ask me anything they fear or hear concerning me.[29]

On the whole, Thornton recognized that participation in a band meeting, with its probing of his spiritual state, could be painful. However, his desire to avoid self-deception helped him continue practicing this "ordinance" that he routinely found to be a blessing.

The Search for Faith and Assurance

One of the reasons that Methodists were willing to submit themselves to such probing of their spiritual lives was because they were often already painfully

---

[26] Ibid., 17.

[27] David Hempton, *Methodism: Empire of the Spirit*, 78.

[28] Thornton's experience in a band is a suggestive example of the ways in which the bands could be a socially conservative force, providing some evidence for both Halévy's famous "thesis" and Thompson's strong rejection of early Methodist communal formation because of the way it placated the proletariat.

[29] Thornton, 40–41.

aware of their separation from God and were seeking peace with Christ. Indeed, one of the most surprising aspects of early Methodist first-person accounts is that the band meeting was often integrally connected to the individual pursuit of justification by faith and assurance. Margerit Austin's account is one particularly vivid example:

> I knew I had Sin enough to Damn me. without the Sins of my parents and here I was in Dispair of finding mercy. . . . I went to the Sacrament and as I took the Cup Satan told me I Should be Damned for all that: but when we had Done receiving and the minister was Covering the Cup I Saw Christ Lay with his open Side. and I thought I Could See his heart bleeding for me: afterward I had a Strong Desire to get into the Bands: I went to ye Rvd Mr John Wesley and he admitted me—and the first we met, hearing the other tell the State of their Souls it was of much Strength to me to Speak of the State of mine.[30]

One of the striking things about Austin's account is that it reveals an area of contrast between popular Methodist practice and John Wesley's conception of the band meeting. In Wesley's conception of the band meeting, there were restrictions that limited who was eligible to participate. The "Rules of the Band Societies" explicitly stated that potential members had to meet certain prerequisites. A potential member, according to these rules, should already have received the gift of justification by faith in Christ and assurance from the Holy Spirit that they were God's children. And yet in Austin's account, she seemed painfully aware that she had neither justifying faith nor assurance. In fact, her pursuit of saving faith led to her "strong desire" to join a band meeting. Austin testified to receiving assurance that her sins had been forgiven *after* her initial involvement in a band meeting, "As I was arising the voice of the Lord Said to me thy Sins are forgiven twice—over I heard it a third time—Daughter be of good Cheer—thy Sins are forgiven thee: then I felt old things passing away and all things become new."[31] This particular account is especially interesting because Austin asked John Wesley himself for permission to be admitted into a band, and he admitted her. Apparently one needs to look no further than John Wesley himself in order to find deviations from his own conception of the band meeting![32]

---

[30] Margerit Austin, EMV 1.

[31] Ibid.

[32] One reason for this exception may have been pastoral considerations on Wesley's part. He may have felt that she was on the cusp of receiving justifying faith and that involvement in a band would have helped her continue moving closer to God. This example also points to one of the reasons that the discovery of the class meeting was viewed by Wesley as "the very thing we have wanted so long." Wesley, "A Plain Account," in *Works* 9: 261.

There are also examples, however, when the "Rules of the Band Societies" appear to have been followed more closely. In May 1740, Sarah Barber described her search for faith, writing, "the Lord Shewed me I had not faith though before I thought I had. yet I was very uneasy knowing I wanting Something but knew not what till then: nor then neither for then I thought I had faith though not Such Strong faith."[33] As a result of her search for faith, Barber revealed "att that time I went to Sister Robinsons to get into the Bands."[34] However, Barber recounted that Robinson did not admit her, "I told her my Case. but She told me. I had no faith which indeed was true."[35]

And yet, even in this case, Barber was allowed to join a band before she had met the requirements outlined in the "Rules of the Band Societies." As Barber's account of her conversion continued, she recounted her continued struggle to find faith, even as she participated in "Sister Robinson's" band meeting:

> The Lord Shewed me more and more my unworthiness and the want of a Saviour then I Saw the Saviour was not mine—for I was not Saved from Sin. neither Could I Call the Saviour mine—then I walked on in a Deep Spirit of bondage—: afterward I was admitted upon tryall and then I was Most time in great Doubts but then hearing the Lord Justifieth the ungodly then I knew I was ungodly but then Satan would Dragg it away again and would make me believe it was not for me. though Sister Robinson would often bid me not believe—him. then I hoped and found Comfort and indeed the band was of great Service to me for I never went away without Some Comforts.[36]

Despite her active involvement in a band meeting, Barber did not receive justifying faith until Charles Wesley was in town. Barber recounted, "att night when we met again in your Prayers the Lord was pleased to give me the Second gift of faith to believe—that Jesus was my Lord....I told Sister Robinson and She glorified god and Said I was Justified."[37] Both Margerit Austin and Sarah Barber, then, are examples of people who experienced justification after their involvement in a band meeting.

The accounts of Methodists such as Austin and Barber point to a lack of nuance in Wesley's "Rules," particularly related to requirements regarding the forgiveness of sins, peace with God, and the witness of the Spirit prior to admission into a band meeting. William Seward's manuscript diary, on the other hand,

[33] Sarah Barber, EMV 7.
[34] Ibid.
[35] Ibid.
[36] Ibid.
[37] Ibid.

does evidence a slightly more flexible approach to the requirements for entry into a band meeting, perhaps reflecting the impact of popular Methodists on the actual practice of the band meeting. According to Seward, none were to be admitted into a band "but Such who know their Sins are forgiven *or are Earnestly Seeking forgiveness.*"[38] Thus, Seward's prescription for involvement in a band meeting would have allowed for Austin and Barber's participation before knowing their sins were forgiven, because they were both earnest in their search for forgiveness.

Mary Thomas's experience is perhaps the most consistent with the conception of the band meeting found in Wesley's "Rules." Thomas wrote to Charles Wesley in May of 1742:

> Mr John Wesley...was telling of the five wounds Christ had receivd for us then I found his Blood aplied to my heart Saying Daughter be of good chear thy Sins are forgiven thee then I found Great Joy and Sweetness in my Soul I then went upon tryal into the bands and there I found Great Love to my band when Mr John Wesley came Last to bristol I was taken in to the publick bands I have not now Such Joy as I had I See my Self the worst of Sinners and Stands amazed to think that I am out of hell I See I can do nothing to the Glory of God I find every immagination of my heart is only evil—continualy but I know when christ Speaketh the word I Shall be made perfectly whole.[39]

In Thomas's account, she first found "Great Joy and Sweetness" in her soul as she was justified and given assurance of her new relationship as a daughter of God. After this experience, which clearly met the requirements for entry into a band, she then "went upon tryal into the bands."[40]

Aside from the role that the band meeting played in lay Methodists finding justification, the band meeting was also frequently discussed as an important context where especially meaningful spiritual experiences occurred. One example of this in the Early Methodist Volume is Elizabeth Downes's description of her participation in a band meeting when her desire to pray during the meeting led to feeling the "power of God" and being "filled with joy":

> In the morning I met the Band being then upon trial I found a more than usual desire to pray, as soon as I began I was led to plead the benefits of Christ's death and sufferings, I felt the power of God in such a manner as I cannot express I was filled with joy and Love wonder and

---

[38] Seward, manuscript diary, September 17, 1740, 59 (italics mine).
[39] Mary Thomas, letter to Charles Wesley, May 24, 1742, EMV 128.
[40] Ibid.

amazement that the Lord should reveal himself in such a distinct manner as I thought then few had seen or felt the like.[41]

In this account, it appears that the act of praying within the context of the band
meeting was a powerful spiritual experience for Downes, causing her to feel
"filled with joy and Love wonder and amazement" by how distinctly and directly
she experienced God.

Elizabeth Halfpenny's account of her spiritual experience to Charles Wesley
offers another example of the way that participation in a band meeting could act
as a catalyst for a deeper experience of God. Halfpenny's account was also generally in sync with John Wesley's ideas about the place of the band meeting in the
Christian life, as she described her experience of justification prior to talking
about her involvement in a band:

> About Two years ago, I went to Rose Glen, where under your ministry
> (Blessed be God) I Received Forgiveness of Sins, Since which I found that
> I Thirsted for Christ more and more, and more of his Love; I found that
> whatever Temptation would beset me, would work together for my Good,
> if I would Cast all my fears on the Lord, and not Trust in my own Strength.[42]

Although Halfpenny did not indicate when she first entered a band meeting,
her first mention of a band was after her description of this experience. In her
account, she also described the specific band meeting where she testified to an
experience of entire sanctification:

> At a certain time in my Band, I received an Extraordinary measure of
> the Love of God, which made me think that I Loved the Lord alone I had
> no love for the World nor the Things Hereof; I counted all Things but
> Dung and Dross for the Excellency of the Knowledge of Christ Jesus
> the Lord; Ever Since, the Word of God Sinks in my heart, with greater
> Power and Demonstration, and I Enjoy a Closer Union with God.[43]

Halfpenny's description of loving the "Lord alone" and counting "all Things
but Dung and Dross for the Excellency of the Knowledge of Christ Jesus and
the Lord" echoes Wesley's emphasis on the goal of the Christian life—entire
sanctification. Halfpenny's testimony, then, provides a concrete example of
the band meeting being a place not only where people pursued holiness, but
where they actually felt that they were becoming holy. It is also significant that

---

[41] Elizabeth Downes, letter to Charles Wesley, April 13, 1742, EMV 53.
[42] Elizabeth Halfpenny, letter to Charles Wesley, May, 1742, EMV 87.
[43] Ibid.

Halfpenny's experience of entire sanctification was closely connected to receiving "an Extraordinary measure of the Love of God." Moreover, she counts "all Things but Dung and Dross" because of the "Excellency of the Knowledge of Christ Jesus the Lord."

As previously mentioned, Wesley's conception of the band meeting preserved the Moravian emphasis on the witness of the Spirit. However, the band "Rules" did not specifically carve out a place for discussing the ways that members had experienced an awareness of God's love and favor. Seward's account of the band meeting, however, did provide a more prominent place for such experiences. The leader, for example, not only confessed her faults and temptations, but she also declared "wt—Communications she has had from above."[44] Seward expected that the leader of a band would have direct "communications" from God that she could relate to the members of her band. Seward also expanded on the role of prayer in the band meeting. In Wesley's "Rules," it is simply stated that the meeting should begin with prayer and end with prayer "suited to the state of each person present."[45] Seward preserved similar wording, but added to it. The meeting was to be concluded with "Extempore prayer wherin every one is desired to Exercise their Gifts & Talents—& to pray as their own & Brethrens States—Require."[46] Seward's account suggests a quasi-Pentecostal time of prayer when people's gifts and talents, as they related to prayer, were exercised in extemporaneous prayer.[47] One way of interpreting Seward's "Rules," then, would be to infer that he created a more communal role for facilitating the experience of the witness of the Spirit of God's love and mercy through a time of corporate prayer within the context of a band meeting.

Upholding the Necessity of the Means of Grace

The final theme of the accounts of early Methodists from 1738 through 1742 that reference participation in a band meeting related to tension about the validity of the practice of the means of grace prior to justification in the Fetter Lane Society. The accounts in the Early Methodist Volume illustrate the extent to which the dispute about the role of the means of grace filtered throughout the bands in London.

In 1741, for example, Thomas Cooper wrote an account of his spiritual experience to Charles Wesley. The disputes between people within the Fetter Lane

---

[44] Seward, manuscript diary, September 17, 1740, 60.

[45] Wesley, "Rules of the Bands," in *Works* 9: 77.

[46] Seward, manuscript diary, September 17, 1740, 61.

[47] Seward's account can also be seen to offer a very early hint that prayer meetings (which are explored in chapter 5 and became much more prominent in the late eighteenth century and early nineteenth century) were one of the factors that led to the decline and replacement of band meetings in popular Methodist practice.

Society about the means of grace are prominent in Cooper's account. According to Cooper, at a private band meeting, "the German brethren came over...mr Huton and a nother they tould me I had not faith but I withstood them and tould them I had and the witnes of the Spirit."[48] According to Cooper, Hutton challenged Cooper to test whether he had real faith by asking "if i Could not go to bed with out prayer and Leave of prayer for a fortnight."[49] To Cooper's surprise at the suggestion, he was told "if i Could not i trusted in my one workes."[50] After the meeting ended, Cooper recounted that "brother price Staid with me and thein the Lord Showed me their adwise was of the devil for i found it was plesing to flesh and blood for I had found often it was contrary to my nature to pray at all."[51]

One way of reading the remainder of Cooper's account is that it provides evidence that directly countered the arguments of "the German brethren."[52] Cooper tested the importance of the means of grace by practicing them, not by giving them up. He "Set a point for fasting and prayer and prayed to the Lord to Sho me is will in these things and the Lord Shoed me that I must keep in all is ordaninces and exort all to go their."[53] This experience seemed to resolve Cooper's concern about the value of the means of grace, as he wrote that "from that time the Lord hath Cept me in is oranancis and i hope will do to the end."[54] Cooper also testified to the ongoing relevance of the ordinances of God as, for example, he brought his "experince to the word of god it would not Stand the trial their for I found my Selves Come Short of it i found pride and worldly mindednes Lust and maney others evels in my heart."[55] Thus, Cooper's experience offered testimony to the value of the means of grace in providing direct experiences of God's presence and in acting as a corrective to self-deception, as Cooper felt that Scripture helped him recognize his true spiritual state.

Aside from giving insight into the Fetter Lane dispute about the role of the means of grace, Cooper's account also testified to the way the band meeting itself was a means of grace that reinforced the others:

> one night after we had been in band i found faith to be held I went to prayer and was determined not to rise from my knees till he forgave me my sin and gave me power ove the unclean Sperit and glorey be to his name for he heard my prayer and ever Since i have found a sweet Calmn in my Soul.[56]

[48] Thomas Cooper, letter to Charles Wesley, 1741, EMV 16.

[49] Ibid.

[50] Ibid.

[51] Ibid.

[52] It is worth noting that Cooper is referring to a *particular* Moravian view that should not be taken at face value as an accurate representation of the general Moravian view.

[53] Ibid. Cooper further recounted that subsequently, the Lord "Sent mr John to town and he Confirmed all that the Lord has Shoed me."

[54] Ibid.

[55] Ibid.

[56] Ibid.

Among other things, Cooper's account offers an example of the impact of Wesley's synthesis of the band meeting being practiced in the beginnings of the Methodist movement. Cooper sought justifying faith and assurance, but was convinced (in part because of the influence of John Wesley himself) that the best way to seek and find God was through a disciplined practice of the means of grace.

Thomas Cooper's influence on early Methodism is further seen in William Barber's account of his spiritual experience. Barber began his account by acknowledging that "the first instrumentt under god of bringing my soull outt Darkness into the marvelous Light, was our Brother Cooper."[57] Barber's account also contains numerous references to "Mr Mulltor" a reference to Philipp Molther (1714–80), who was one of the key advocates of stillness among the Moravians in the Fetter Lane Society.[58] Molther was featured prominently in Barber's first experience with a band meeting:

> about this time i was putt upon the triall Band & in the time appointed i was admitted into the bands i was putt into our Brother Edmunds Band we went on very well for some time together butt itt was nott Long befor Mr Mulltor Came over & he used to attend our band almost every time we mett i remember the first time he Came amongst us there was nothing done butt he telling us his own Experience.[59]

Eventually, Barber decided to ask Molther for his advice on whether or not he should receive the sacrament of Communion. Barber wrote to Charles Wesley that at the next band meeting, he asked Molther "the question whether or nott such a one as me Should go to the Sacromentt he tould me itt was onely for them that had attained to the Liberty of the gosple."[60] Barber recalled that a few people in his band were persuaded by Molther's advice. However, Barber also suggested that this was in part due to a low valuing of the sacrament of Communion: "i remember very well there was two or three in band that Readily received his Saying & said they Chould as well Stay away as go itt was Equally the same to them."[61]

[57] William Barber, letter to Charles Wesley, 1741, EMV 20. Barber's account offers further evidence that the publication date of the "Rules of the Bands" is plausible. Barber stated that Cooper invited him to attend a meeting at the Fetter Lane Society where Charles Wesley was "Expounding the Scriptures." Barber noted that he could not remember the topic of Wesley's sermon, "for this is about three years ago." This letter was initially dated 1742, but a line was drawn through the 2 and a 1 was written next to it, in what appears to be the same ink. This is far from conclusive, but offers another piece of evidence.

[58] For a sympathetic account of Molther's role in the Fetter Lane Society, see Podmore, 59–71.

[59] Barber, EMV 20.

[60] Ibid.

[61] Ibid.

Barber struggled with the temptation to turn away from the means of grace and confided in Cooper again, "i tould my mind to my old freind our Brother Cooper & he advised me to keep Close to the ordinances wich by the grace of god i did."[62] In attending to the ordinances, Barber wrote that he "found my Lord again for i know he is to be found in the ordinances for i have had many seewt [sweet?] & precious promises brought to me in the Sacroment."[63] Thus, the same sacrament that Molther advised Barber to avoid until he had proper faith, Barber found to be a key means of grace in his ongoing search for peace with God. Barber's testimony was a rebuttal of the Moravians who taught still-ness, because when Barber repented and recommitted to "Seeking him in his own appointed ways," he found that "the Lord as returned to me again."[64]

A final example of the tension related to the role of the means of grace prior to justification and the new birth is found in a letter from Samuel Webb to Charles Wesley. Webb appeared to have been aware of the tension and disagreements related to the practice of the means of grace. Yet, he also seemed to have been less interested in taking sides:

> I found out fetterlane Society were I attended ye word Constantly Twice a week And one thing is very Remarkable Although I heard them Preach their Still Doctrine yet for as much as I went with a Sencere Desire to Know Christ all their Warnings against the Ordinances where taken by me that we must Not depend any thing we did as Meritorious.[65]

Webb's account is interesting because it expressed an understanding of the means of grace that was consistent with John Wesley's understanding (the means of grace are not meritorious); however, it was not in line with Wesley's judgment about what Moravians like Molther were teaching about the means of grace.[66]

Further information on the importance of the band meeting is found in return-ing to Henry Thornton's account of his spiritual experience. Thornton described the discipline of meeting in a weekly band meeting as an "Ordinance," which is the term Wesley used for the means of grace that are listed in the third rule of the

---

[62] Ibid.

[63] Ibid.

[64] Ibid.

[65] Samuel Webb, letter to Charles Wesley, November 20, 1741, EMV 18.

[66] In his *Journal*, Wesley described his understanding of Molther's position on the means of grace prior to faith and his own: "As to *the way to faith*, you believe, That the way to attain it is to *wait* for Christ, and be *still*, i.e., Not to use (what *we* term) the 'means of grace.'... Whereas I believe, The way to attain faith is to *wait* for Christ and be *still*, In using 'all the means of grace.'" *Journal* for December 31, 1739, in *Works* 19: 132–133 (parenthesis original). Further, Wesley commented on the "fruits" of Molther's teaching, stating that he believed "that very little good, but much hurt, has been done by it." Ibid., 133.

"General Rules."[67] In one sense, Thornton actually expands the understanding of ordinances found in the "General Rules" so that it includes the practice of communal confession of sin that constituted the band meeting. Thus, Thornton's account provides evidence that the Anglican side of the Wesleyan synthesis was preserved and perhaps even accentuated in the popular practice and experience of the band meeting.[68]

In the period before the advent of the class meeting, then, the band meeting played a vital and visible role in the efforts of Methodists to support one another in the common pursuit of holiness. In this period, Wesley's conception was, for the most part, effectively put into practice. This is not altogether surprising, given that this section has considered only the four years after Wesley's creation of a particular set of "Rules" to order the bands. However, a few notable exceptions or additions to his conception of the bands have also been noted. The most significant ones are the presence of a band leader and the admission of men and women into bands before receiving justifying faith and being born again.

The Band Meeting in Popular Methodist Experience (ca. 1743–ca. 1765)

> Last night our Lord was in the bands.
> —Charles Wesley***

In 1742, the class meeting began to be used throughout the Wesleyan movement, even becoming a requirement for membership in a Methodist society. From 1743 through 1765, the class meeting became increasingly visible in Methodist primary source materials.[69] However, the primary sources from this period also contain frequent references to band meetings. The key sources for this period are from the

*** Epigraph is from Charles Wesley, letter to Sarah Gwynne, Jr., March 1748, MAM, Ref: MAM DDCW 6/92F.

[67] Thornton, 17. See Wesley, "General Rules," in *Works* 9: 73.

[68] That Thornton was on Wesley's "side" in the Fetter Lane dispute is seen in this account where Thornton referenced "the day we separated from ye fetter lane Brethren." Thornton, 17.

[69] A thorough discussion of this is beyond the scope of the present work. For a more detailed study of the class meeting in the early Methodist period, see David Lowes Watson, *The Early Methodist Class Meeting*, 93–116 (although Watson does not focus on the popular experience of the class meeting in its initial period with particular detail); and Andrew Goodhead, *A Crown and a Cross*, 145–187. There are some significant problems with Goodhead's account. His argument lacks a sophisticated account of the differences between the classes and bands. Moreover, Goodhead's argument that band material could be appropriated for a study of the class meeting makes even less sense in light of his conclusion that "the class meeting was the zenith of eighteenth-century piety, unlike anything that preceded it." Ibid., 185. Like David Watson, Goodhead did not thoroughly explore the primary source materials for the early Methodist period. Finally, see William Dean, "Disciplined Fellowship," 172–183. Again, Dean did not focus on the popular Methodist experience of the class meeting, primarily citing Wesley's accounts of the class and its purpose. Dean even asserted that "We know practically nothing about the class meeting before 1770 except through the references to them in

Early Methodist Volume,[70] the *Arminian Magazine*, manuscript letters to John Wesley, manuscript letters from Charles Wesley, and an unpublished manuscript by Samuel Roberts, a disillusioned former Methodist. Each of these sources provides further insight into the early Methodist experience of the band meeting and allows for further comparison of the practice of actual band meetings in the eighteenth century to Wesley's conception of the bands.

Several themes emerge related to the popular experience of the band meeting from these primary sources. First, these materials illuminate the organization and conduct of the bands in this period. Second, the writings of early Methodists demonstrate that the band meeting was a place where Methodists sought a direct encounter with God's grace that would enable them to become more holy, even leading to entire sanctification. Third, the accounts referenced show that the band meeting was a place where searching, blunt conversation occurred. And finally, the primary source materials contain references to the band meeting being a place where the means of grace were reinforced, as well as to the band meeting being a means of grace itself.

The Organization and Conduct of Band Meetings

The source materials related to the band meeting provide significant contributions to the understanding of what occurred in actual band meetings and the way that they were organized. The bands continued to be led by a lay leader, who often served to nurture leadership for the early Methodist movement, helping Methodists gain experience as spiritual leaders before beginning to preach.[71] There are also several examples of early Methodists who discerned and wrestled with their sense of calling to preach in their band meetings.

Wesley's *Journal*, letters, and tracts." Ibid., 181. This overlooks the substantial collection of primary source materials at the Methodist Archives in Manchester.

[70] The EMV contains fewer references to the band meeting in the period from 1743 to 1765 than it does in the period from 1738 to 1742. In the period considered in this section, there are five documents in the collection that contain references to band meetings. Two of the references are in relation to a person who has died (James Jones, letter to Charles Wesley, December 24, 1759, EMV 95; and "Jane Cowper's death" letter to Charles Wesley, 1763, EMV 45). Two of the references are about personal experiences in bands, but do not offer extensive insight into those experiences (Mary Maddern, letter to Charles Wesley, June 29, 1762, EMV 105; and William Ellis, letter to Charles Wesley, December 23, 1762, EMV 56). Finally, one account contains frequent references to band meetings, with particular attention to conflict related to the Wesleyan understanding of Christian perfection (John Walsh, letter to Charles Wesley, August 11, 1762, EMV 134). Chronologically, the five references in the EMV occur quite close together, from the end of 1759 to 1763.

[71] John Wigger, e.g., references Francis Asbury's (1745–1816) involvement in a band meeting and suggests that he was the leader of a class meeting as his initial steps in involvement and leadership in Methodism. Wigger, *American Saint*, 33–35.

Though Wesley did not describe the presence of a leader in band meetings, there are multiple examples of Methodists naming or referring to the presence of a leader in bands in the period from 1743 through 1765.[72] Richard Viney's manuscript diary, excerpts of which were published in the *Proceedings of the Wesley Historical Society* (*PWHS*), contains multiple references to band leaders. On February 26, 1744, Viney wrote: "went back to ye Foundery about 2 o'clock, was at a Conference of ye Bandleaders."[73] Viney's reference on May 26, 1744, to "a Meeting of some of ye Bandkeepers" is likely another reference to band leaders.[74]

Further references to the presence of leaders in early Methodist band meetings can be found throughout the period surveyed in this section. Margaret Wood recalled the role a band leader played in her spiritual development in a letter to John Wesley.[75] Similarly, Sampson Staniforth recounted to John Wesley that around 1763, he was "Leader of the Bands and Classes."[76] Finally, John Walsh's account of his spiritual experience in the Early Methodist Volume contains a reference to a disagreement related to Christian perfection between one of the members of the band who professed to have been made perfect in love and "Mr. Vardin, the Leader."[77] Ultimately, the references to band leaders in the period from 1743 through 1765 significantly reinforce the evidence from 1738 through 1742 that band leaders were a common fixture of band meetings.

One of the most important sources that indicate the presence of leaders in the Wesleyan bands during this period is George J. Stevenson's *City Road Chapel London and its Associations* (ca. 1872). Stevenson cited "a complete list of the Band Society" that was "from Mr [John] Wesley's manuscript."[78] This source also provided important demographic information about the Foundery Society bands in the mid-1740s. According to Stevenson, the bands were a significant presence in the Foundery Society in the mid-1740s. Stevenson recorded eighty-five different bands in the Foundery Society in 1745 alone! The list confirms one aspect of Wesley's organization of the bands, as the Foundery bands were divided by married women, single women, married men, and single men. There were just

---

[72] One important exception in this period is a letter Wesley wrote in 1757 to Dorothy Furly: "The great point is to pick out in Bristol (as in all places) such acquaintance as have a deep fear of God, a continual consciousness of His presence, and a strong thirst after His whole image. Such I take most of the leaders of bands to be." John Wesley, letter to Dorothy Furly, May 18, 1757, in *Letters* (Telford), 3:214.

[73] Richard Viney, manuscript diary, February 26, 1744, in "Richard Viney's Diary, 1744, VIII," ed. M. Riggall, in *PWHS* 14 (1923–24): 51.

[74] Ibid., May 26, 1744, in "Richard Viney's Diary, 1744, XI," ed. M. Riggall, in *PWHS* 14: 193.

[75] Margaret Wood, letter to John Wesley, January 7, 1772, in *Arminian Magazine*, 8: 58. Wood recalled that on September 22, 1761, "when I went to my Band, my dear Leader said…."

[76] "A Short Account of Mr. Sampson Staniforth: in a Letter to the Rev. Mr. Wesley," in *AM* 6: 295.

[77] John Walsh, letter to Charles Wesley, August 11, 1762, EMV 134.

[78] Stevenson, *City Road Chapel*, 32.

over twice as many bands for women as there were for men (fifty-seven female bands and twenty-eight male bands). There were also significantly more married bands (fifty-one) than single bands (thirty-four). The Foundery bands consisted of thirty-two bands for married women, twenty-five for single women, nineteen for married men, and nine for single men.[79]

The preponderance of women in the Foundery Society band lists confirms the prevailing assumption among Methodist historians that women made up the majority of early Methodists. In fact, the number of women in the Foundery bands provides empirical evidence of women's importance not only in early Methodist communal formation, but also in embracing and advocating Wesley's emphasis on holiness. The role of women in band meetings is further underscored by the number of women who wrote of their experiences in bands in the extant primary source materials referenced throughout this volume.

The bands, then, open a window into the experience of women in early Methodism and their pursuit of social holiness, showing the ways that the band meeting created a place for women to be alone together and to mediate God's sanctifying grace to one another.[80] In many instances, it was within the context of the band meeting that women were able to give voice to their experiences of God.[81] Thus, the band meeting is significant for the study of gender in Methodism, not only because it was a place where women were leaders, but also because in the bands, women ministered to each other by hearing confessions, praying for each other, and offering the forgiveness and healing they believed was promised in James 5:16.[82]

---

[79] Ibid., 33–38.

[80] "A Method of Confession," cited in chapter 3 (see also appendix E) complicates this picture, as it provides an example where the leader of a female band meeting appears to have been a male (either John Wesley or George Whitefield). Moreover, a prominent topic of the band meeting described in "A Method" was the male leader pressing the women on the proper objects of their love, which further calls for gender analysis. The fact that this practice (men leading women bands) was not continued in the band meeting at City Road may mean that there was a recognition that the female band meetings should be led by a woman and not a man.

[81] See, e.g., Margaret Wood's experience of sanctification and the way that her band leader seemed to help her testify to her experience by observing a visible change in her appearance and through prayer. Wood's experience is discussed in this chapter in the section "Seeking Growth in Holiness."

[82] The standard study of the experience of women in early Methodism is Phyllis Mack's exceptional *Heart Religion in the British Enlightenment*. Mack provided a particularly needed corrective to the tendency of historians to "insist on the centrality of feminine (or anti-masculine) elements in the movement while almost totally ignoring the thinking and behavior of actual women," 19. Mack further argued that historians and feminist scholars have neglected early Methodist women because of the strong "impression that we know about the gender of Methodism without needing to know about Methodist women," 20. Mack's survey of women's experience within Methodism contains multiple references to women's participation in bands. David Hempton noted the "disproportionately female following" in eighteenth-century British Methodism in "Women and Evangelical Religion in Ireland, 1750–1900," in *The Religion of the People*, 180–183. While Hempton discussed the significance of women class leaders in early Methodism, their role in leading and attending

The list of Foundery bands in 1745 also further demonstrates the presence of band leaders. For each band in the list, with the exception of two of the eighty-five, the word "Leader" is written next to the name of one of the people in the band.[83] Twenty-two of the eighty-five bands listed also contain the words "on trial" written next to one or two of the members' names. This suggests two interesting details that are not found in Wesley's "Rules of the Band Societies," "Directions given to the Band Societies," or "A Plain Account of the People Called Methodists"—namely, the presence of band leaders and the practice of admitting members on a trial basis.

In fact, the Foundery band lists suggest that parts of the Fetter Lane Society rules continued to be practiced in the Foundery Society. After asking a prospective member a series of questions and receiving their consent to the Fetter Lane "orders," the Fetter Lane Rules further outlined the process for joining the bands:

> 20. ... That those who answer these Questions in the Affirmative, be proposed every Fourth Wednesday.
>
> 21. That everyone then present speak clearly and fully, whatever objection he has to any Person proposed to be a Member.
>
> 22. That those against whom any Reasonable Objection appears, be acquainted with that Objection, & the admitting them upon Trial postponed, 'till that Objection is removed.
>
> 23. That those against whom no Reasonable Objection appears or remains, be in order for their trial, immediately formed into distinct Bands, & some Person agreed on to assist them.
>
> 24. That if no New Objection then appears, they be after a month's Trial admitted into the Society.[84]

band meetings is almost entirely absent from his account. In a later work, Hempton argued that Methodism "was predominantly a movement of women, who formed a clear majority of society members almost everywhere Methodism took root." He also noted that in American Methodism, women were a clear majority of participants in class meetings (by a ratio of nearly three to two). Hempton, *Methodism: Empire of the Spirit*, 30–31, 78. For his most extensive discussion of gender in Methodism, see *Methodism: Empire of the Spirit*, 137–150. On John Wesley's relationship with women and the band meeting, see Rack, *Reasonable Enthusiast*, 267–269. On women preachers in early Methodism, see Paul Wesley Chilcote, *John Wesley and the Women Preachers of Early Methodism* (Metuchen, NJ: Scarecrow Press, 1991).

[83] The two exceptions are the last single male band listed, which only contains two names (John Jones and Thomas Scipio) and one of the bands for single women (the members were Ann Graham, Hannah Butcher, Ann Parker, Sarah Orange, and Ann Broad).

[84] "Rules of the Fetter Lane Society," in *PWHS* 17 (1929): 32.

Thus, the Foundery band lists, which were apparently recorded by John Wesley's own hand, show a divergence from the conception of the band meeting as found in his own published writing on the bands.

Another key source for information on the organization and conduct of band meetings is a 261-page manuscript by Samuel Roberts. This manuscript is the most detailed and longest account of a Wesleyan band meeting during this period and of the Methodist approach to communal formation in general. Roberts's account is also unique among the sources that have been considered thus far, because the ultimate concern of it was to show that John Wesley and his followers were not Christians and that Methodism was actually harmful to Christian faith. Thus, Roberts testified that "It has pleased God in his Goodness towards me to Open mine Eyes, and to turn me from Darkness to light."[85] Roberts further wrote that he believed that "Mr John Westlay himself is Quite a Strainger to ye Saving knowledg of Jesus...he is nothing but a blind man."[86]

Roberts had experienced Methodism firsthand, as he "was led on by ye Doctrin of Mr John Westlay, for 16 years."[87] Roberts was also a leader in early Methodism, as he "was joined in thare Sociaty from ye year 1741 to 1759...having been in many classes, & having been a classleader, at Severl Plases & also a bandleader."[88] Roberts asserted that he was so "well acquainted with all thare affares, insomuch that if God's truth was Not My hindernce, I Could go & Preach thare Docktring in ye Manner thay Doe & am Porswaded that I Could give them Satisfaction."[89] Roberts, then, described the band meeting based on his experience as a member and leader of a band.

Perhaps surprisingly, Roberts actually provides evidence that confirms one aspect of Wesley's conception of the band meeting that prior sources have suggested was not consistently practiced: justification as a prerequisite for entry into a band meeting. Roberts wrote that "When any Man or woman Say & Spreds it a Broad that thay have found ye Pardon of all thare Past Sins & yt thay Now Can beleve yt thare Justifyed by Xt ye Preacher. Puts them into a band."[90] Roberts also wrote that the bands were divided based on gender and age (as opposed to marital status).[91] Roberts argued that "ye Proper number of a band" was three or four people, but bands often had five or six people, "because of a scarceness of leaders."[92] Finally, Roberts confirmed that the bands met weekly

---

[85] Samuel Roberts, manuscript, vol. 1. A transcription of Roberts's account of the band meeting can be found in appendix F.

[86] Ibid., 2.

[87] Ibid., 8.

[88] Ibid., 109.

[89] Ibid., 109.

[90] Ibid., 201.

[91] Ibid.

[92] Ibid.

and he described their basic activity as telling "how thare Souls Prospers, & how often thay have conqurd or been Concerd. by ye world flesh or ye Devil."[93] The key differences in Roberts's account regarding the organization and conduct of a band meeting as compared to the previous sources, then, are that justification was often a prerequisite for joining a band and that three or four people were considered to be ideal, though of necessity, there were often five or six people in a group.

The band meeting also appears to have nurtured leadership in early Methodism. Thomas Olivers (1725–99) and Alexander Mather (1733–1800) both particularly wrestled with their sense that God was calling them to preach within the context of their bands. In the accounts of both men, the members of their bands took very seriously the role they played in helping a member discern God's calling. Thomas Olivers recalled his initial sense of calling to preach and the support of the members of his band:

> From my first awakening, I had a great desire to tell the world, what God had done for my soul. And as I grew more experienced, this desire grew stronger and stronger. At last, I thought I was called to preach; this I communicated to the young men that met in band with me. They proposed a day of solemn fasting on the occasion; which we accordingly kept. They then advised me to make a trial: I did so; and many approved of my gifts; but others thought I ought to be more established.[94]

Olivers was supported by the members of his band, but they were honest with him about the possibility of failure. Olivers recounted that "it was often said, that I was too earnest to hold it long: and instances were produced, of some who had been exceeding earnest for a season, but afterwards fell away."[95]

Alexander Mather's account of his sense of calling to preach is remarkably similar to Olivers's. Mather's discernment began due to "strong impressions upon my mind, that God had called me to preach."[96] Mather, like Olivers, "mentioned this to my Band."[97] However, Mather noted that he only broached the subject with his band after he had "often sought God by fasting and prayer."[98] He and the members of his band then "set apart some days for the same exercises

[93] Ibid.

[94] Thomas Olivers, "An Account of the Life of Mr. Thomas Olivers, written by Himself," in *AM* 2: 129.

[95] Ibid.

[96] Alexander Mather, "An Account of Mr. Alexander Mather: in a Letter to the Rev. Mr. John Wesley," in *AM* 3: 146.

[97] Ibid.

[98] Ibid.

[fasting and prayer]."[99] An important difference in Mather's case was that the band referred him to John Wesley.

Mather's conversation with Wesley provides an example of the way in which the band meeting was seen as a training ground for leadership in Methodism:

> You [Wesley] said, "This is a common temptation among young men. Several have mentioned it to *me*. But the next thing I hear of them is, that they are married, or upon the point of it." I said, "Sir, I am married already." You said, "Care not for it; but seek God by fasting and prayer." I answered, This I have done. You strongly recommended patience and perseverance therein; and said, you doubted not, but God would soon make the way plain before my face.
>
> Soon after you appointed me to be the Leader of a Band, and in a little time, of a Class. And God blessed me in both: this did not at all alter my Conviction that I must preach; nay, it grew stronger and stronger, 'till having no rest day or night, I was constrained to come to you again and tell you just what I felt.[100]

After undergoing a rigorous discernment process, and persisting in his sense of calling, Mather was finally given a chance to preach, which began his entrance into itinerant preaching.[101] In both Olivers's and Mather's accounts of their callings to preach, their band meetings served as the hub or central place where they tested and prepared for their callings.

The way that early Methodists examined their sense of God's calling in bands is an example of the seriousness with which they took the more general task of searching their own hearts and one another's hearts in band meetings. In some cases, one Methodist probing her own heart for sin could lead others to recognize the depths of sin in their own lives. John Oliver's account provides an example of when this occurred within the context of a band meeting. Oliver recounted the growth of one Methodist society and his being invited to join a band meeting:

> Our society was now much united together, and did indeed love as brethren. Some of them had just began to meet in band, and invited me to meet with them. Here, one of them speaking of the wickedness of his heart, I was greatly surprised; telling them, I felt no such things, my heart being kept in peace and love all the day long. But

---

[99] Ibid.

[100] Ibid., 146–147 (emphasis original).

[101] Mather reported that Wesley gave him an opportunity to preach at Snow-field Chapel, then at Wapping Chapel, and then at the Foundery. Not long after these trials, Wesley invited Mather to go to Ireland as a traveling preacher in March 1756. Ibid., 147–148.

it was not a week before I felt the swelling of pride, and the storms of anger and self-will: so when I met again, I could speak the same language with them. We sympathized with each other, prayed for each other, and believed, God was both able and willing to purify our hearts from all sin.[102]

In Oliver's account, he recognized the presence of sin in his own life in a new way, primarily because of the confession of one of his fellow band members. In this example, one person's searching of his own spiritual condition led another person to recognize his need for further repentance and growth in holiness.

Another example of frank and searching conversation is seen in the diaries of John Bennet. After preaching in Baildon, Bennet searched for the cause of the "deadness" there.[103] Bennet discovered that a Methodist who was a class leader and a member of a band meeting "lived in sin."[104] As a result of this discovery, Bennet confronted the man: "I sent for him, and spoke plain but he co'd scarce bear it, began to excuse himself, until he condemned himself out of his own mouth."[105] Bennet then expressed what seems to have been one of the benefits of this kind of "plain" speaking: "Thus God bring all hidden things to light & will make manifest the secrets of every heart."[106] For sanctification to occur, hidden sins and the secrets of the heart first had to be brought to the light.

In a letter to John Wesley in 1749, Bennet further expressed his understanding of the value of "mutually exhorting and encouraging one another" in Christian community. Bennet asked Wesley to "Pray that a Sense of his gracious dealings towards Us, be a means of enlargeing our Hearts in Fervency of Affection one towards another, that we may mutually exhort & encourage each other to a steady Perseverance in the Path of Truth & Righteousness."[107] Bennet further reported to Wesley the progress in Methodist societies in "Cheshire, Derbyshire, and Lancashire" where people were

> brought to an inward Fellowship & Communion in the one Lord, one Faith, one Baptism; by which they are become Sensible not only of their own inward State, but have also a Sympathy & Concern raised in them, for the wellfare of others, watching over one another for Good,

[102] John Oliver, letter to John Wesley, June 1, 1779, in *AM*, "An Account of Mr. John Oliver, Written by Himself," 2: (1779), 419–420.

[103] John Bennet, diary for December 21, 1747; published in Simon Ross Valentine, "Significant inroads into Satan's Seat: Early Methodism in Bradford: 1740–1760," in *PWHS* 51 (1997–98), 147.

[104] Bennet, diary for December 22, 1747, ibid.

[105] Ibid.

[106] Ibid.

[107] John Bennet, letter to John Wesley, April 25, 1749, MAM, Ref: FL BNNJ(25/04/1749) Clm. box.

and in Christian Freedom & Plainness of Speech exhorting the Remiss, reprove the Offenders, encourageing the weak, and bringing forward the hindermost of the Flock; Which Brotherly Concern conduces to the gathering of Many.[108]

In this quotation, Bennet offered a profound summary of the goals of the Methodist pursuit of social holiness. One of the reasons that searching, plain conversation was important in the band meeting, then, was that exhorting, reproving, encouraging, and "bringing forward the hindermost" was necessary for the growth in holiness that the bands sought to facilitate.

The value of plainness of speech and searching conversation could also lead early Methodists to confront the members of their band meeting for not pressing them hard enough. In Sarah Ryan's spiritual memoir, she recounted her struggle to give up an idol that "lay concealed" in her heart.[109] She realized that "this was the thing that stood between God and my soul, and, that if I would give it up, my soul should grow like a cedar in Lebanon. And I was earnestly desirous so to do, to break through, and forsake all for God."[110] However, Ryan was unable to succeed in so doing; she recalled that she "could no more do it" than she "could cease to breathe."[111] She then recounted the conversation with her band meeting: "In this condition I was, when one day coming into the room to meet my band, I said, 'None of you shall deceive me any longer; I will not believe I have a grain of living faith.'"[112] In this example, Ryan held her entire band accountable for failing to speak truthfully to her concerning the state of her soul.

One of the major themes of Samuel Roberts's account of the Wesleyan bands was the central role of searching conversations by the leader of each band meeting. In order to give his reader a better sense of what happened in a band meeting, Roberts actually provided a hypothetical band meeting that "is a true & clear account of ye Nature of a band Meeting."[113] There are six people in Roberts's imagined band meeting: Brother Hate ye Truth (the leader), Brother Knowlittle, Brother Mizarable, Brother Fretful, Brother Slippery, and Brother Lofty. As their names suggest, Roberts uses each person to caricature various problematic aspects of Methodism. Brother Knowlittle, for example, when asked by Hate ye Truth how he is doing, responds, "I hardly know at Present."[114] In Roberts's account, one of the primary roles of the band leader was to ask searching, even invasive, questions of each member of their band. The leader's questioning of

[108] Ibid.
[109] Sarah Ryan, March 19, 1760, "Account of Mrs. Sarah Ryan," in *AM* 2 (1779), 303.
[110] Ibid.
[111] Ibid.
[112] Ibid.
[113] Samuel Roberts, 202.
[114] Ibid., 205.

members was exemplified, in Roberts's account, by Hate ye Truth's interaction with
Brother Lofty:

HATE YE TRUTH (H): Well Br. Lofty. How Doe you Doe.

BROTHER LOFTY (L): O bless ye Lord I am vary joyful. I have had swete
Comfort, Since we met to Gather.

H: Prase ye Lord...how longue Br. have you know ye Lord?

L: 3 hole years. & I find his ways to be ways of Pleasant Ness, & all his Pasths.
to be Paths of Peace.

H: what Doe You Never find No temtations

L: Yes but it is vary Seldom yt thay over Come me. & when thay do I Doe Not
Yeald to them wilfully.

H: But when your overtaken are you not Sorrowful then.

L: Yes I am Grevd. but then before I Sleep I Confess my folt to god....

H: have you Never no Cloudy Days. whear ye Sperit. hides his face. from you. &
you find you Soul Could Ded lifeless & barron.

L: O Yes, but Never longe tagether. for by. keeping Cloce to ye Means. Praying
& watching. & Meditating on ye Promisis of God: Setting ye Crown before.
my vue. I goe on Rejoysing. Reckning Every Day yt Goes over my hed, yt
I am a Day Nier Everlasting happyness....

H: but Br. are You Satisfyed in ye State your in, Dont you Want to be More
Holy. in Inward holyness. Good by inward Goodness. Jentel by in ward jen-
tilness. (that is) Dont You want to be holy throughout body Soul & Sperit

L: O yes. & I believe I Shall be one Day. before I Depart this fife. but this
work is ye Lords. & I'll leave it for him to Doe. according to his own
Will....

H: And houd Doe you find your Self in your Marridg bed.

L: formily. ye Ennimy Made a Great Snare of it but by ye blessing of God
I have Overcumd him at Last. for I Never lay with my wife after She is
with Child. but when She is not. then i Lay with hor. & Use my liberty.
but after it apears yt She is with Child, then I lay with my tow boys.
& ye Girls lay with thare Mother, & So I Now keep my Contiance in yt
Respect.[115]

At the end of his account of a typical band meeting, Roberts offered some nuance
to his account: "Some [band meetings] are Not Quite So Strict in Aczamining
into Every Porticalar Matter yt I have treated Upon...because Some Do not like
to be under So Cloce a tye...but those are Such yt walk Contrary. to what is
Mr Westlay. Skeam in Matters of this kind."[116] In fact, Roberts wrote that one

[115] Ibid., 209–212.
[116] Ibid., 216.

Methodist preacher did ask him "how I found my Self in my Marridg bed...& inded ye band yt I was in, & ye band yt I was leader of Was as Strict as Could be. & in this vary Method."[117] Though Roberts acknowledged that some Methodists did not want to be examined too closely, he was clear that when the leader failed to probe deeply into the lives of the members of their bands, they failed to live up to Wesley's standards, and they were doing so out of impure motives, such as "hugging thare darling evils, & Not Devulg Every thing yt thay Doe amiss."[118]

"Directions Given to the Band Societies"

The primary source materials on the popular experience of the early Methodist band meeting also offer insight into the development, availability, and appropriation of John Wesley's "Directions given to the Band Societies."[119] Richard Viney's diary and Thomas Willis's letter to John Wesley both provide references to the "Directions" that offer evidence that they were actually written and circulated among Methodists prior to the publication date.

Richard Viney's manuscript diary contains two entries that are of particular interest for the "Directions given to the Band Societies." On May 30, Viney recorded his presence "at ye Meeting of ye Band members who meet every Wensday night, at which was read ye new Band orders."[120] The next day, Viney reflected further on the "new Band orders" that had been presented. He wrote, "Thinking on the absurdities of some of Mr. Wesley's private Band orders."[121] Viney does not elaborate on what he considered to be "absurd" about the new, private Band orders. However, given that the "Rules of the Band Societies" had been available for several years before these two entries, it is most likely that Viney's reference to "new Band orders" is the "Directions given to the Band Societies." Viney's diary provides evidence that the "Directions" were available some six months before their publication date, which was "Dec. 25, 1744."[122]

A letter from Thomas Willis to John Wesley provides further evidence that the "Directions" were being used by Methodists before December 25, 1744. Willis's letter, which was written on November 13, 1744, begins, "If any man should ask me whether I am in the Band Society, I should answer yes; and should he ask me if I did follow all the directions given to the Band Societies, I must answer no."[123] Here, Willis appeared to refer not to general directions for the

---

[117] Ibid.

[118] Ibid.

[119] For the full text of the "Directions given to the Band Societies," see appendix D.

[120] Richard Viney, manuscript diary, May 30, 1744, in "Richard Viney's Diary, 1744, XI," ed. M. Riggall, in *PWHS* 14: 199.

[121] Viney, manuscript diary, May 31, 1744, in ibid., 200.

[122] Wesley, "Directions given to the Band Societies," in *Works* 9: 79.

[123] Thomas Willis, letter to John Wesley, November 13, 1744, in *AM* 1 (1778), 273.

bands, but to the actual document, which he referred to by name. Willis not only mentioned the "Directions" by name, he then accurately and extensively quoted from the document.

In fact, Willis used the text of the "Directions given to the Band Societies" to structure his report to Wesley of his spiritual progress. He wrote, "Now, Sir, I will tell you as plain and short as I can how far I do keep the rules, and where I do err."[124] The remainder of the letter consists of Willis citing each rule in the "Directions" and then describing how he has kept or failed to keep it. Willis's approach is particularly interesting because it is an example of critical engagement with Wesley's conception of the bands by an early Methodist that shows both agreement and disagreement, which is of further interest for class dynamics in early Methodism, as Willis was clearly in a subordinate position to Wesley. Yet, Willis felt comfortable challenging the "Directions" that Wesley had issued for his participation in the bands. The document is of further interest because at the end of several of Willis's comments, a response was written in parenthesis, most likely made by John Wesley who was the editor of the *Arminian Magazine* at the time this letter was published.

In this literary back-and-forth, Wesley agreed with one of Willis's critiques of the "Directions," granted another, and seems to have disagreed with one. To the first rule, "Neither to buy nor sell any thing at all on the Lord's day," Willis professed that he kept the rule with one exception:

> I do perform this rule exactly, except selling milk on Sunday mornings, which, I believe, is a work of necessity and mercy; but if it is not, I could easily strike all that off at one stroke. But there are some people in our class, which make it their business to sell milk, and to carry it to Bristol Sunday mornings. The cross seems to lie heavy upon them, since these rules are given out. The laws of the nation do allow selling milk on Sunday mornings. The cows must be milked on Sundays; children must be fed with the milk, and if it is not used, it will not keep good from Sunday morning till Monday.[125]

Wesley apparently accepted Willis's analysis as the parenthetical response is "Quite right."[126]

In the second example, Willis addressed the rule that those in bands were "to be at a word both in buying and selling."[127] Willis affirmed the spirit of the rule, as he sought "to speak the truth with my neighbour"; however, he could

[124] Ibid., 274.
[125] Ibid.
[126] Ibid.
[127] Ibid., quoted in.

not literally adhere to the rule because "a man cannot tell what he shall have for his goods before he goes to market, neither can he tell what he shall give for goods till he come there."[128] Here, Wesley seemed to grant Willis's analysis, albeit rather lukewarmly, as the parenthetical response of "All right" was less affirming than the previous one.[129]

The final example concerned the rule "To pawn nothing; no, not to save life."[130] Initially, Willis seemed to be willing to give his wholehearted endorsement to this rule as he responded, "This rule I keep to perfection, for I hate extortion of any kind."[131] However, Willis then took issue with the second part of the rule, "not to save life," writing, "I believe it is better to save life than to destroy. We read what David did, and they that were with him, and what Christ's disciples did to save life, and both were blameless."[132] In this instance, Wesley was unwilling to grant Willis's concern. Instead, he offered a bit of a rebuke: "You need take the phrase literally."[133]

The exchange between Willis and Wesley in this letter is interesting for several reasons. First, Willis's letter was written a month before the publication date of the "Direction given to Band Societies." Willis's letter, which cited every one of the rules found in the "Directions," provides strong evidence that the document was available before the publication date. Second, the concerns that Willis raised provides a window into the kind of exchanges that would have occurred between band leaders and those in their bands. Wesley attempted to add another level of oversight by providing guidelines, such as the "Rules of the Band Societies" and the "Directions given to the Band Societies," and by corresponding directly with Thomas Willis and many others. Yet, Willis's letter demonstrates that the guidelines had to be put into practice in particular contexts and that the application unavoidably involved interpretation.

Seeking Growth in Holiness

A major theme of popular accounts of the band meeting from 1743 through 1765 is the pursuit of growth in holiness. In bands, early Methodists sought direct encounters with God and discussed those encounters, or the lack thereof, with the members of their bands. The band meeting was also a central location for the pursuit of Christian perfection and conflicts related to it. The band meeting was not a closed system, as it was often an entry point for people on the cusp of justifying faith and assurance. Participation in band meetings also led others

128 Ibid.
129 Ibid.
130 Ibid., quoted in.
131 Ibid.
132 Ibid.
133 Ibid.

to the pinnacle of the Methodist structures for communal Christian formation, the select society.

Samuel Roberts described the purpose of the band meeting in his account of the errors and dangers of early Methodism. Despite his clear distaste for Methodism, Roberts's description of the band meeting's purpose appears to be fairly accurate:

> A band is a Company of People who joynd to gather in church falowship (should be) & when thay meet together thay reveal all thare Consarns, speritual & tempral to one another, thare Disined End is in this to help & Strengthen one another, to over Come ye world ye flesh & ye Devil. & to walk as Xt walked. til thay arive to be holy in thought word & Deed. & to have ye Sperit of God to abide with them for Ever. in thare inmost Souls ye Same as ye apostels had.[134]

In Roberts's account, then, the goal of the band meeting was for Methodists to support each other in order to overcome sin and become like Christ, holy in all things as Christ is holy. Roberts's account of the goals of the band meeting is largely in harmony with similar accounts from those who continued within the Methodist movement.

Further, early Methodist references to the band meeting often directly connected the desire for an initial experience of assurance, or further experiences through the Spirit of God's loving presence, to their involvement in bands. Even key leaders of Methodism, such as Charles Wesley, continued to seek ongoing assurance of God's love. Charles himself, particularly at the end of the 1740s, often described his experiences of God in the context of band meetings and select bands. In 1748, Charles Wesley wrote to Sarah Gwynne, Jr., who would become his wife, about one particularly memorable band meeting:

> Last night our Lord was in the bands as I have seldom, if ever known Him. O! what a spirit of prayer, what a flame of desire & love did he kindle among us! We lay weeping at his feet and washing them with our tears. And strong confidence He gave us all, (not excepting me).[135]

Not quite a year later, Charles again wrote to his future wife about the way that the band meeting led him to a deeper fellowship with other Christians. He also included the testimony of one of the other band members, who found a fuller sense of the love of God during the meeting. Charles wrote, "Another half hour I passed in yet closer and sweeter Fellowship with the W. Bands. Col. Gumley

---

[134] Samuel Roberts, 201.

[135] Charles Wesley, letter to Sarah Gwynne, Jr., March 1748, MAM (emphasis original).

was admitted, & filled with the Presence of Divine Love. He told me He had never known such a Day since He knew Christ."[136]

Nearly twenty years after Charles Wesley wrote the previous letters, Elizabeth Johnson wrote a letter that expressed a similar sense of an increase in fellowship and unity through participation in bands. Johnson wrote to Sarah Ryan:

> ye wednesday Nights Bands; & men bands, meet all to gather, where every one Speaks freely, & any prays as will, this God has greatly Bless'd to ye removeing of prejudices & increasing Union amongst us, we have bin forward to Speak of ye Loveing kindness of ye Lord in ye midst of them, & many there is whose eyes are opening.[137]

Johnson's account highlighted not only the way that the band meeting often served to increase "Union" among early Methodists, it also pointed to the practice of one aspect of Wesley's conception of the band meeting. In "A Plain Account of the People Called Methodists," Wesley described the gathering together of the bands at different levels for quarterly love-feasts. The male and female bands would each come together for a love-feast once a year, and once a year all of the members of the bands would come together for a love-feast.[138] In her account, Elizabeth Johnson described a love-feast of all the band members, where people testified to the ways that they had experienced God's presence and activity in their midst.

While people often testified to experiencing God more deeply through their involvement in bands, there are also examples where people strongly desired a deeper encounter with God, but did not immediately have such an encounter. Methodists would sometimes observe other Methodists' experiences of God, leading them to desire a similar experience for themselves. A letter published in the *Arminian Magazine* described a man who was searching for justification by faith and assurance:

> My soul thirsted for God. My wife prayed with and for me; and all the remainder of the day was spent in prayer, with scarce any intermission. I was not now distrest: I called God *my Father*. And knew, he *could* save me *now*. I went to the chapel, and my desire still increased. When you met the Bands and prayed with them, my thirst increased even to agony; yet I returned without the blessing.[139]

---

[136] Charles Wesley, letter to [Sarah Gwynne, Jr.], [January 24, 1749], MAM, Ref: MAM DDCW 5/22.

[137] Elizabeth Johnson, letter to Mrs Rien [Sarah Ryan], July 3, [ca. 1765], MAM, Ref: MAM Fl 4/5/3.

[138] Wesley, "Plain Account," in *Works* 9: 267–268.

[139] Letter to John Wesley from an unidentified correspondent, January 25, 1762, in *AM* 4: 163 (emphasis original).

This account demonstrates that the search for salvation was sometimes an ago-nizing and prolonged process for Methodists who searched for justification and inward witness of their new status as God's children.

Another example of the prolonged search for peace with God is found in the Early Methodist Volume. Mary Maddern wrote to Charles Wesley in 1762 that she "hapend one day to Meat with your Brother he adwisd Me to meat a Band wich I did for sumtime, before I found any relife from that deep distress of Soul."[140] Maddern's account also illuminates one aspect of the early Methodist experi-ence. The search for salvation might require extended seeking, but Maddern's example offered hope that persistence in the search for "relife from that deep distress of Soul" would not be fruitless.

Methodists not only searched for justification and assurance, they also pur-sued the ultimate goal of Methodist spirituality, Christian perfection or entire sanctification. Lawrence Coughlan's letter to John Wesley in 1762 provides an example of the pursuit of holiness through the bands, as well as an example of how that search could culminate in an experience of full deliverance from the power of sin. Coughlan described the deliverance of "Old Mr. Pritchard" from sin and the way in which his deliverance seemed to be contagious:

> In the meeting of the Bands, several of our Friends spoke. Old Mr. *Pritchard* was the first. He said, "For some time I have been longing for a clean heart; yet I thought God would not give it to so vile a sinner. And the first night Mr. *W.* preached, I felt something across my heart, like an iron bar, cold and hard. But hearing Mr. *W.* insist on the word *now*, I said, Lord, here I am, a poor sinner. I believe thou canst save me *now*, and give me a clean heart. In that moment Jesus said to my soul, *I will: be thou clean*. Immediately that bar was broken, and all my soul was filled with love: nor could I doubt but Jesus had made me clean, through the word which he had spoken to my soul." And three more were enabled, before we parted, to declare the same.[141]

Pritchard was given a "clean heart" during a sermon that "Mr. W" preached (presumably John Wesley, but it could also indicate Charles). It is significant that Pritchard spoke of his experience of being cleansed from sin during "the meeting of the Bands," which was likely another reference to a love-feast. As a result of Pritchard's speaking of his experience, three more band members were entirely sanctified before the meeting was over. Coughlan's account, as well as Elizabeth Johnson's, suggest that another reason the band meeting was

---

[140] Mary Maddern, letter to Charles Wesley, June 29, 1762, EMV 105.

[141] Lawrence Coughlan, letter to John Wesley, April 12, 1762, in *AM* 4: 337–338 (emphasis original).

meaningful to early Methodists was that it was an entry point to the love-feasts, where Methodists particularly anticipated encountering God.

Margaret Wood wrote of her experience of sanctification, which came, in part, as a result of John Wesley's preaching.[142] Wood recalled that on September 21, 1761, after hearing John Wesley preach a sermon, when she went home and prayed, the following words came to her mind: "I will cleanse thee from all thy filthiness."[143] The next day, when Wood heard Wesley preach on 1 Samuel 17, she recounted, "Glory be to God, that night my Goliath was slain! But I thought, I would not tell it to any body: but when I went to meet my Band, my dear Leader said, 'Sister W. the Lord has done great things for you: your very countenance tells me so.'"[144] At this point, a difference between Wood's experience and Pritchard's can be seen. Pritchard came to the love-feast ready to testify to the work that God had done in his life. In Wood's case, however, her band leader played an important role in helping her give voice to her experience. Wood wrote that her band leader, "went to prayer, and O what a fire of love did the Lord kindle in each breast! I was constrained to cry aloud, Jesus is my King! my God and my All!"[145] When Wood claimed this experience, her testimony seemed to act as a spark, which led many of the women who heard about her experience to experience the love of God more deeply. Wood concluded her account of this band meeting: "O what a testimony did the Lord give us of his love! We could not part: but continued four hours praising our dear Emmanuel."[146] The experiences of both Wood and Pritchard suggest that testimonies were often contagious in early Methodism. When one person spoke of their experience of God, other people who heard the testimony often had a similar experience.

The bands were not only a place where people yearned for and often experienced entire sanctification, they were also a focal point for disputes about the doctrine of entire sanctification and the range of practices that could appropriately be claimed by those who had been made perfect in love. These disputes were especially evident during the early 1760s when George Bell, after claiming to have been entirely sanctified, prophesied that the world would end on February 28, 1763.[147] For his part, John Wesley was concerned that Bell had become an enthusiast, placing too much value on "*feelings* and *inward impressions*; mistaking the mere work of *imagination* for the voice of the Spirit; expecting the end without the means."[148] Wesley, concerned to "do nothing hastily,"

---

[142] The reference in the quotation is from Margaret Wood, letter to John Wesley, January 7, 1772, in *AM* 8: 58.

[143] Ibid.

[144] Ibid.

[145] Ibid.

[146] Ibid.

[147] See Wesley, *Journal* for January 7, 1763, in *Works* 21: 402.

[148] Wesley, letter to Thomas Maxfield, November 1, 1762, transcribed in Wesley, *Journal* for November 1, 1762, in *Works* 21: 396 (emphasis original).

decided to allow Bell to preach one more time at West Street chapel and the Foundery. Ultimately, Wesley concluded that Bell had become an enthusiast, and "desired" that Bell "would come thither no more" because he "spoke as from God, what I knew God had not spoken."[149]

One of the reasons John Wesley discussed George Bell so much in his published *Journals* from November 1762 through April 1763 was because Bell, and his approach to Christian perfection, had already attracted significant attention among popular Methodists during this period. John Walsh, for example, wrote an extended account of his spiritual experience to Charles Wesley on August 11, 1762. At the center of Walsh's account was his involvement in band meetings, his pursuit of further growth in holiness, his interaction with several band members who claimed to have been made perfect, and the ministry and teaching of George Bell.

Walsh's account is of particular interest because of his frequent references to the bands, and because he does not appear to have been enamored with the band meetings, especially due to his observations of the hypocritical actions of those who were participants and professed to have been made perfect in love. One example of the kind of occurrence that cast doubt on the integrity of those who claimed to have been entirely sanctified illustrates Walsh's concern:

> I think it improper to name the next young Woman; who had not long declared herself perfect, when she desired me to give 2 Shils on her account to another; for she had no change, & wd return it the next time we met. I did so, & often saw her afterwards without receiving it: whereupon I said at last, "I gave what you desired me." "No, said she, for I gave it myself." ...I return'd to the perfect one; who then said, "If I did not give her 2 S:, I am sure I gave one." & so ended this trifling Affair. I made no reply; but cod never since think her perfect, tho' probably justified.[150]

Walsh also provides insight into disputes about entire sanctification in Methodism during the early 1760s. Walsh included in his account to Charles Wesley what appears to be a transcription from his diary of a band meeting at West Street in London on February 25, 1761: "The Men Bands at West Street were a greater number than usual, & disputed much about Perfection; which I counted a false Doctrine, founded on spiritual Pride. they who pleaded for it were many, & show'd much warmth; their Opponents were few & cool."[151] In July of the same year, Walsh recorded:

---

[149] Wesley, *Journal* for December 26, 1762, in *Works* 21: 401.
[150] John Walsh, letter to Charles Wesley, August 11, 1762, EMV 134.
[151] Ibid.

Out of 8 men, with whom I met in private Band, six declared they had clean hearts; and the chief of them, Mr. Langshaw, to whom I said, "Let him that standeth, take heed lest he fall and be not high minded but fear." tho' he seem'd to like these & most of my Words, call'd me afterwards, in his Prayer, *An Advocate for the Devil*. & likewise bro't Accusations against Mr. Vardin, the Leader, who had no otherwise contradicted him than by recommending Caution.[152]

Generally, Walsh appeared to be quite suspicious of the ease and confidence with which people professed to have been entirely sanctified. Walsh's hesitancy to endorse entire sanctification is especially interesting because he himself appeared to have experienced it, or at least something very similar to it. And yet, George Bell was one of the central figures in Walsh's own experience of entire sanctification. On February 17, 1762, Walsh recorded: "A Man at West Street Bands declared, he had been made perfect by Mr Bell's laying his hand upon him & on the 23d: much the same thing befell me."[153]

Despite his own experiences, Walsh continued to be very restrained in his evaluation of the doctrine of Christian perfection and fairly critical of those who "count themselves perfect."[154] Walsh provided a concise summary of his concerns about Christian perfection in a transcription of a letter he wrote to "Mr. Berridge" on July 1, 1762:

Now I will tell you what I think of all who count themselves perfect. They have tasted something of divine Joy; but neither been used to it, nor felt it a 10th part so strongly or ineffably as I have. They are neither buffeted by Satan, nor have a Thorn in their Flesh like me; but are absolutely at ease in Sion. Pleasing as that State is, I believe it lays the Soul open to the greatest Snare of Satan, which is spiritual Pride. Alas for me! that very State would be my choice, if I did not fear God.[155]

Walsh's negative experience with people who professed to have been entirely sanctified occurred within the context of band meetings. Among other things, then, Walsh's account suggests that the bands were one of the key places where disputes about Christian perfection were played out, which reinforces the arguments of earlier chapters that the band meeting was the key place that focused on growth in holiness in the early Methodist structures for communal Christian formation.

---

[152] Ibid. (emphasis original).
[153] Ibid.
[154] Ibid.
[155] Ibid.

The band meeting can be seen as an important context where Methodists not only pursued further growth in holiness, but wrestled with competing visions for what the possibilities of holiness were and how such holiness should be pursued. John Wesley was an active participant in these conversations; however, his voice was often competing with others to persuade Methodists that his understanding of the bands and of holiness continued to deserve their allegiance. Ultimately, Wesley objected to George Bell's message not only because he believed that Bell was an enthusiast, but also because Bell's enthusiasm detracted from the Methodist approach to Christian communal formation. Thus, Wesley complained of Bell and Thomas Maxfield "spending so *much time* in several meetings, as many that attend can spare from the other duties of their calling, unless they omit either the preaching or their class or band. This naturally tends to dissolve our society by cutting the sinews of it."[156] Wesley disliked Bell and Maxfield setting up meetings that were focused on the pursuit of a deeper experience of God that competed with the band meeting because the band meeting was already focused on further growth in holiness.

The early Methodist experience of the band meeting also provides evidence of functioning select societies in early Methodism.[157] Stevenson's *City Road Chapel* provided a list of the members of the select society in the Foundery Society from February 1744 in the same section where he listed the members of the bands. According to this list, which Stevenson says was again from "Mr Wesley's manuscript," there were seventy-seven people in the select society (twenty-eight single women, ten single men, twenty-five married women, and fifteen married men).[158] In letters to his wife from 1749 to 1760, Charles Wesley also frequently mentioned his participation in a "Select Band."[159]

Popular references further point to the existence of select societies in early Methodism. In 1757, Benjamin Biggs described being "admitted into the Select Society: by being present at which, I saw things in such a light as I never had done before."[160] Another early Methodist, John Walsh, in his extended account

---

[156] Wesley, letter to Thomas Maxfield, November 1, 1762, transcribed in Wesley, *Journal*, November 1, 1762, in *Works* 21: 396 (italics original).

[157] Select societies were introduced in chapter 2, "The Band Meeting."

[158] Stevenson, *City Road Chapel*, 33.

[159] See Charles Wesley, letter to [Sarah Gwynne, Jr.], January 16, [1749], MAM DDCW 5/20; Charles Wesley, letter to [Sarah Gwynne, Jr.], [January 24, 1749]; Charles Wesley, letter to Sally, July 9, 1759, MAM DDCW 7/18; Charles Wesley, letter to S. W., July 24, [?1759], MAM DDCW 5/96; Charles Wesley, letter to Sarah Wesley, March 2, 1760, MAM DDCW 7/57; Charles Wesley, letter to S. W., March 17, [1760], MAM DDCW 5/108.

[160] Benjamin Biggs, "Christian Experience," in *AM* 3 (1780): 495. This account is signed "B.B." However, the entry for Benjamin Biggs in the Methodist Archives, Manchester Biographical Index lists this passage from the *AM* as one of the references for information on Biggs. This account is somewhat perplexing, as Biggs also wrote that as a result of joining the select society, he "saw my want of inward holiness." Exploring this, however, is beyond the scope of the present volume.

of his involvement in band meetings in London Methodism, wrote that after having an experience of entire sanctification, John Wesley "had S. S. put upon my Ticket," likely a reference to membership in a select society.[161] Later in 1762, Walsh again referred to participation in the "Friday Meetings of the S. S."[162] Finally, in Jasper Robinson's account of his spiritual experience, he recalled that "in the year 1763, I received a large effusion of the Holy Spirit, and seemed changed throughout the whole man. I then joined the select band."[163] Robinson's and Walsh's accounts both confirm Wesley's conception of the select societies, as both men had an experience of entire sanctification, of being "changed throughout." They were then invited to join the deepest level of the Methodist communal structures for Christian formation, the select society.

The Band Meeting as a Means of Grace

Wesley's distinct conception of the band meeting was characterized by a synthesis of Moravian and Anglican pieties. This section considers the extent to which Methodists also endorsed or affirmed the Anglican emphasis on a disciplined practice of the means of grace, which was the other side of Wesley's synthesis.

Perhaps the most explicit affirmation of Wesley's understanding of the significance of the Anglican emphasis on a disciplined practice of the means of grace is seen in the published extracts of the journal of "Mr. G— C—." In November 1757, G. C. wrestled with his desire to "overcome my evil heart at last."[164] G. C. was hopeful that his desire would be fulfilled because of his ability to pray consistently; as he put it, he "seldom turned aside from prayer."[165] G. C. found prayer to be a means of grace. As he opened "the secrets of my soul to the Lord," he found that he was "strengthened to endure and to conquer."[166] Immediately after this discussion, G. C. explicitly connected the band meeting to the practice of the means of grace: "Indeed I find great help in the means, particularly my Band and Class; for which I cannot sufficiently bless God."[167] Here, then, the writer explicitly identified participation in a band meeting as a means of grace.

In James Jones's letter to Charles Wesley in 1759, Jones referred to the recent death of Sally Sparrow. One of the things that Jones emphasized as a key quality of a faithful Methodist was never missing "Band or Class upon any Consideration."[168] Although this passage did not explicitly connect the band

---

[161] John Walsh, EMV 134.

[162] Ibid.

[163] Jasper Robinson, "A Short Account of Mr. Jasper Robinson, Written by Himself," in *AM* 13 (1790): 576.

[164] G. C., journal for November 17, 1757, in *AM* 5 (1782): 641.

[165] Ibid.

[166] Ibid.

[167] Ibid.

[168] James Jones, letter to Charles Wesley, December 24, 1759, EMV 95.

meeting to the means of grace, it did resonate with Wesley's emphasis on the importance of consistent participation in Christian communal structures for growth in holiness.

Another interesting source that points to the ways in which the bands reinforced the importance of a disciplined practice of the means of grace is a letter identified as being from "Miss P. T." that was written to John Wesley. P. T. wrote to Wesley while in a state of "desperate misery" and told Wesley that she hoped "that the Lord would have mercy on me, and deliver me from the power of the Devil."[169] However, P. T. "could not pray" for herself and so she wrote to Wesley, asking for intercession on her behalf.[170] P. T.'s request for intercession is intriguing because she seemed to take for granted that earnest Methodists consistently practiced the means of grace. She requested, "that you, dear Sir, and such of your happy people who meet in Band, and ever heard the name of that miserable wretch P. T. would join in fasting and prayer on a Tuesday, the day on which I was born."[171] Her hope was that through their prayers and fasting, "the Lord may change my state, and have mercy on me; for the sake of his people's prayer."[172]

Samuel Roberts's extensive account of the band meeting also provides evidence that the means of grace were reinforced within the context of the Wesleyan bands. In fact, the means of grace were a key focus in Roberts's account of the types of conversations that took place within the band meeting. In introducing the bands, Roberts wrote that after someone received "Pardon of all thare Past sins," they would then be placed in a band meeting, "being thought then that Now thare more capable of Reseving more Privalegs, In ye use of ye Means."[173] Further, in his constructed account of a representative band meeting, the band leader (whom Roberts named Brother Hate ye Truth) testified that he was "in abled to stick Close to Prayer. & to ye use of all ye Means."[174] Hate ye Truth then encouraged the men in his band to make sure they relied on the means of grace. Hate ye Truth exhorted "Brother Mizarable" to "be on your guard wach & Pray. And keep Close to ye Means."[175] "Brother Fretful" was also implored to "watch & Pray keep cloce to ye Means. & you Must get ye Brethren to Pray for you."[176] "Brother Lofty" twice testified that he was sustained and refreshed by "keeping Close to ye Means."[177] In reading through the constructed band meeting in its entirety, one of the most prominent themes was the leader's concern about

[169] Miss P. T., letter to John Wesley, November 28, 1764, in *AM* 6 (1783): 216.
[170] Ibid.
[171] Ibid.
[172] Ibid.
[173] Samuel Roberts, 201.
[174] Ibid., 204.
[175] Ibid., 207.
[176] Ibid., 208.
[177] Ibid., 209, 211.

ensuring that each person was consistently practicing the means of grace, which suggests that Roberts wanted to highlight that the means of grace were, from his perspective, an annoyingly consistent and predictable focus of the bands.

The primary source materials related to the early Methodist experience of the band meeting from 1743 through 1765 show many references to the presence of leaders in band meetings and that the bands themselves were a place that nurtured leadership within Methodism. The bands were also a place where plain speech and searching conversation were valued and expected, which was consistent with Wesley's own conception of the band meeting, and where people were expected to be willing to have their hearts searched to the bottom.[178] Early Methodists also participated in band meetings because they continued to search for direct experiences of God; such encounters particularly occurred within the context of the gathering of all of the bands in a society at a love-feast. The testimonies given in band meetings and at love-feasts were often contagious and led other Methodists to a deeper experience of God's loving presence. The band meeting was also a place where the importance of the means of grace was reinforced, with many Methodists even adopting the band meeting itself as a significant means of grace.

The primary source materials from 1738 through 1765 show that the popular experience of band meetings was rich and complex. There were ways that the actual practice of band meetings diverged from Wesley's intentions for them, as well as indications that his understanding was appropriated in popular practice. Two notable exceptions to Wesley's intentions for the band meeting are that people, especially in the early period, who were particularly earnest in their search for salvation were often allowed to join a band meeting before receiving justifying faith, the new birth, or the assurance of the forgiveness of their sins. Another notable difference from the "Rules of the Band Societies" was that the bands appeared to have leaders who functioned similarly to the class leaders, inquiring into the lives of each member of the band.

The previous chapters argued that Wesley's conception of the band meeting was informed by the conviction that holiness was necessary to the Christian life and holiness was best nurtured through communal formation. It was further argued that Wesley's conception of the band meeting built upon these convictions and created a unique synthesis of Moravian and Anglican piety. The evidence from primary source accounts provides further confirmation that the Wesleyan synthesis of Moravian and Anglican piety was preserved in the bands. Though there were differences, these fundamental aspects of the Wesleyan band meeting were present in the early Methodist experiences of bands.

---

[178] John Wesley, "Rules of the Bands," in *Works* 9:78.

5

Transition in the Popular Practice of the Bands

We had a heaven among us!

—John Pritchard*

According to primary source material from 1766 through the beginning of the nineteenth century, the band meeting continued to be present and functioning in popular Methodism. There are signs of both the decline of the band meeting and a shift in the organization and practice of bands during this period. In the latter half of the eighteenth century, unpublished manuscripts, particularly diaries of early Methodist preachers, continue to reference the band meeting. Two other significant sources that provide documentation of the experiences of early Methodists come from *The Arminian Magazine*, which began publication in 1778, and *The Proceedings of the Wesley Historical Society*, which began publishing the research findings of historians of the Wesleys and early Methodism in the early twentieth century, frequently including transcriptions of eighteenth-century manuscripts from early Methodists. Contrary to what some scholars have suggested, there are significant manuscript references to bands that provide insight into the Methodist experience of the band meeting from the mid-1760s and beyond.[1]

The Band Meeting during the Maturation of Methodism (ca. 1766–ca. 1784)

Our hearts were united together in love.

—Zechariah Yewdall**

---

* Epigraph is from "Some Account of Mr. John Pritchard, Written by Himself," in AM 8 (1785): 567.

** Epigraph is from Zechariah Yewdall, "The Experience of Zechariah Yewdall," in AM 18 (1795): 218.

[1] John Wigger, e.g., has argued that "the distinction between the two meetings [classes and bands] became imprecise and classes largely replaced bands. But in the 1760s both were still in operation." Wigger, *American Saint*, 34.

During the period of the maturation of Methodism, prior to Wesley's decision to ordain preachers for North America, the band meeting continued to serve a visible role in Methodist piety. Charles Perronet wrote a summary of "the right Method of meeting Classes and Bands in the Methodist-Societies," which reinforced the value of the pursuit of social holiness, particularly by asking and answering probing questions about the state of one's devotion to God. An unanticipated finding was the extent of references to functioning select societies. As a result, the presence of these groups is also briefly considered.

The Organization and Conduct of the Bands

In 1781, Charles Perronet's (1723–76) summary of "the right Method of meeting Classes and Bands in the Methodist-Societies" was published in *The Arminian Magazine*.[2] In his account, Perronet began by blurring the distinction between classes and bands, arguing that, "in general, the method proper for meeting the one is proper for meeting the other."[3] However, the vast majority of the remainder of Perronet's "Method" focused on the band meeting. Rather than describing the details of how the band meeting was organized or how it functioned, Perronet devoted the entire section on the band meeting to the ways in which the bands should inquire into the lives of their members. The following specific questions were included among the types of inquiries that should be made:

> Whether they now believe? Now enjoy the life of God?
>> Whether they grow herein, or decay?
>> Whether they aim at being *wholly devoted* to God; or would keep something back?
>> Whether they take up their cross daily? Resist the bent of Nature?
>> Whether they can cordially love those that despitefully use them!
>> How they conquer Self-will, in its spiritual forms?
>> Whether they are simple, open, free, and without reserve in speaking?
>> Whether they have a clear, full, abiding conviction, that without inward, compleat, universal Holiness, no man shall see the Lord?[4]

---

[2] Wesley's publication of Perronet's work and his endorsement of it at the end is intriguing as Perronet had been an itinerant preacher and subsequently withdrew from Methodism. A. Skevington Wood, "Perronet, Charles," in *Dictionary of Evangelical Biography*, ed. Donald M. Lewis (Oxford, UK: Blackwell Publishers, 1995), 2: 876.

[3] Charles Perronet, "Of the right *Method* of meeting *Classes* and *Bands*, in the Methodist-Societies," in *AM* 4 (1781): 604. The entire document is included in appendix G (italics original).

[4] Ibid., 604–605 (italics original).

One characteristic of the band meeting that is particularly prominent in this account is that it was intended to be a place where direct and searching conversation took place. And, as the last question made explicit, the various inquiries were directed toward helping people seek further growth in holiness. Interestingly, the goals or values of the band meeting were not made explicit, but were rather implied in the ways that the questions were asked. Perronet did not say that the purpose of the band meeting was to facilitate the growth of its members in holiness. Nevertheless, the final set of questions evidence Perronet's belief that holiness was necessary for the Christian life.[5]

Perronet's account of the bands and classes is also interesting because it was significantly different than Wesley's previous "Rules" and "Directions" for the bands. However, the fact that Wesley published this document after Perronet's death showed Wesley's implicit endorsement of this vision for the bands. More important, Wesley explicitly endorsed Perronet's "Method" when it was published in *The Arminian Magazine*, writing at the end of the document, "I earnestly exhort all Leaders of Classes and Bands, seriously to consider the preceding Observations, and to put them in execution with all the Understanding and courage that God has given them."[6]

A more detailed look at the conduct of one particular band meeting is found in James Hall's description of his band, which met in the 1770s. His experience, however, more clearly revealed a dependence on Wesley's conception of the bands. In contrast to Perronet's account, Hall described what his involvement in a band meeting was actually like. His narrative was not a theoretical explanation of how a band meeting should function. Hall began by testifying, "What greatly helped me forward in the ways of God, were our band meetings."[7] Hall then outlined the basics of how his band functioned:

> We strictly attended to the Band Rules; each of us had one, to examine and try himself by all the week. We searched each others hearts faithfully; not one temper, word, or work, contrary to holiness, as far as we could discern, were suffered to escape unnoticed, or unreproved.[8]

Hall's initial description, then, highlighted the importance of examining oneself and then searching each other's hearts in the band meeting in order to remove

---

[5] The final question was "Whether they have a clear, full, abiding conviction, that without inward, compleat, universal Holiness, no man shall see the Lord? That Christ was sacrificed for us, that we might be a whole burnt-sacrifice to God; and that the having received the Lord Jesus Christ will profit us nothing, unless we steadily and uniformly walk in him?" Ibid., 605.

[6] Ibid.

[7] "An Account of Mr. James Hall, Written by Himself," in *AM* 16 (1793): 287.

[8] Ibid.

anything that was opposed to holiness. Next, Hall detailed the fruit or results of his involvement in a band meeting:

> This [the process of searching just described] made us watchful over the thoughts and desires of our hearts, and circumspect in all our outward conduct. It was our only desire to live to the glory of God, and to help each other forward in true Religion. The Lord remarkably crowned our little meetings with his presence and blessing. Our souls increased daily in love and unity. We enjoyed a heaven upon earth. I believe each of us were penetrated with the most lively gratitude for these seasonable opportunities; and the return of them filled us with more gladness, than the appointed times for our daily food.[9]

Thus, Hall testified that the discipline of a weekly band meeting facilitated a deeper experience of the "presence and blessing" of God, which led to growth in holiness, or an increase "in love and unity."

Zechariah Yewdall wrote of his involvement in a band meeting during the same period as Hall's. Yewdall wrote that the band helped to preserve him "from the snares incident to youth."[10] Moreover, the members of Yewdall's band also

> became better acquainted with each other's state, temptations, and besetting-sin. Our meetings were managed with faithfulness and decorum, and a conscientious regard to the real welfare and prosperity of our souls. We met in the fear of God, and our hearts were united together in love.[11]

Among other things, Yewdall's description provides further evidence that the bands were a place where searching conversation took place with the goal of the "prosperity of souls."[12]

Samuel Bardsley's manuscript diary is another important source for information on the bands. From the middle of July through the end of August 1766, Bardsley recorded the number of people who attended his band meeting each week. During these seven weeks, five people attended once, four people came twice, two people were present three times, and once Bardsley was the only one who showed up for the meeting.[13] Interestingly, Bardsley's assessment of the

---

[9] Ibid.

[10] Zechariah Yewdall, "The Experience of Zechariah Yewdall," in *AM* 18 (1795): 218.

[11] Ibid. Yewdall's highlighting of the "decorum" of the bands likely expressed sensitivity to the accusations that Methodists were enthusiasts, particularly after George Bell's excesses.

[12] The emphasis on close, searching conversation is discussed further at the end of this section.

[13] Samuel Bardsley, manuscript diary, July 18–August 29, 1766, JRUL, Ref: MA BRD (1977/205). The attendance at each meeting was as follows: July 18–five, July 25–four, August 1–two, August 8–four, August 15–one, August 22–two, and August 29–two.

earnestness of his band was not directly connected to the number of people who attended. On one of the occasions when there were four people at the meeting, Bardsley wrote, "I fear my Band is not So Earnest as it Should be I Pray God to Stirr them up."[14] Each time only one other person met with Bardsley, he recorded something positive about the meeting. After the August 29 meeting, for example, Bardsley wrote, "In the Evening I Expected my band Would have met but there was only Thos Greatrex and me I Had to tell him how I had been Labouring under a Tryal for Some Days and Indeed it was a tryal which was Very Close."[15] Thus, on Bardsley's account, one could have a profitable band meeting even with only one other person.

The primary source material for this period also contains multiple references to the presence and importance of band leaders. After having the nature of sanctification explained to her by a preacher, Christiana Malenoir testified that her band leader "who was a witness of this blessing, was also very useful to me; I saw it was my privilege, and determined to seek till I attained."[16] On August 31, 1766, Samuel Bardsley also recorded in his diary that he "met with The Band Leaders."[17] A letter from Mary Bosanquet Fletcher to John Wesley in 1782 discussed her role in organizing and leading a band. Fletcher wrote, "We have now also a Band, into which I gather the most lively; all that are newly blest, or that have any light into sanctification; and indeed we have much of the presence of God with us."[18] The final reference is perhaps the most interesting, as it points to how significant the role of the band leader could be. Hester Ann Rogers (1756–94), in a letter to John Wesley, described the decline of the band meetings that she led during a prolonged absence caused by an illness: "Hearing that my bands never met during my confinement...I said, 'Lord, if thy unworthiest servant can be a blessing to their precious souls, remove this affliction,' it is enough; 'and I will praise thee.' And the prayer was heard."[19] Rogers's miraculous account suggests that the success of bands in popular Methodism was strongly connected to, and in some sense dependent on, the quality of the leaders of the bands.

The source material also demonstrates how intimately connected the band meeting was to the other parts of the Methodist ecosystem. An account of the death of Catharine Lions pointed to the way that a trial band was the initial step for someone who "had many tastes of the love of God; but could not say, He was

[14] Ibid., July 25, 1766.

[15] Ibid., August 29, 1766.

[16] Christiana Malenoir, "The Experience of Christiana Malenoir, Written by Herself," in *AM* 15 (1792): 531.

[17] Samuel Bardsley, manuscript diary, August 31, 1766.

[18] Mary Bosanquet Fletcher, letter to John Wesley, July 7, 1782, in *AM* 13 (1790): 390.

[19] Hester Ann Rogers, letter to John Wesley, January 6, 1782, in *AM* 13 (1790): 108–109. The letter is published as "From Miss H. A. R.," which is highly likely to be Hester Ann Rogers.

reconciled to her."[20] As a result, Lions was advised, with "another young woman, to meet in a trial band."[21] In Duncan Wright's narrative, the two women had not met together in the trial band for long "till they both could rejoice in the love of God."[22]

Popular accounts also point to the close connection of the band meeting to public bands, love-feasts, and prayer meetings. Indeed, throughout this period, it is sometimes difficult to differentiate these meetings from one another. In October 1782, Mrs. M. Ward described her experience at the "public Bands" to John Wesley. Ward recounted that she

> was enabled to witness a good confession, and to tell the people, that through grace, I loved the Lord my God with all my heart, with all my soul, and with all my strength. The fire of his love constrained me to declare all that I experienced; that the efficacy of the Saviour's blood is powerful to cleanse from all unrighteousness.[23]

In a letter she wrote to Sarah Ryan about a meeting of all of the members of the bands, Elizabeth Johnson recounted:

> The Wednesday Night Bands; & men bands, meet all to gather, where every one Speaks freely, & any prays as will, this God has greatly Bless'd to ye removeing of prejudice & increasing Union amonst us, we have bin forward to Speak of ye Loveing kindness of ye Lord in ye midst of them, & many there is whose eyes are opening.[24]

Johnson's description was similar to Ward's; however, Johnson did not specifically name this meeting where "every one Speaks freely & any prays as will." Was it a love-feast, a public band, or a prayer meeting? Or were these terms synonymous in some contexts?

In the early 1770s, John Pritchard narrated a similar way that the band meeting was connected to these larger corporate gatherings of prayer and testimony to the work of God's grace in the lives of individual Methodists. Pritchard started a band of single men, which "increased every month" until it became so large that he divided it into four different bands.[25] The people in these groups

[20] Duncan Wright, "A Short Account of the Death of Catharine Lions," January 15, 1773, in *AM* 9 (1786): 138.

[21] Ibid.

[22] Ibid.

[23] M. Ward, letter to John Wesley, October 28, 1782, in *AM* 13 (1790): 610.

[24] Elizabeth Johnson, letter to Sarah Ryan, July 3 [ca. 1765].

[25] John Pritchard, "Some Account of Mr. John Pritchard, Written by Himself," in *AM* 8 (1785): 566.

had become so close to one another that they were "unwilling to be parted."[26] As a result, the members agreed to "meet altogether once a month, and to make it a Prayer-meeting."[27] Pritchard testified to the power of these monthly meetings, where "God was with us of a truth. We had a heaven among us! and a paradise within us! We lived as the Christians of old, having all things common: so that few, if any, counted any thing that he possessed his own."[28] Pritchard described this meeting as a prayer meeting, but it is not clear exactly how it would have been different from what happened in the public bands. In fact, the gathering together of all of the bands seems to have been one of the most constitutive aspects of the public bands.[29]

Bennett Dugdale's manuscript diary also contains references to a "Band Love Feast" and public bands. On April 7, 1778, Dugdale (1756–1826) wrote: "Glory be [to] God who has visited me in many and gives me to taste of his loving kindness, particularly at the Band Love Feast which I found to be solemn and profitable."[30] Five months later, Dugdale recorded his "desire to speak at public band of the abundance of the heart what I then felt of the love of God."[31] Finally, in January 1780, Dugdale noted that "we had a comfortable band love feast, at which I spoke a few words."[32] From these comments, it is not possible to clearly differentiate the public bands from the love-feast or the prayer meeting. These references do suggest, however, that an important part of the early Methodist experience of the band meeting was involvement in the larger gatherings of all of the bands of a specific society. These meetings were often times when Methodists particularly experienced the presence of God. The previous citations also support the argument of the previous chapter that the bands were an important entry point into the love-feasts and public bands.

Searching conversation was an important aspect of the practice of early Methodist band meetings, and this theme continued to be evident in the primary source materials from 1766 through 1784. Searching conversations were often a source of comfort for Methodists, as people realized they shared similar struggles. In 1766, Samuel Bardsley, for example, who "had been Labouring under a Tryal for Some Days" seemed to find some comfort in confiding in a member of his band meeting about this "tryal which was Very Close."[33] Nearly two decades later, John Goodfellow similarly wrote in his diary that he "rec'd a

[26] Ibid., 566–567.

[27] Ibid., 567.

[28] Ibid.

[29] Samuel Bardsley's manuscript diary also contains references to "Body Bands," which seem to be synonymous with "public bands." Bardsley, August 25, 1766.

[30] Bennett Dugdale, manuscript diary, April 7, 1778, MAM, Diaries Collection, Ref: MA 1977/216.

[31] Ibid., September 8, 1778.

[32] Ibid., January 18, 1780.

[33] Samuel Bardsley, manuscript diary, August 29, 1766.

little comfort, from hearing one of my Brethren had gone thro' the like grievous trials & temptations; and by looking to the Lord, my burthen was somewhat Removed before we parted from each other."[34]

As noted in the previous chapter, the standard of searching conversation could also have unhelpful consequences. Robert Wilkinson, for example, recounted that someone told his band leader that he was "prejudiced against the doctrine of Perfection."[35] Wilkinson's band leader then made indirect comments that Wilkinson realized were aimed at him. Wilkinson then asked the leader, "It is me you mean? He answered, 'What I have said, I have said.'"[36] As a result of this confrontation, Wilkinson found "violent prejudice" against the leader of his band, and he found that his "peace was gone. My soul was torn in pieces within me."[37] Wilkinson was so upset that he violated the confidence of the group and "told one of our people" about the actions of his band leader.[38] Wilkinson wrote that he "did not regard breaking the Band-Rules, because I was determined never to meet in a Band any more."[39]

The evidence considered in this section does not show a major shift in the popular experience and practice of the band meeting. There are significant references to band meetings that were written by the Methodists who were active in them. The band meeting continued to be led by a leader, and close conversation was valued. The bands were also an important entry point to the public bands, love-feasts, and prayer meetings. In short, the material considered in this section largely fills in the picture that was sketched in the previous chapter, rather than dramatically altering it.

The Search for Faith and Assurance

To what extent did the popular practice of the bands from 1766 through 1784 continue to evidence the influence of Moravian piety, particularly the importance of justification by faith and the witness of the Spirit? A common characteristic of accounts of the popular early Methodist experience during this period was that Methodists searched for peace with God through the witness of the Spirit. These experiences were often pursued with desperate determination. One of the key ways that the band meeting was connected to this search was by providing a location where Methodists could both express their yearning for peace with God and testify to occasions when they had tasted God's amazing grace.

---

[34] John Goodfellow, manuscript diary, November 16, 1784, MAM, Methodist Diaries, Box 15, Ref: MA 1977/236.

[35] "A Short Account of Mr. Robert Wilkinson," in *AM* 5 (1782): 236.

[36] Ibid., 237.

[37] Ibid.

[38] Ibid.

[39] Ibid.

Samuel Bardsley, for example, wrote in his diary in 1766 that he found his soul "Happy this Evening Particularly in Band."[40] As a result, Bardsley resolved to "never give oer wrestling with god Untill he gives me a Clean Heart."[41] Bardsley's diary shows how the band meeting facilitated the ongoing search for holiness and continued assurance of God's love and favor.

Another primary source account provides an example from 1773 of a woman who came to a band meeting "like one that had lost all hope."[42] This woman's honesty about her spiritual condition in band seemed to help her find peace with God. The writer of the letter, who is identified as "Miss B. C.," wrote:

> I attempted to pray for her, but my mouth was stopped. So sacred was the place, no one could utter a word. The silent language of our hearts was, Speak Lord, for thy servants hear! Before we parted, she found peace beyond all our expectations. She now waits for the witness of the Spirit, that she is his. O that her example may stir up those who are old and careless! that they too, may be in earnest for salvation.[43]

Though we do not have a record of this woman actually receiving the witness of the Spirit of her adoption as a child of God, the typical response to receiving such assurance would have been to testify to the experience. There are multiple examples of such testimony in the primary source materials from the 1770s and '80s. For example, one Methodist recorded that "on Sunday I told my Band what God had done for my soul."[44]

James Wigget's experience evidently followed Wesley's ideal more closely than most, as in 1780, "he obtained a gracious answer to his petitions; he found redemption through the blood of Jesus, even the pardon of all his sins; and a clear witness of his adoption into the family of God, through the merits of the Lord Jesus Christ."[45] "Soon" after, Wigget began meeting "in band, and was able to give a scriptural account of the hope that was in him, His soul was filled with peace and joy through believing, and his conscience was exceeding tender."[46] Interestingly, the narrator included the qualifier "scriptural" in this account, which seemed to legitimize Wigget's experience of God. The observation that Wigget subsequently had peace, joy, and a "tender" conscience after receiving

---

[40] Samuel Bardsley, manuscript diary, July 18, 1766.

[41] Ibid.

[42] "From Miss B. C. to the Rev. J. Wesley," October 13, 1773, in *AM* 9 (1786): 459.

[43] Ibid.

[44] "Miss E. R. to the Rev. J. Wesley," May 23, 1774, in *AM* 10 (1787): 49.

[45] William Ashman, "An Account of the Life and Death of Mr. James Wigget, of Norwich; Who departed this life October 3, 1792," in *AM* 16 (1793): 154.

[46] Ibid.

the gift of his assurance as a child of God further validated the prior "witness of his adoption into the family of God."

In his preaching and writing, John Wesley insisted that justification and sanctification both occurred by faith.[47] A similar emphasis is also seen in early Methodist accounts. In Henry Moore's "Life of Mrs. Fletcher," Moore preserved Fletcher's account of a young man who "was a Leader of a Band of young men, all desirous of giving their whole hearts to God."[48] Initially, the members of the band "could not see the way Clearly" for how to give their whole hearts to God.[49] The leader of the band then had a dream that beautifully illustrated the strong desire that Methodists had for peace with God through assurance, as well as providing insight into the theology that informed this desire:

> One night he dreamed he was at the bottom of a deep but dry well, with his little Company. He told them if they remained there they must Perish, and Exhorted them to Strive hard to get out. Accordingly they exerted all their strength endeavouring to get up, but all in Vain. At last they were quite discouraged, and said, what must we do? Truly said he I know not—but looking up he saw in the sky a little bright spot which did not appear larger than half a Crown. He looked at it for some time, when feeling himself move, He looked down into the Well, and found to his surprise he was Risen some feet from the bottom. As soon however as he looked down he began to sink again. O said he, now I have found the way out of the Well! It is by looking Steadily on yonder bright spot; On which fixing his Eye, he was brought up in a short time, and his feet was set on firm ground.[50]

The dream was a blessing to both the leader of the band and the members, as Fletcher recorded that "this discovery of the way of Faith, was greatly blest both to him and his Brethren."[51] Fletcher then added her own postscript to this dream, "I am convinced could I constantly look by the Eye of my mind to him, as the author and finisher of my faith, the work of sanctification would be going on without hindrance."[52]

Methodists not only discovered "the way of Faith" in band meetings, but it was also a place where people experienced growth in holiness, or sanctification. The weekly meeting was a place where Methodists continued to receive

---

[47] For one example, see Wesley, "The Scripture Way of Salvation," in *Works* 2: 163ff.

[48] Henry Moore, Life of Mrs. Fletcher, manuscript, JRUL, Fletcher-Tooth Collection, Ref: MAM Fl.22.

[49] Ibid.

[50] Ibid.

[51] Ibid.

[52] Ibid.

assurance of God's love and favor. Sarah Ryan, for example, emphasized this when she exhorted those who had been members of the classes and the band that she led to continue attending them, reminding those under her direction "How often our Lord Hath meat us with a blessing."[53] Similarly, another Methodist reported in 1764 on the state of the Dublin Society, noting in particular that "The Bands and Classes meet well, and are increasing in the knowledge and love of God."[54] Another example of the way that the band meeting was found to facilitate sanctification is seen in a letter written in 1773, wherein the writer testified, "I see more than ever how our Love-feasts, Classes and Bands are adapted to increase our union with God and each other."[55] Further, Bennett Dugdale wrote in his diary in 1778 after one band meeting: "My Soul also was abundantly refreshed...this evening at preach and in meeting my Band."[56] Finally, the author of Sarah Roberts's spiritual experience wrote that in 1782 she "received a clear witness that God, for Christ's sake, had blotted out all her sins, and adopted her into his family."[57] Immediately after this, she began meeting in a band, where she "often experienced...the divine presence and much consolation."[58] Therefore, many Methodists testified that when they met their band, they experienced assurance of God's love and favor (not necessarily for the first time). These encounters with "the divine presence" empowered early Methodists' pursuit of sanctification.

The band meeting was also a place where a more general revival could occur. In 1782, Mrs. Ward wrote to John Wesley that there was "a universal revival in our Bands and Classes: God is in the midst of us, and all feel that uniting principle of life exciting us to provoke one another to love and good works."[59] When the select bands or societies are considered, it will be seen that they were also a place where such revival occurred.[60]

There were also times when the blessings that occurred in band meetings overflowed into contexts beyond the bands. A letter to Mary Fletcher in 1782 contained an account of a woman who experienced entire sanctification as her soul had been set "at perfect liberty."[61] As this story was being told, another woman, on hearing it, was convicted "of the want of this blessing."[62] When she

[53] Sarah Ryan, letter to My Bands and Classes [n.d.], MAM, Fletcher-Tooth Collection, Ref: MAM Fl 6/9/9.

[54] "Mr. J. D—, to the Rev. Mr. Wesley," November 21, 1769, in AM 6 (1783): 275.

[55] "From Miss A. B. to the Rev. J. Wesley," April 16, 1773, in AM 9 (1786): 284.

[56] Bennett Dugdale, manuscript diary, August 31, 1778.

[57] George Button, "Experience and Happy Death of Sarah Roberts, of Brambly, near Sheffield," in AM 20 (1797): 590.

[58] Ibid.

[59] "From Mrs. M. Ward, to the Rev. J. Wesley," December 22, 1782, in AM 13 (1790): 566.

[60] See esp. "From Miss A. B. to the Rev. J. Wesley," February 13, 1772, in AM 8 (1785): 277.

[61] "Mrs Smith to Mary Fletcher," September 25, 1782, MAM, Fletcher-Tooth Collection, Ref: 6/10/14.

[62] Ibid.

was convinced, the woman who was relating the story said, "Mrs Smith the Lord intends to bless you to day for I think he hath sent me & all the way I came I had such faith for you and the Lord was so present he doeth not often disopoint his poor drest."[63] Soon after, the woman prayed for Mrs. Smith, who recalled, "I found my Self so penetrated with the power of God that I tremble'd in shuch a maner she was obl'd to hould me while the tears run down my face so fast and those words where applied thou are all fair my love there is no spot in the then was my Soul filled with love."[64] This meeting provides a vivid example of the ways that the pursuit of holiness was social for early Methodist women.

The band meeting was also a place where Methodists looked for the strength to persevere in the face of various trials and challenges as they pursued entire sanctification. John Valton (1740–94) recorded in his diary in 1765 the experience of "Mr Colly" who told "his experience" in a band meeting of being "most grievously assaulted by the Enemy."[65] Colly "felt so much Enmity against God, that he thought it impossible to hold out any longer, and that he must entirely have given it up."[66] Valton found consolation in Colly's account, writing, "How like to my Experience is this Ministers! I have had a desire to spend a whole night in prayer and singing with him, in hopes of finding the blessing."[67] In hearing about another person's struggles, Valton found comfort and a desire to persevere in his search for holiness.

The ongoing search for the witness of the Spirit of God did not always have positive or unambiguous results. The desire for an immediate sense of God's loving presence could lead to excess, and often led to the charge of enthusiasm. Charles Wesley was especially sensitive to this charge, particularly in the wake of George Bell's actions, which culminated in his prophesy that the world would end on February 28, 1763.[68] Although there is significant evidence that Charles Wesley was actively involved in bands and select societies in the period covered in the previous chapter, he seemed to regard them with more ambivalence later in his life.[69]

A particularly suggestive, though not unproblematic, account of Charles Wesley's thoughts on the band meeting in the latter half of his life comes from a letter Thomas Coke (1747–1814) wrote to him in 1779. Coke recounted a

---

[63] bid.

[64] Ibid.

[65] John Valton, manuscript diary, November 15, 1765, MAM, Diaries Collection, Box 26, Ref: MA 1977/293.

[66] Ibid.

[67] Ibid.

[68] See, Wesley, *Journal* for January 7, 1763, in *Works* 21: 402. For Wesley's record of his actions on the prophesied day, see ibid., 407.

[69] On the difference between John and Charles Wesley's reactions to George Bell's excesses, see Gareth Lloyd, *Charles Wesley and the Struggle for Methodist Identity* (New York: Oxford University Press, 2007), 80–81.

conversation he had with Charles "about the false fire, which sometimes breaks out in our Band-meetings."[70] According to Coke, during this conversation, Charles said, "I abominate those Band-meetings."[71] Coke acknowledged that at the time that Charles made the comment, "I put the worst construction on his words, and repeated them afterwards to others."[72] Thus, Charles's comment and Coke's subsequent gossip attracted enough attention that Coke wrote a letter to John Wesley explaining his recollection of what Charles Wesley said, the context in which it was said, and his sense of what Charles meant. Coke admitted, in hindsight, that he could not know whether Charles "abominated" the bands "at the Foundery *only*, or the *institution itself*"; though he speculated that Charles "meant the former."[73]

While Coke was willing to acknowledge that Charles may have meant that he "abominated" the "false fire" in a particular band meeting, he still left open the possibility that Charles Wesley meant that he "abominated" the band meeting itself. Coke, in other words, suggested that Charles Wesley may have seen the band meeting as part of the cause of the outbreak of enthusiasm in Methodism. In his letter to John Wesley, Coke wanted to reaffirm that he supported the Methodist approach to communal Christian formation with no hesitation. Coke's support of Methodist discipline was particularly seen in a passage where he commented on Charles Wesley giving his wife permission to stop attending her class meeting. Coke simultaneously affirmed his loyalty to John Wesley's conception of Methodism, while further calling into question Charles's loyalty:

> What was the full meaning of his heart, when he spoke these words, he alone can satisfy you. As to myself, I have such sincere and unfeigned attachment to the Methodist Discipline, that, highly as I love and respect your Brother, I would rather withdraw myself from that friendship, with which he has lately honoured me, than to sacrifice or abandon the Discipline.[74]

This passage highlights the complexity of the early Methodist experience, as it places three of the key leaders of Methodism in the 1770s in tension with one another, as Coke inserted himself between the Wesleys by calling into question Charles's loyalty to his brother's vision for Methodism. It also points to the richness and variety of experiences in popular Methodism. For some Methodists,

[70] Thomas Coke, letter to John Wesley, December 15, 1779, MAM, Ref: MA 1977/610/48. Also published in *AM* 13 (1790): 50–51. Lloyd discussed the tension between Coke and Charles Wesley in 193–195.
[71] Ibid.
[72] Ibid.
[73] Ibid. (emphasis original).
[74] Ibid.

the band meeting was a blessing as it helped them find assurance. For others, the band meeting led to excesses and enthusiasm. Regarding John Wesley's conception of the band meeting, however, there is significant source material that points to the preservation of the key aspect of Moravian piety that Wesley wove into his understanding of the band meeting. The band meeting was a place where Methodists either had already experienced justification by faith and the witness of the Spirit and sought further growth in holiness, or they were yearning for these experiences and joined a band in hopes that it would help them encounter God.

The Band Meeting as a Means of Grace

In John Wesley's understanding, the band meeting not only affirmed the Moravian emphasis on a direct experience of God's love, particularly through the witness of the Spirit. Wesley also intended for the band meeting to hold this aspect of Moravian piety in tension with the particularly Anglican understanding of the importance of a disciplined practice of the means of grace. Was this aspect of Wesley's synthesis of Anglican piety preserved in the popular Methodist experience of the band meeting?

From 1766 through 1784, there is evidence that Methodists considered the band meeting itself to be a means of grace, as well as a place that supported the practice of the means of grace as defined by the "General Rules." The source materials show that Methodists were committed to the consistent practice of meeting weekly in bands, though some Methodists acknowledged that they were tempted to stray from their investment in a weekly meeting. Accounts of participation in band meetings also contain references to the importance of relying on the "ordinances" or the "means." These references point not only to the importance of the means of grace, they also point more generally to the importance of discipline in the Christian life. Nevertheless, there are less explicit references to the band meeting as a means of grace, or to accountability for practicing the means of grace, in this period than in the periods previously discussed.

There are multiple primary sources where Methodists discuss their commitment to the weekly practice of meeting in a band. Samuel Bardsley's manuscript diary, which contains weekly references to his attending bands in 1766, has been previously cited.[75] In his account of his spiritual experience from the 1770s, which was also previously cited, James Hall pointed to the way that the practice of meeting weekly in a band meeting and "strictly attending to the Band Rules...greatly helped" him "forward in the ways of God."[76] Hall's description

---

[75] Samuel Bardsley, manuscript diary, July 18–August 29, 1766.
[76] James Hall, *AM* 16 (1793): 287.

contained the key qualities of a prudential means of grace, a practice that an individual finds to be reliable in bringing them into God's presence.

In his account of the "Right Method" for conducting a band meeting, Charles Perronet suggested that the band leader should inquire into the prayer life of each person in their band and the ways that their prayers had been answered.[77] Although prayer was certainly considered to be a means of grace, this was the only question related to the means of grace in Perronet's list of questions. Though it was shown earlier that John Wesley himself endorsed Perronet's "Method" when it was published in *The Arminian Magazine*, Perronet's approach did not emphasize commitment to the practice of the means of grace as clearly as Wesley's "Directions given to the Band Societies" did. Wesley's "Directions," which were organized similarly to the "General Rules," contained three sections, the third of which was "Constantly to attend on all the ordinances of God." This section, then, explicitly named attending church, receiving Communion, attending the public meeting of the bands, the ministry of the Word, private and family prayer, reading the Scriptures, and observing fast days as means of grace that the members of bands should attend.[78] Interestingly, in the "Directions," Wesley listed the "public meeting of the bands" as an ordinance, but not the weekly meeting of individual bands.[79]

An account of the life of Lucy Walton from the 1780s included an unusual format for a band meeting. Walton "met in band every week with her husband."[80] This is the only known example of a husband and wife forming a band meeting by themselves. However, this band gave the couple "a profitable opportunity of speaking freely to each other of the state of their souls, and their various trials and temptations."[81] The author of Walton's spiritual biography testified that through this band, husband and wife "mutually exhorted each other to keep close to God, and persevere in his good ways: By these means they walked hand in hand towards their heavenly home."[82] Thus, the band meeting functioned as a prudential means of grace for the Waltons.[83]

---

[77] Charles Perronet, "Of the right Method of meeting Classes and Bands," 605.

[78] Wesley, "Directions given to the Band Societies," in *Works* 9: 79.

[79] Most likely this was because Wesley assumed the importance of the weekly meeting for those who were observing the "Directions."

[80] "An Account of the Experience of Mrs. Lucy Walton, of Newcastle-upon-Tyne," in *AM* 16 (1793): 209.

[81] Ibid.

[82] Ibid.

[83] This account of a married couple "mutually exhorting each other" points to a potentially fruitful area of further research regarding the role of gender in early Methodism. Did the band meeting create new possibilities for women and men to interact and relate to one another that transcended dominant eighteenth-century gender roles? Mack further opens this line of enquiry in *Heart Religion*, 91, 129.

Methodists were at times tempted to abandon the discipline of a weekly band meeting. In 1774, when John Wesley asked Mary Jones, for example, "What are the temptations you have been delivered from?"[84] Jones responded, "Awhile ago, it was strongly imprest upon me, 'That now I had no need of ordinances: in particular, not of Band or Class: that these were only the shadow, the outward form; and that I was to feed on Christ, who is the substance.'"[85] Ultimately, Jones "was not suffered to keep from my Class or Band: but I was so bound up, that sometimes I could hardly speak a word. I then saw it was a temptation, and intreated the Lord to give me patience, till it was his will to deliver me."[86] It is significant that Jones both admitted that she thought about discontinuing attending her band and that she interpreted this desire as a temptation that she should resist.

In George Shadford's spiritual memoir, he provided a cautionary tale from the late 1760s of what could be the consequences of abandoning the means of grace. Shadford's account of a backslider provides such insight into the importance that Methodists placed on keeping the means of grace that it is worth quoting at length:

> I was much affected this year with a remarkable instance of the sudden death of a backslider, who lived between *Truro* and *Redruth*. He had known the love of God, and walked circumspectly in the light of his countenance for seven years; and was diligent in every means of grace. But he began to give way to lightness, and a trifling spirit. After this he refused to meet his brethren in band, and seldom met in Class, until at length he entirely gave up both. He came to preaching sometimes, but began to be very free with his carnal neighbours, and shy with the people of God; till at last he fell into his old besetting sin, drunkenness, which he had conquered for seven years. One Sabbath-day he went with some carnal men to an ale-house, or gin-shop, and continued there until they all got drunk. At last they resolved to go home though it was dark. Two of them lay down in the road; but the backslider was determined to go home alone; and as there were pits along the road side about fifteen or twenty fathoms deep, he dropped into one of them and was crushed to death leaving a wife and children in deep distress.[87]

Shadford's account was a particularly arresting example of the possible consequences of neglecting the means of grace—death! The logic of Shadford's account is important, as the backslider first turned to "lightness and a trifling

---

[84] Mary Jones, letter to John Wesley, June 7, 1774, in *AM* 9 (1786): 57.

[85] Ibid.

[86] Ibid.

[87] George Shadford, "A Short Account of Mr. George Shadford, Written by Himself," in *AM* 13 (1790): 236 (emphasis original).

spirit" and away from the means of grace. Then, he refused meeting in band and gradually abandoned his class meeting, which were both places where he would have been held accountable for keeping the means of grace. Eventually, he stopped attending the preaching services, until he ended up going to an ale house on the Sabbath instead of attending worship. The result is that he fell into his former "besetting sin" of drunkenness.

This account is especially significant because the backslider, according to Shadford, went almost directly in reverse through the steps that Methodists would have seen as marks of progress in the Christian life. The exception is that the means of grace were considered basic for all people, from those who were seeking initial forgiveness of their sins and peace with God, to those who had experienced Christian perfection. A decreased dependence on the means of grace led to abandoning the band, then the class, and finally any contact with the Methodists. And yet, even here Shadford's story of the backslider was not only tragic. It ended in hope, as other backsliders repented and turned back to God as a result of his death: "Many were greatly affected at this alarming case, and some backsliders, who were acquainted with him, were stirred up to return to him, from whom they had revolted."[88]

The band meeting itself was also referred to by some Methodists as a means of grace. In his diary, Bennett Dugdale described a day when he found that he "felt a thirsting after God, liberty to pour out my soul before him, and a delight in his ordinances especially band."[89] Similarly, Richard Rodda wrote to John Wesley in 1784 about Methodists at Wednesbury who "desired I would join them in a select band. I told them I rejoiced at the proposal, and exhorted them to use every means for gaining and retaining all the life of God."[90] The band meeting, then, was understood by many Methodists to have been a practice that God reliably used to convey grace to those who were seeking it.

Nevertheless, the general impression from the primary source materials studied from 1766 to 1784 is that the means of grace were not discussed as frequently within the context of the band meeting as they were in the earlier period. One possible explanation for this is that the conflict with the Moravians that initially occurred within the Fetter Lane Society was in the deep background by the period this section has considered. Methodists may have continued to assume that a committed practice of the means of grace was important, but no longer needed to explicitly make the case for a disciplined practice of the means of grace, because such practices were no longer challenged by people

---

[88] Ibid.

[89] Bennett Dugdale, manuscript diary, June 5, 1779.

[90] Richard Rodda, letter to John Wesley, May 7, 1784, in *AM* 14 (1791): 555. There is admittedly some ambiguity in Rodda's use of "means" here. However, early Methodists often used "means" as an abbreviation for "means of grace." It is plausible that Rodda was using means in more than one sense here, but very likely that he was referring to the means of grace.

within Methodism. In the early 1740s, Wesleyan Methodists were concerned that the Moravians were threatening the practice of the means of grace. In the late 1760s and 1770s, this threat was no longer as immediate. Nevertheless, the primary source materials do provide evidence that Methodists in this period were more passionate about their search for a clear sense of forgiveness of their sins and the witness of the Spirit than they were about consistent, habitual spiritual practices.

The Select Society

While the band meeting is the primary focus of this volume, one surprising result of the research from 1766 through 1784 was the number of references to select bands or select societies that were encountered. Hester Ann Rogers in 1782 provided one of the most detailed pictures of a select band during this period:

> The Select Band is now the most precious meeting in which I ever assembled; there are forty eight members, all truly and happily walking in the narrow path; thirty five, I have no doubt, enjoy perfect love. About six have enjoyed it before, and are now seeking it afresh, and the rest who never enjoyed it, are thirsting for it more than gold or silver. We are all too united in one spirit: all in this little company are helpers of each others joy.[91]

Rogers's account offers a window into a select band that, with forty-eight members, was evidently thriving. Her description also offers evidence of Wesley's conception of the Methodist structures of communal formation being powerfully brought to life, as members who were growing in holiness were actually made perfect in love and joined together at the deepest level of communal support, the select band. Rogers also reported that six people who had lost a previous experience of entire sanctification were seeking it again, and seven more were earnestly seeking to receive the gift of perfect love. In an earlier letter to Wesley, Rogers described the same "Select Band," writing, "I have just been there, since I began my letter, and find another soul has received the witness of sanctification under Mr. L. this morning."[92]

Nearly a decade before Rogers's narrative, in 1773, a woman identified as Mrs. P. N. wrote to John Wesley about her involvement in a select band. She first prayed for such a group, which resulted in "a few of us meeting constantly."[93] The

---

[91] Hester Ann Rogers, letter to John Wesley, November 21, 1782, in *AM* 14 (1791): 218.
[92] Hester Ann Rogers, letter to John Wesley, January 6, 1782, in *AM* 13 (1790): 108–109.
[93] Mrs. P. N., letter to John Wesley, February 21, 1773, in *AM* 9 (1786): 171.

result of the regular meeting of this group was that the members could "bear testimony that we love the Lord our God with all our heart, and our neighbour as ourselves."[94] Thus, Mrs. P. N. provided further evidence that the select band did facilitate the ultimate goal of Wesleyan Methodism, Christian perfection.

Like the band meeting, the select band was sometimes perceived by its participants as a time of particular revival. Miss A. B. described one such experience in a letter to John Wesley:

> We had a profitable opportunity in the select Band last Monday night. I believe I may say for each, it was such a time as we never before experienced. Glory be to God! he did fulfil his promise, by pouring out his Spirit upon us. Within these last four days, five have received a clear sense of God's pardoning love; and appears to hold fast whereunto they have attained; and blessed be God, the dead in sin likewise hear his voice, and enquire the way to Zion.[95]

This account is significant because the select band was composed of people with a broader range of experiences than one would expect. Particularly based on Wesley's conception, one would not anticipate the presence of people in select bands who were seeking "God's pardoning love." However, in this account, the select band appeared to be able to simultaneously help some people find pardon while helping others grow further in holiness.

Another way that the popular experience of the select bands was similar to that of the band meeting is that both appeared to have helped Methodists acknowledge their need for further growth in holiness. John Pawson (1737–1806), for example, wrote in his diary in 1783 that he met his select band "and found power to acknowledge my state of poverty and dependence upon Christ."[96] John Valton experienced room for growth as a result of his struggle with pride that was related to the fact that he was a member of a select band. Nearly two decades before Pawson, Valton wrote in his diary: "I was in the Select Society.... I found many Temptations to pride, 'That I had met the Select Society, That the people would admire me, That it was a sign that I should be a Preacher.'"[97] Valton's experience of the select bands was somewhat ambivalent. On the one hand, his participation in a band meeting helped him to be more sensitive to his own sins and his need for forgiveness, as well as to the room in his life for further growth in holiness. On the other hand, his participation in the select society itself caused him to struggle with pride.

---

[94] Ibid.

[95] Miss. A. B., letter to John Wesley, February 13, 177, in *AM* 8 (1785): 277.

[96] John Pawson, manuscript diary, October 1, 1783, MAM, Diaries Collection, Ref: 1977/276.

[97] John Valton, manuscript diary, September 19, 1766.

Samuel Bardsley's manuscript diary also contains multiple references to meeting the "Select Society."[98] However, his accounts were not as detailed as some of the ones we have previously considered. A representative entry is Bardsley's reference to the select society that he met on August 6, 1766. He wrote, "In the Evening I was at Select Society We had An agreeable meeting there Seem'd to be an Openness And freedom amongst us in Some measure."[99] These references suggest the need for further research into the role of the select society, or select bands, in the early Methodist experience, particularly in their connection to the doctrine of entire sanctification. The previously cited sources suggest that such research is feasible and promises to be fruitful.

The Continuation and Adaptation of the Band Meeting (ca. 1785–ca. 1801)

The sacred fire spreads!
—Elizabeth Ritchie[***]

This section concludes the exploration of the popular Methodist experience of the band meeting in the era of John Wesley's immediate influence. The general organization and conduct of the bands from 1785 through the early 1800s is considered. Then, the extent to which the search for justifying faith and the witness of the Spirit continued to be an important part of the experience of being in band is explored. Next, the opposite side of Wesley's synthesis in the bands is considered, the extent to which Methodists continued to emphasize the importance of a disciplined practice of the means of grace as a part of their experience in bands. Finally, the primary source references to select bands or select societies are surveyed.

The Organization and Conduct of the Bands

In 1796, *The Arminian Magazine* published a lengthy letter by Disney Alexander that contained valuable information on the structures of Methodism, with particular focus on the band meeting. In turning his attention to "the Institutions or Discipline of the Methodists," Alexander wrote that, "Besides the ordinary service performed at the Preaching House on the Sabbath, and occasional preaching in the course of the week, they have their Classes, Band-Meetings,

---

[***] Epigraph is from Elizabeth Ritchie, letter to Mary Fletcher, December 20, 1787, MAM, Fletcher-Tooth Collection, Ref: MAM Fl 6/6/14.

[98] Bardsley's manuscript diary for 1766 contains references to meeting the "Select Society" on July 23, August 6, August 20, August 27, and September 3.

[99] Samuel Bardsley, manuscript diary, August 6, 1766.

Love-Feasts, and Watch-Nights."[100] When Alexander turned to the conduct of the band meeting, he quoted liberally from "a sermon written in defence of Methodism" by Samuel Bradburn (1751–1816). After Bradburn described the class meeting, he turned to the bands:

> Where this company [the class meeting] is thought too large to speak their minds freely, many meet also once a week in smaller companies called Bands, consisting of four or five persons, men with men, and women with women. Nothing can be more simple than these meetings. And we think the Apostle James's words are best understood, by supposing something of this kind,—"Confess your faults one to another, and pray one for another that ye may be healed."[101]

This description of the bands is interesting for many reasons. Bradburn described the necessity of the band as a solution to the problem of some class meetings being too large for everyone in a class to "speak their minds freely." On one hand, Bradburn's description was consistent with Wesley's own description of the development of the band meeting in "A Plain Account of the People Called Methodists," where he described the bands as arising out of a need that people meeting in class expressed for "some means of closer union."[102] However, Bradburn's explanation that the bands were for people whose classes were too large goes beyond Wesley's own account. For Wesley, the bands arose because of a desire for deeper intimacy and support, not because of a lack of time in class meetings. And yet, when Bradburn described the actual conduct of the band meeting, it did not function in his conception as simply a smaller class meeting. Instead, Bradburn quoted James 5:16, the quintessential Scripture passage for the purpose of the band meeting. This distinction is further highlighted when Bradburn's description of the class meeting is considered. The kernel of the class meeting for Bradburn consisted of the class leader conversing "with each member about Christian experience, giving suitable advice to all."[103] The classes and bands, then, had different functions. One important implication of Bradburn's account, nevertheless, was that the classes were more active than the bands during this period.

Bradburn's account also provides insight into the purpose that lay behind the confession of specific sins, especially as it related to the Catholic practice of confession. In fact, nearly half of Bradburn's discussion of the band meeting is dedicated to dispelling the notion that the band meeting was the same as penance:

---

[100] Disney Alexander, letter to "A Friend," January 1, 1796, in *AM* 19 (1796): 315.

[101] Ibid., 316, quoting Samuel Bradburn.

[102] Wesley, "Plain Account," in *Works* 9: 266.

[103] Disney Alexander, quoting Samuel Bradburn, 315.

But let it be well observed, there is nothing in these assemblies like the confession of sin to a priest, in order to obtain absolution from him; but the speaking freely of their state of mind to one another, that they *may* know how to rejoice with those that rejoice, and to weep with those that weep, which they could not do without some acquaintance with each others condition.[104]

According to Bradburn, the purpose of the band meeting was not for the members to obtain absolution, but to know what people were actually going through in order to appropriately rejoice or weep as people's spiritual conditions required. Yet, Bradburn's account is perplexing, as his description of the rationale of the band meetings was fairly shallow and does not ring true with the testimonies of popular Methodists about their experiences of bands. Methodists were not merely seeking to know more clearly what others were going through. Rather, they were seeking freedom from bondage to sin. They wanted to encounter God's sanctifying grace and be made holy. One suspects that Bradburn's narrative was more concerned with defusing accusations that the bands were "Catholic" than accurately describing their purpose.

Another general account of the conduct of the band meeting in this period comes from the memorandum book of Frances Pawson (1736–1809), who wrote a detailed description of one band meeting. During this meeting, the leader and others gave Pawson advice on seeking further growth in holiness. Because of the details that Pawson preserved and the insight that her account gives into a band meeting in 1787, particularly the way a leader conversed with those in the band, it is worth quoting at length:

She advised me, not to be uneasy if I did not as yet come up to ye full light which ye Lord shewed me. Whilst I was [illegible word] after it my Soul was growing all the time—To those who were young in grace—she often does not shew much light to them lest they should be discouraged but only just point to them what they stood in need of.

She thought set forms of prayer was not setting as it were a proper value upon ye influence of ye holy Spirit who has promised to help our infirmities—Both Mrs Yoder and her—said that they always found it best simply when they went to prayer not to meditate beforehand but look unto ye Lord at *that* time to help their infirmities. The same Mrs O-s observed when she went to her Class.

She spoke of our looking for ye Glory of ye Lord at our Meetings.— Mrs. Yoder spoke of never having seen this Word as she now saw it "rejoice in hope" as a command of God.

---

[104] Ibid. (emphasis original).

Mrs Downe recommended Mrs. M[illegible] to wait upon ye Lord for him to shine upon his Work—not to look to [illegible word] by putting these aside we gathered strength.

She said few people that was seeking the Lord was years before they found peace if Unbelief was ye only hindrance because when that was ye only hindrance we generally [illegible word] mightily to have it removed—She remembered that when she was seeking Sanctification that Mrs. Coley who was her band Leader—Upon telling her that she felt her self bound with Unbelief as with bars of Iron—answered that she was glad of it; the Lord would soon give her the blessing.

Speaking of ye Intention being pure she observed that what our Words and actions were to men being all that they could discover our hearts—So our eye being single was what ye Lord looked at and if this was [illegible word] He made more allowance for our infirmities than Mand did.[105]

Based on this account, Pawson's band meeting appears to have been more of a consultation on growth in holiness than a rigid meeting where people took turns confessing sins. The women in Pawson's band searched together for ways to advise, encourage, and support Pawson in her search for holiness. The tone of Pawson's band leader was pastoral and compassionate. Pawson's account suggested that she was comfortable being vulnerable with the women in her band, and that the meeting felt like a safe place to her.

Pawson's account reinforces a theme of both this chapter and the last regarding the organization and conduct of the early Methodist band meeting—the importance of the role of the band leader. Early Methodist accounts often highlighted the way that the band leader would diagnose the true spiritual condition of someone in their band, or ask someone a question that helped them articulate something they were feeling but had been unable to express.

Alexander Mather's account of the spiritual biography of Elizabeth Richardson provides yet another example of the band leader as spiritual director. Mather wrote of Richardson's experience of joining a married women's band meeting in 1785: "her Leader, after some time, took an opportunity of speaking to her about her particular exercises; to whom she opened her mind freely, though she had been reserved before."[106] Here, the leader asked questions that were especially useful and helped Richardson to "open her mind freely" despite

[105] Frances Pawson, manuscript memorandum book, ca. 1782–ca. 1805, MAM, Diaries Collection, Box 24, Ref: MA 1977/275 (emphasis original).

[106] Alexander Mather, "An Account of the death of Elizabeth Richardson," in AM 13 (1790): 297.

the fact that she had previously struggled to do so. On Mather's account, the band leader's ministry bore significant fruit, as Richardson

> began to understand the way of expecting and receiving all she felt the need of from God, and an instantaneous deliverance from all the evil in her heart, by simple faith in the Lord Jesus Christ. She also saw that she was not to expect this deliverance first, and then to believe it, as she had formerly done; but to believe now on the Lord Jesus, and then be saved from what she felt, or from whatever burden she brought to the Lord, desiring to be delivered from it. She had not waited long in this way, before she was made a happy partaker of *that* salvation.[107]

It was the band leader's attention to Richardson that helped her come to a deeper understanding of entire sanctification, and ultimately led her to be saved from "all the evil in her heart."

A further result of Richardson's experience of entire sanctification was that she no longer found it difficult to speak in her class and band meetings. From the point of being entirely sanctified, "she was no longer reserved; but spoke in Class, Band, Select Society, and in conversation, as freely and chearfully as any of her brethren, of the things pertaining to God, and her own experience."[108] This highlights one of the important aspects of the popular Methodist experience of communal Christian formation—the band meeting helped many people express themselves and find their voices, even as the bands often had clear expectations as to what a proper way to express oneself was. Thus, the bands both helped Methodist women and men exercise their agency at the same time that they acted as a form of socialization, putting pressure on Methodists to conform to certain basic patterns in their spiritual lives.[109]

Multiple sources also pointed to the band leader's importance in maintaining Methodism's commitment to holiness. Frances Pawson preserved the remarks of someone who said that "he looked upon a Band worth nothing if the Leader did not urge holiness—or a Salvation from ye remains of sin."[110] Similarly,

---

[107] Ibid., 297–298 (emphasis original).

[108] Ibid., 298.

[109] Phyllis Mack particularly discussed the dynamics of gender, agency, and social pressure within Methodism in *Heart Religion in the British Enlightenment*.

[110] Frances Pawson, manuscript memorandum book, April 24, 1785. Pawson's account appears to be notes from a society meeting. The same memorandum book frequently mentioned "Mr. Mather," so Alexander Mather may be the one who spoke the words that Pawson recorded.

Alexander Mather encouraged George Marsden (1772–1858) to ensure that new converts

> meet in band with one who will prove a nursing father or mother to them. By these means they will be established in the grace received; especially if their Leader is a friend to holiness,—and, as soon as they have the least sensibility of the evil yet remaining in their hearts, points them directly to the fountain open for sin and uncleanness.[111]

Mather further connected the band meeting to the importance of growth in holiness by reminding Marsden, "It is your bounden duty, to shew young converts, before their zeal and first love are abated, that full sanctification is attained by faith; and that they are to seek it and expect it now."[112] Isabella Mather's diary provides a final example of the way in which the band meeting was connected to growth in holiness: "Went & met my own Band, I see more & more need to press Believers to lay hold on full Salvation."[113]

Similar to the first period this chapter considered, the band meeting was also closely connected to public bands (also called body bands), love-feasts, and prayer meetings from 1785 through 1801. In fact, the final section of this chapter suggests that these larger groups began to replace the small band meetings in the late eighteenth and early nineteenth centuries. Bennett Dugdale, for example, wrote that he "was quickened and comforted at the publick bands."[114] After describing Love Lovegrove's "delight" in her band meeting, her experience of public bands was also discussed. The writer of Lovegrove's spiritual experience testified, "I have seen her in the public meeting of the Bands...so overwhelmed with divine love, that she fell back on the chair while attempting to speak of the goodness of God!"[115]

James Wood's account of Matthew Whiting demonstrates the connection of the various parts of the Methodist structures for communal formation to one another. Wood described Whiting's involvement: "He frequently expressed his gratitude to God for preserving mercy, in a very feeling and affecting manner, in his Class, in the Bands, and in Love-feasts."[116] Disney Alexander also included the love-feast in his discussion of the "Reasons for Methodism," which also listed the class meeting, band meeting, and watch-nights as a part of Methodist discipline.[117] From 1738 to 1784, a theme of the band meeting was the value placed

---

[111] Alexander Mather, letter to George Marsden, January 29, 1796, in *AM* 20 (1797): 515.

[112] Ibid.

[113] Isabella Mather, manuscript diary, 1800–12, April 21, 1801, MAM, Methodist Diaries Collection, Box 21, Ref: MA 1977/264.

[114] Bennett Dugdale, September 10, 1792, manuscript diary.

[115] "The experience & happy Death of Love Lovegrove," in *AM* 19 (1795): 406.

[116] James Wood, "A Short Account of Mr. Matthew Whiting," in *AM* 21 (1798): 175.

[117] Disney Alexander, "Reasons for Methodism," in *AM* 19 (1896): 315.

on it as a place where searching and direct conversation occurred. This theme continued from 1785 through 1801. The way in which it was most prominently expressed during this period was through the importance of speaking freely to one another. Eliza Beecroft wrote to Mary Fletcher in 1794 that she met in a band meeting where the members "communicated our thoughts freely."[118] Similarly, George Marsden wrote in his journal about a band meeting in 1803 where "the people spoke in a free lively manner, two or three Souls appeared to be visited with Salvation at the conclusion of the meeting."[119] Finally, Isaac Bradnock (1774–1833), a missionary to the West Indies, wrote in his journal that Sunday, September 12, 1802, "concluded with hearing the dear people speak with simplicity in the Bands."[120]

The Search for Deeper Faith and Assurance

The primary source materials from the mid-1780s onward provide significant insight into the popular piety of early Methodists. These sources demonstrate not only the continued presence of band meetings in many Methodist societies, but also that bands were a place where people were especially focused on their growth in holiness. From 1785 through 1801, many Methodists earnestly prayed and interceded for one another in the search for entire sanctification or Christian perfection. Most typically, a person felt that he or she was instantly delivered or cleansed from sin.

Alexander Mather's account of Elizabeth Richardson's involvement in a band meeting was considered in the previous section. The account, however, also highlighted the role of faith and the search for an experience of entire sanctification that would instantly deliver her "from all the evil in her heart."[121] In this account, Richardson's new understanding that sanctification happened "by simple faith in the Lord Jesus Christ" contributed to her receiving such faith.[122] Mather testified that not long after searching for sanctifying faith, Richardson "was made a happy partaker of *that* salvation."[123] It was thus within the context of the band meeting that Richardson learned about the importance of faith in Christ for deliverance from sin. It was also within the context of the band meeting that she received this faith.

---

[118] Eliza Beecroft, letter to Mary Fletcher, November 21, 1794, MAM, Fletcher-Tooth Collection, Ref: MAM Fl 1.2/15.

[119] George Marsden, manuscript journal, 1801–20, April 18, 1803, MAM, Methodist Diaries Collection, Box 21, Ref: MA 1977/267.

[120] Isaac Bradnock, manuscript diary, September 12, 1802, MAM, Ref: 2002/001 MA 9769.

[121] Mather, "Account of the death of Elizabeth Richardson," 297.

[122] Ibid.

[123] Ibid., 298 (emphasis original).

John Allen testified to a similar experience of entire sanctification in John Parkinson's life. Allen described an especially significant experience of Parkinson's in a band meeting in 1791:

> while he was meeting his band, and engaged in earnest prayer, the Lord graciously manifested himself in a more powerful manner than ever. He was so affected with the divine goodness and mercy, that he cried out, "Lord, thou dost draw near indeed! and brings us to the very borders of heaven!" The power of the holy Spirit, that from that time rested upon his soul, was fully evidenced in every part of his conduct; he enjoyed a serene uninterrupted peace; and his will was entirely subdued to the will of God.[124]

In this account, "the Lord graciously manifested himself" to Parkinson, which enabled him to experience "uninterrupted peace" and have his will "entirely subdued to the will of God." Allen closely connected this experience and its immediate impact on Parkinson's conduct with the lasting fruits of Parkinson's life. The power of the Holy Spirit was with Parkinson "from that time," and the peace that he experienced was "uninterrupted." Allen's account, then, was not only a testimony to the initial impact of a specific experience of God's grace, but also to the ongoing effects that this encounter with God had on Parkinson's life, namely, ongoing growth in holiness.

The manuscript journals of George Marsden are another illuminating source into the ways in which the band meeting continued to be a place where Methodists searched for justification, the witness of the Spirit, and sanctification. On August 1, 1801, for example, Marsden wrote, "At the Band meeting several spoke well, and during prayer the Lord was particularly present; several received the cleansing Spirit of God; and some the pardoning mercy of God."[125] On January 22, 1802, Marsden wrote about a band meeting during which "at the conclusion of the meeting," a woman "informed us, that while we were on our knees, God had given her faith in the cleansg efficacy of the Redeemers blood."[126] This account of the gift of justifying faith shows that experiences of God's presence were not always obvious to all who were present, as the other people who were there did not know about the woman's experience of justifying faith until she testified to God's work in her soul.

Marsden not only described particularly powerful band meetings, he also noted when a band meeting was not effective. On August 28, Marsden wrote, "Met the Band a good many persons were present, but the meeting was not very

---

[124] John Allen, "A Short Account of Mr. John Parkinson," March 24, 1792, in *AM* 16 (1793): 305.

[125] George Marsden, manuscript journal, August 1, 1801.

[126] Ibid., January 22, 1802.

lively the people were backward to speak."[127] This provides a helpful insight, as Marsden evidently did not consider simple attendance to be the most important factor in a band meeting's success. It was more important to him that the people who did show up "spoke well" and that people encountered the grace of God in ways that helped them make progress on the Way of Salvation.

The band meeting was also viewed by Methodist missionaries as a helpful tool that could guide new converts closer to God. Isaac Bradnock, a missionary to the West Indies, described his attempts to revive Methodist discipline during his missionary work. He frequently referred to public bands, noting on July 4, 1802, the "great simplicity" of those who met in the public bands, "in begging of God to wash them with his Son's blood & make them quite clean."[128] The public bands also appear to have been a means of grace in Bradnock's own pursuit of sanctification. On July 11, he noted that "when meeting the publick bands, my mind was much happier, & my body stronger, then in the morning. my earnest desire is to be made holy: O Lord give me grace, for every trying hour."[129] In this instance, the public bands led him to rededicate his own search for holiness.

In Bradnock's account, the bands and public bands were one of the key places where his ministry bore fruit. On one occasion, he wrote that the public bands "appear'd to be the gate of heaven to all present."[130] Just over a week later, he described a meeting with the bands, noting his thankfulness at hearing "such a breathing after holiness amongst the people."[131] Though Wesley had been dead for more than a decade, Bradnock's phrases beautifully captured the key reason for Wesley's emphasis on the importance of the bands; they were originally created and continued to be used because of their value in helping people pursue entire sanctification, or keep "breathing after holiness."[132]

Finally, Bradnock also described the way that encounters with God's grace within the bands could lead to reconciliation among members of a band meeting. Bradnock recorded in his diary on December 26, 1803: "in meeting the Bands my Soul was much drawn out for an outpouring of God's spirit, & I felt great love to him who had done me the evil. O may God forgive him."[133] Bradnock's entry provides one example of the way in which the band meeting was not just a place where individual Methodists gathered together in the hopes of personally tasting God's grace; the band meeting was also a place where Methodists testified that God's grace drew them closer together and connected them more deeply to one another.

[127] Ibid., August 28, 1801.

[128] Isaac Bradnock, manuscript diary, July 4, 1802.

[129] Ibid., July 11, 1802.

[130] Ibid., July 25, 1802.

[131] Ibid., August 8, 1802.

[132] Though, as the concluding section of this chapter discusses, the process or method for "breathing after holiness" in bands may have changed considerably.

[133] Isaac Bradnock, manuscript diary, December 26, 1803.

Through their participation in band meetings, Methodists also recognized their continued room for growth in holiness. However, a realization of a lack of holiness was not necessarily resolved by an immediate infusion of grace that led to deeper holiness. A letter published in *The Arminian Magazine* in 1786, for example, shows how the band meeting could lead to a realization of the need for further growth in holiness:

> My dear wife says, when her Band met on Tuesday, they were led to speak of being so fixed on God, as not to be moved, however things happened or appeared. It then occurred to her mind, that there wanted a degree of this faith, when she found herself so exercised on account of a Letter not coming (as expected) from Mr. P—: but I trust that both of you have since found more of what it is to have the mind kept in perfect peace and stayed upon God; your trust more invariably fixed upon him, however unfavourable circumstances might seem at the time.[134]

It was through her participation in a band meeting that the writer's wife recognized her need for the faith that was discussed. It was also in this context that she realized that she did not "invariably" trust God.

Previous sections of this book have discussed the body bands, or public bands, where individual band meetings came together and testified to the ways that God had been at work in their lives. The final primary source related to the band meetings as a location for the search for entire sanctification provides an example of how the body bands, individual class meetings, and band meetings all contributed to the pursuit of Christian perfection. Elizabeth Ritchie wrote to Mary Fletcher in 1787 about her experience at a meeting of the body bands where she "felt it right to speak freely."[135] Ritchie further described this experience and its results:

> Satan wd have hindered [her from speaking], but I broke through, & found the approbation of God abundantly. Since yt time ye hearts of ye are open to me; & Classes & Bands pour in upon me: I have found one or two who really enjoyed ye pure love of God, & several who are truly athirst for purity of heart. Blessed by God the sacred fire spreads! 3 or four have found full Deliverance, & many seem all athirst to be renewed in love. The Preachers are kind indeed; & to strengthen ye hands of those who are determined to be wholly the Lords, have begun a Select Band, & we have had some good simple meetings: pray for us.[136]

---

[134] Mr. M., letter to Mrs. P., May, 1786, in *AM* 20 (1797): 47.

[135] Elizabeth Ritchie, letter to Mary Fletcher, December 20, 1787.

[136] Ibid.

Ritchie interpreted her experience at the body bands as a catalyst that led several others to open their hearts to her. As a result, some people experienced entire sanctification, and others became more serious in their search for "purity of heart." The work that began in the body band, then, was shored up by starting a select band in order "to strengthen ye hands of those who are determined to be wholly the Lords." This pattern was not always followed in early Methodism; nevertheless, Ritchie's account provides an excellent example of the ways Methodists searched for further growth in holiness, and instinctively sought deeper levels of mutual support and accountability in order to support their growth in holiness.

The Band Meeting as a Means of Grace

In his diary, John Goodfellow described one experience of his band meeting that suggests that he viewed it as a means of grace: "The band meeting was a blessed means to my Soul this day, and the more so, as we all seem'd to be of one heart, determined to seek for the whole mind that was 'also in Xt Jesus,' The Lord."[137] Goodfellow's comment was not unambiguous, as it did not clearly say "means of grace." In the absence of another qualifier, however, it is likely that Goodfellow was referring to the means of grace. Goodfellow used the word "means" at least two more times in his diary in reference to the band meeting. On January 29, 1786, he wrote, "Found the Lord very precious at the Band meeting this morning; this is a blessed means indeed! I feel myself fixed on God at present, yet I desire to be wholly given up to him; to rejoice evermore, and in all things to be thankful."[138] On July 14, 1786, Goodfellow lamented missing out on the opportunity to meet in his band: "This was a day of heaviness to me; I waited for my Brethren to meet in Band, but none came; this hindered me from meeting Class at Athamton, so that I was deprived of both means."[139] The immediate context of both of the previous references to the band meeting as a "means" most naturally fits with the ways that Methodists typically talked about means of grace. Finally, in his reference to his participation in a band meeting on September 10, 1786, Goodfellow used the entire phrase "means of grace." He wrote:

> I awoke this morning in the spirit of prayer, thankfully accepting another day of rest; & hoping to profit in the means of grace.—At Band meeting we took sweet council together, and the Lord was graciously present with us. We appointed wednesday, to be set apart for a day of fasting, & prayer, for God to revive his work among us; and unite us closer to himself, & to each other; that we may ever live in the unity of the Spirit.[140]

[137] John Goodfellow, manuscript diary, October 9, 1785.
[138] Ibid., January 29, 1786.
[139] Ibid., July 14, 1786.
[140] Ibid., September 10, 1786.

This passage further increases the likelihood that Goodfellow was simply abbreviating the phrase "means of grace" to "means" in each of the previously cited passages. The passage is perhaps even more significant because it demonstrates both that Goodfellow considered the band meeting to be a means of grace and that the band meeting was a place where other means of grace were reinforced, as time was "appointed" for fasting and prayer during the band meeting. Further, Goodfellow and his colleagues looked for God "to revive his work among us; and unite us closer to himself, & to each other" through their practice of these means of grace. Thus, Goodfellow provided strong evidence that what has been referred to as the Anglican aspect of the Wesleyan synthesis was preserved as late as 1786.

Another example of the preservation of Wesley's emphasis on the importance of a disciplined practice of the means of grace at the popular level of Methodist experience is seen in Hiram William Lovegrove's account of his sister's spiritual experience:

> Among the various means of grace, with which we are highly favoured in this place, she particularly loved and delighted in her Band-meeting; and in this she was peculiarly favoured, being blest with a suitable and pious companion, one after her own heart, who earnestly panted after the whole mind of Christ.[141]

Of particular interest in this passage is that Lovegrove suggested that there were several means of grace available to the Methodists in Nova Scotia, and of these means of grace, the band meeting was the one that Love Lovegrove most valued and "delighted in." One of the key reasons the band meeting was a means of grace was because of the way the bands brought two or more people together in order to "pant after the whole mind of Christ." Thus, Methodists such as Lovegrove found Wesley's insistence that there was "no holiness but social holiness" to be true in their own experience.[142]

The final reference to the band meeting as a means of grace comes from the Fletcher-Tooth Collection, where Mr. Cranage's private papers are quoted. In 1794, Cranage wrote a list of rules to guide his life. The seventh rule was "I am determined to keep as close as possible to the Means of grace Such as hearing the word preached, Society-meetings, prayer-meetings, Band-meetings, etc."[143] It is interesting in this list that every means of grace that Cranage cited was a form of

---

[141] Hiram William Lovegrove, "The Christian Experience and happy Death of Love Lovegrove, of Halifax, in Nova-Scotia; who departed this life, January 19, 1795, aged 28," in *AM* 19 (1796): 406.

[142] For this quote, see Wesley, "Preface," *Hymns and Sacred Poems, 1739,* in *Works,* Jackson, 14: 321.

[143] Mary Tooth, personal papers, September 28, 1823, quoting Mr. Cranage's personal papers from 1794, MAM, Fletcher-Tooth Collection, Ref: MA Fl 33.1.

communal formation. And yet, "hearing the word preached" was the only means of grace that Wesley listed under "ordinances of God" in the "General Rules."

Cranage's papers were quoted in Mary Tooth's journals in 1823, the year Cranage died. After citing his diary directly, she added her own comments on Cranage's spiritual practice: "if we may judge by his conduct all must conclude that he walked by these rules to the end of his life."[144] Thus, Tooth added not only her own endorsement of Cranage's spiritual practice, but she also affirmed the importance of the means of grace and band meetings for Methodist practice through 1823.

Throughout the period that this volume is concerned with, early Methodists do seem to have upheld the part of Anglican piety that Wesley attempted to synthesize with Moravian piety in the band meeting. If there was a change in popular Methodist spirituality related to the means of grace within the band meeting, it would seem to be that early Methodists often expressed their value of the practice of the band meeting, and the importance of consistently attending their bands, by defining the band meeting itself as a means of grace. This is not inconsistent with Wesley's understanding of the means of grace, especially when he talks about Christian conferencing as a means of grace. However, it does seem to be a bolder appropriation of the band meeting as a means of grace in its own right than is typically found in Wesley's discussions of the means of grace.[145]

The Select Society

Early Methodists also sometimes referred to select bands as a means of grace from 1785 through 1801. Sarah Crosby, for example, wrote to Mary Fletcher in 1787 in order to give her an account of the spiritual progress in Leeds:

> I wish to give you Some Idea, of how we are going on: as I think it will be agreeable to you, to hear of our Temporals, & Spirituals: These I trust, we are living to Improve; alltho it Seems but Slowly. Indeed if I were to judge

---

[144] Ibid.

[145] In the sermon "The Means of Grace," e.g., Wesley listed prayer, searching the Scriptures, and receiving the Lord's Supper as the "ordinary" means of grace; in *Works* 2: 381. In the "General Rules," public worship, "the ministry of the Word," and fasting or abstinence were also included as "ordinances of God." *Works* 9: 73. One of the key places where Wesley came particularly close to describing the band meeting as a means of grace was in the "Large Minutes" where "Christian conference" is listed as the last of five instituted means of grace. The band meeting would certainly have been considered a form of Christian conferencing by Wesley and Methodists, though it is not explicitly named as such. The band meeting is explicitly mentioned under practices that are prudential means of grace for Methodists, where the question is asked, "Do you never miss your class, or Band?" Wesley, *Works* 10: 856–857. Ted A. Campbell described Wesley's development of the means of grace in *Wesleyan Beliefs*, 30–32.

of My Improvement, by My attendance on what is call'd *means of Grace*, it w'd be Small indeed: for I have not been able to go to the Select Band of a Sat: Night, these 4 Months past. Nor to preaching Many Times, from Sund. To Sunday this winter.[146]

Crosby's letter to Mary Fletcher provides one example of a Methodist who viewed the select bands as a means of grace. If the appropriation of the band meeting as a means of grace was an unanticipated finding of this book, another unexpected result is the frequency of references to functioning select societies, such as the one Sarah Crosby mentioned, which were most commonly referred to as select bands.

The diaries of Frances Pawson contain multiple references to her participation in select bands. On March 5, 1785, Pawson recorded what appeared to be her advice to the members of a select band on how to receive sanctifying faith:

We may have ye love of God & our whole hearts given up to God in a state of Justification without our having looked for Sanctification [illegible word] if from a view of our Inbred sins we look up to the Lord for Sanctification, & he sheds his love abroad in our hearts, we may then exercise faith that he has give us ye blessing.[147]

In June of the same year, while "At ye select Band," Pawson recorded her understanding of the truth that Christians may be tempted after being entirely sanctified, but they need not give in to temptation: "The Enemy can mimick what was in our hearts before we was clean from Inbred sin. We may likewise feel his temptations but we need not give way to them."[148] The struggle with temptation was evidently ongoing for Pawson and the members of her select band, as more than a year later, she recorded the following reflection from a meeting of her select band: "Never to reason with Temptation *give it no place*."[149]

The spiritual memoirs of Elizabeth Taylor provide further insight into the conduct of select bands:

One of her brethren, with whom she met in the Select Band, enquiring into the state of her mind, was answered, "That she had not known one dark or unhappy hour for about twelve months;" and lifting up her eyes, she added, "I have now such views of the heavenly world, that dying seems no more to me, than passing out of one room into another." She had an unfeigned concern for those who did once run

[146] Sarah Crosby, letter to Mary Fletcher, March 26, 1787, MAM, Fletcher-Tooth Collection, MAM Fl 2.5A/18 (emphasis original).

[147] Frances Pawson, manuscript memorandum book, March 5, 1785.

[148] Ibid., June 23, 1785.

[149] Ibid., September 27, 1786 (emphasis original).

well, but were now walking in the ways and spirit of the world: often saying, "What will become of poor backsliders?" And when any of them came to see her, she intreated them with all her might, to return again unto the Lord.[150]

The account of Taylor's select band confirms that select bands were not divided by gender, as were the regular bands. Taylor's concern for backsliders also provides evidence that, in the early Methodist experience, receiving entire sanctification did not guarantee that one would continue in this state from that point forward.[151] Finally, this account suggests that the questions asked at the select bands were not that different from those asked at the regular classes or bands. Rather than the questions being dramatically different, the distinction between classes, bands, and select bands related to the depth and spiritual maturity with which members were expected to be able to answer the questions. Taylor, for example, reflected on her readiness for death in the context of her select band.

There are also references to select bands in the journals of Thomas Coke and the diaries of Isabella Mather. These two sources, however, are primarily valuable because of the confirmation they provide of the existence of select bands, rather than in providing detailed information about them. For example, Coke wrote toward the end of 1792 that, "In the meeting of the Select Society, I was much satisfied indeed."[152] Mather's diary contained many references to select bands. However, they nearly always consisted of either "Went to ye Select Band" or "at ye Select Band."[153] Mather's diary is nevertheless of value because it shows that her select band was functioning and meeting regularly.

The final example of a reference to select bands is found in a letter from Elizabeth Ritchie to Mary Fletcher. Ritchie wrote to Fletcher that subsequent to the outbreak of a small revival where several people experienced the "pure love of God" and more were seeking this love, a select band was started in order to

---

[150] "An Account of the Conversion and happy Death of Mrs. Elizabeth Taylor, of *Halifax* in *Yorkshire*," anonymous, in *AM* 16 (1793): 472.

[151] It is also interesting that this account does not mention a penitent band, as Taylor's concern for backsliders would seem to have naturally led her to form a penitent band if that had been an option for her. This points to a general lack of source material relating to penitent bands. I do not recall finding any evidence of functioning penitent bands in the sources I consulted for this book; this suggests that they may have been the key piece of Wesley's structure that failed to take hold in popular Methodist practice.

[152] Thomas Coke, journal for November/December 1792, in *AM* 16 (1793): 388. Citation is also published in *Journals of Dr. Thomas Coke*, ed. John A. Vickers (Nashville, TN: Kingswood Books, 2005), 176–177.

[153] For examples, see Isabella Mather, manuscript diary, March 19, 1801; April 18, 1801; July 25, 1801; August 8, 1801; August 22, 1801; August 31, 1801; March 6, 1802; March 20, 1802; April 3, 1802; and April 17, 1802.

"strengthen ye hands of those who are determined to be wholly the Lords."[154] Ritchie's reference is of particular relevance because it provides an example of the kind of progression of Christian communal formation that Wesley envisioned. Already a member of both a class meeting and a band meeting, Ritchie had a particular desire to "speak freely" in this meeting, which led to the "sacred fire" spreading. In order to "strengthen the hands" of those who had experienced entire sanctification, or were on the cusp of it, the preacher formed them into a select band. Though Ritchie's description does not fill in all of the gaps, such as when and in what context she herself experienced justification and the new birth, the material in this account is in harmony with Wesley's narrative in "A Plain Account of the People Called Methodists."

Ultimately, the sources from 1785 through 1802 related to the select bands or select societies further confirm the earlier observation that there is enough material on them to warrant further study. A focused study would provide insight into the select societies and clarify the function of the band meeting in comparison to the select bands. To what extent were they different? How meaningful were these differences? Were these differences consistent?

Continued Remnants of the Band Meeting (ca. 1802–ca. 1843)

> We have many blessed times together in our band.
> —Eleanor Dickinson[****]

One of the biggest surprises of this study was the number of primary source references to band meetings in the first half of the nineteenth century. References to bands were found in British Methodism up to 1843, suggesting that the band meeting at least lingered in Methodist consciousness until the middle of the nineteenth century.

The Continued Presence of the Bands

Although finding the outer boundary of functioning bands within British Methodism was not a major goal of this book, the research for it nevertheless encountered multiple references to band meetings in the early nineteenth century, even as late as 1837. The *Proceedings of the Wesley Historical Society* also published the "Rules of the Original Methodists" from 1843, which included

---

[****] Epigraph is from Eleanor Dickinson, letter to Mary Fletcher, March 20, 1813, MAM, Fletcher-Tooth Collection, Ref: MAM Fl 2.11/11.

[154] Elizabeth Ritchie, letter to Mary Fletcher, December 20, 1787; previously cited in "The Search for Deeper Faith and Experience of God" in this chapter.

band meetings under the question "What meetings for worship are authorized among us?"[155] However, as we discuss at the conclusion of this chapter, this source also provides evidence that the understanding of the band meeting had undergone a significant shift.

From the 1800s through the 1830s, there is evidence that the band meetings were declining and not functioning as effectively as they had been, as well as evidence that bands were in some places still viewed as an important part of the Methodist approach for growth in holiness.[156] Earlier in this chapter, the role of the bands and public bands in Isaac Bradnock's missionary work in the West Indies at the beginning of the nineteenth century was considered. In 1803, Bradnock noted on several occasions his continued advocacy of bands and public bands. On January 9, he wrote, "I met the society & the bands and felt much of the presence of the Lord."[157] And on February 20, he described a meeting of the public bands where "many gave a clear account of the work of grace in their Souls that much pleas'd me."[158]

There are references to several functioning band meetings over the next several decades. In 1813, Eleanor Dickinson wrote to Mary Fletcher about the value of her band meeting: "We have many blessed times together in our band."[159] Another decade later, in 1825, Ann Jordan wrote to Mary Tooth about her sense of the work of God in the public bands: "I feel the Lord is among us we have Souls brought to God and a very good feeling in the publick band."[160] In a letter from Frances Bourne to Mary Tooth in 1828, Bourne twice referenced her participation in bands. After one band meeting, she wrote, "I trust the people were stirred up."[161] She wrote of the second meeting, "they had a very excellens band meeting yesterday morning."[162]

Aside from references to band meetings that establish their presence, there are also references that suggest that some Methodists continued to turn to the band meeting after a revival, or in hopes of continuing a revival. In 1826, Sarah Jenkins described an occasion when, instead of having a class meeting, a band

---

[155] Donald M. Grundy, "A History of the Original Methodists," in *PWHS* 35 (1965–66): 192–193, citing "Rules of the Original Methodists," 1843.

[156] William Dean argued that the band meeting was in serious decline by the end of the eighteenth century. Dean cited letters from John Wesley and the *Minutes* from the end of the eighteenth century to the beginning of the nineteenth century as evidence of this decline. Dean, Ph.D. diss., 165–168. However, Dean also noted that "References to private bands in the diaries of the nineteenth century indicate that such bands did not disappear entirely until about mid-century." Ibid., 168.

[157] Isaac Bradnock, manuscript diary, January 9, 1803.

[158] Ibid., February 20, 1803.

[159] Eleanor Dickinson, letter to Mary Fletcher, March 20, 1813, MAM.

[160] Ann Jordan, letter to Mary Tooth, February 9, 1825, MAM, Fletcher-Tooth Collection, MAM Fl 4/7/7.

[161] Frances Bourne, letter to Mary Tooth, February 4/5 [1828], MAM, Fletcher-Tooth Collection, MAM Fl 1.11/4.

[162] Ibid.

meeting was held that "was indeed a season of refreshing from the presence of the Lord I believe every soul felt the spirit two were set at perfect liberty."[163] Similarly, in 1828, Rebecca Longmore wrote to Mary Tooth about the visit of a superintendant who "for the second time in the afternoon he held a Band meeting and a prayer meetng after preaching at night. And it will give you pleasure to learn that there is at last something like a shaking of dry Bones even at Oswestry."[164] Longmore attributed the practice of holding band meetings and prayer meetings to the initial stirrings of revival.

The final example comes from Henry Stormont, who wrote:

> I have lately felt my soul quickened & my desire, strengthened. The Lord has sent among us a truly pious & heart searching Preacher whose labours have already been made a blessing to many & there seems a general revival through the circuit. Some of us have begun to think of meeting in band so that I hope this helpful mean [sic] of grace will in a short time be observed by many who seem till lately to have scarcely known its name.[165]

Stormont's account is of interest for several reasons. First, the decline of the band meeting in this context can be seen, as Stormont reported that many had "scarcely known its name." However, the band meeting was in the consciousness of Stormont and a few other people so that they viewed it as a way to further and strengthen the general revival that had begun in the circuit. Finally, Stormont referred to the band meeting as a means of grace, providing evidence that this aspect of Wesley's synthesis was preserved into the 1820s.

One cannot generalize too much from the previous references to band meetings, particularly because all of the references that have just been cited, with the exception of the material from Isaac Bradnock's manuscript diary, are from the Fletcher-Tooth Collection. Because the materials consist of letters to Mary Fletcher and Mary Tooth, the correspondents represent a somewhat narrow angle of vision restricted to these two women's circle of correspondence. Nevertheless, they are of value because each reference provides documentation that there were at least some band meetings functioning in this period, even if we cannot be certain how many bands there were. What can be said with confidence is that the band meeting was not extinct in the early nineteenth century.

---

[163] Sarah Jenkins, letter to Mary Tooth, July 5, 1826, MAM, Fletcher-Tooth Collection, Ref: Fl 4/4/25.

[164] Rebecca Longmore, letter to Mary Tooth, November 5, 1828, MAM, Fletcher-Tooth Collection, Ref: MAM Fl 4/13/15.

[165] Henry Stormont, letter to Mary Tooth, October 27, 1823, MAM, Fletcher-Tooth Collection, Ref: MAM Fl 6/12/3.

Some key Methodist leaders, such as Mary Fletcher and Mary Tooth, advocated for the use of band meetings and kept them alive in Methodist consciousness.

Transition to Prayer Meetings?

An excerpt from George Marsden's manuscript journal in 1802 points to what may have been a key transition in popular Methodism. Marsden wrote, "We had intended having a Band meeting after preaching, but on account of the distress of several we held a prayer meeting for an hour and a half during which several appeared broken down, & several found peace with God."[166] A passage such as this would have been unthinkable in earlier periods of Methodist practice of the band meeting, particularly because Marsden's journal suggests that there was general agreement that conducting a regular band meeting would have been insufficient to meet the needs of those who were in distress. It also does not fit with the early Methodist practice of the band meeting to have numerous people in a band meeting who are seeking "peace with God."[167] When Marsden's journal entry is considered with other references to prayer meetings and to later accounts of band meetings, it appears that the band meeting increasingly came to resemble the prayer meeting, until the two were nearly indistinguishable. One explanation for the decline of the band meeting, then, is that the prayer meeting changed the practice of the bands and ultimately replaced them.

The seventh rule of Mr. Cranage's "rules for his own conduct" was previously cited.[168] In this rule, Cranage not only spoke of the band meeting as a means of grace, he also referred to the prayer meeting as a means of grace.[169] In the same year, 1794, Mr. Moon wrote a letter to Thomas Coke about the value of both band meetings and prayer meetings:

> Last Thursday night, the meeting of the Bands was a particular season; it lasted from nine o'clock, till near one in the morning: during which time, I am told, four or five persons were enabled to love God with their whole heart; and the rest were abundantly refreshed and strengthened in this way. Even little boys and girls have now prayer-meetings among themselves; and one company of lads, meet constantly in the evening, when the weather is fine, in a field; they form a circle, and pray for each other, till they have some signal answer of divine approbation. In this

---

[166] George Marsden, manuscript journal, November 22, 1802.

[167] In chapter 4, though, it was pointed out that this was not unheard of in the earlier period of the band meeting.

[168] See Mary Tooth, personal papers, September 28, 1823, quoting Mr. Cranage's personal papers from 1794.

[169] September 28, 1823, personal papers of Mary Tooth, MAM, Fletcher-Tooth Collection, Ref: MA Fl 33.1.

meeting, simple as it may appear to some, two or three have sometimes been set at liberty before they parted.[170]

In Moon's account, it is difficult to distinguish the band meeting from the prayer meeting. This particular band meeting was said to last nearly four hours, apparently because the search for the ability "to love God with their whole heart" was of such urgency. In the prayer meetings, a "company of lads" prayed together "till they have some signal answer of divine approbation," which at least at times led those praying to be "set at liberty."

The prayer meeting was important enough, and of a significant enough source of controversy, that a defense of it was published in *The Arminian Magazine* in May 1798 by someone identified as "A Well Wisher to Zion." The author acknowledged that there were opponents of prayer meetings, and that they argued that prayer meetings were most similar to the "extravagancies" of George Bell in 1761.[171] However, the author made a distinction between "the former revival" and "the case at present." Under George Bell's enthusiasm, people were encouraged to turn away from the preachers, and some "became wise above what is written" so that "they laid aside the Bible."[172] In contrast, in prayer meetings, people "are remarkable for an affectionate attachment to their Preachers; they constantly attend all the means of grace; they ardently love their Bibles; and steadily adhere to the Methodist doctrines and discipline."[173] In other words, the author agreed that George Bell was not faithful to Wesley's vision for Methodism, but then argued that the prayer meetings were faithful because they upheld Wesley's deepest ideals for Methodism: obedience to the preachers, attendance on the means of grace—including searching the Scriptures—and keeping Methodist doctrine and discipline.

When the author described the way a prayer meeting should be conducted, he described it as beginning, in typically Methodist fashion, "with singing a few verses, and solemn prayer."[174] After the meeting was opened in this way, the heart of the prayer meeting was described:

> Then let two or three pray in succession, short and lively, while the congregation continue on their knees. If any persons are perceived to be in distress, some one should, in a low voice, enquire into their state; and if they be earnestly seeking pardon, or holiness, after giving them proper advice, and suitable encouragement to look unto Jesus in faith,

[170] Mr. Moon, letter to Thomas Coke, August 22, 1794, in *AM* 18 (1795): 417–418.

[171] Anonymous (A Well Wisher to Zion), "Thoughts on the Revival of Religion in the Prayer-Meetings," in *AM* 21 (1798): 240.

[172] Ibid., 241.

[173] Ibid.

[174] Ibid., 243.

and to venture their souls wholly upon him, let one pray for them, but not in too loud a manner; and others likewise should assist by prayer and animating exhortations, till the blessing of God descends upon the penitent mourners. In a little time, probably, there may be several companies engaged in the same manner, in different parts of the meeting; and while they are thus employed, a proper person should preside in the meeting, and occasionally address the congregation at large, intermixing hymns proper for the occasion, in which all may join, except those who are praying with the distressed. When there is good reason to believe that any of the mourners have found divine consolation, the person who conducts the meeting should be made acquainted with it, in order that he may inform the congregation, when all will unite in praising God for his mercy and grace. Attention to these circumstances will conduce to keep the people in their places, the different parties may go quietly on with those that are in distress, and all the congregation will be encouraged to persevere in prayer and thanksgiving.[175]

At first glance, this account does not appear to have much of anything in common with the early Methodist band meeting. In fact, the prayer meeting appeared to be more similar to an early Methodist society meeting than the more intimate band meeting that was focused on confession of sin.

However, many of the references to band meetings in the nineteenth century more closely resembled the above account than they resembled Wesley's "Rules of the Band Societies," or even the accounts of popular Methodist experiences of bands in the 1740s and 1750s. This is seen in a passage in George Marsden's manuscript journal at the end of 1804. Marsden's description of a newly formed band meeting appeared to indicate a meeting that had undergone a significant shift in practice from the bands that John Wesley organized:

Had a most precious season at the Band meeting, which has been established about two months. Several persons were in deep distress for want of holiness, and while 3 or 4 persons prayed one after another the agony of some who were in distress was very great indeed, and 3 or 4 profess'd to receive that invaluable blessing purity of heart. The Band has been of much use the short time it has been established, and through the divine blessing seems as though it would be a real and lasting blessing to this Society.[176]

---

[175] Ibid., 243.
[176] George Marsden, manuscript journal, December 8, 1804.

In this meeting, the primary goal was finding relief from distress for those who realized their "want of holiness." The primary activity of the groups was prayer, which led people to experience the "invaluable blessing" of "purity of heart." This band meeting, then, was more like a small prayer meeting than a mid-eighteenth-century band meeting.

Finally, the 1843 "Rules of the Original Methodists" further point to a significant shift in the conception of the band meeting. According to these "Rules," the Original Methodists authorized the following meetings: "Preachings, prayer meetings, class meetings, band or fellowship meetings, lovefeasts, the sacrament of the Lord's supper, and camp meetings."[177] A shift in understanding of the band meeting is suggested simply by the fact that it was listed as a band *or fellowship* meeting. A change is further seen in the description of these meetings, which "are frequently held once a month in our societies, and are conducted similarly to lovefeasts, only the bread and water is not partaken of, and must be concluded within the hour."[178] Aside from the name, there is not much in this description that is connected to John Wesley's conception of the band meeting. It appears that at least among the Original Methodists, by 1843, there were no longer private band meetings. Instead, the term "band meeting" had become associated with what used to be called the "public bands" or "body bands," which were the larger gatherings of all of the band meetings in a particular location.[179]

In these shifts, there are suggestions of a move away from an approach to communal Christian formation focused on "watching over one another in love" through close and searching conversation in order to know the state of the soul of each person in the society and to foster the kind of intimacy that Wesley believed led to growth in holiness. Thus, the decline of the band meeting, in part, points to a move toward larger scale revivalism. The prayer meeting may have marked an initial step away from Wesley's approach to social holiness toward the revivalism found in the camp meetings, which the 1843 "Rules" also reference.[180]

From 1766 through 1801, the band meeting did largely adhere to Wesley's conception. There is significant evidence that Methodists participated in bands

---

[177] "Rules of the Original Methodists," in Donald M. Grundy, "A History of the Original Methodists" *PWHS* 35 (1965–66): 192.

[178] Ibid., 193.

[179] This is supported by Dean, who found in his Ph.D. dissertation that "Far more Methodists around the turn of the century enjoyed or saw value in the public band than they did in the private bands." Dean, 169.

[180] Demonstrating such dependence is beyond the scope of this volume. However, I have noted it here to suggest the interdependence of the various forms of the Methodist structures on one another. This book suggests that the prayer meeting cannot be adequately understood without some consideration of the class and band meetings as crucial background. Further, the bands and classes would likely be more fully understood in light of a more complete study of the prayer meeting and its connection to the camp meeting. Dean made a similar argument in his Ph.D. dissertation, though neither the bands nor the prayer meetings were the particular focus of his study. Dean, 172.

as a result of searching for or experiencing the witness of the Spirit, and that they sought further confirmation of God's love in this context. Wesley's emphasis on the importance of a disciplined practice of the means of grace was also developed by Methodists in this period. Methodists appeared to take the importance of the means of grace for granted. When they talked about the means of grace in relation to band meetings, most often it was in order to point to the importance of the band meeting itself as a means of grace.

Yet, there also appears to have been a shift in understanding of the band meeting; some of the references to band meetings point to their transition to prayer meetings. One explanation for the decline of the band meeting, then, is that as individual bands became less common, the larger gatherings of bands (public bands or body bands) gradually came to be known as band meetings. Combined with the rise and development of the prayer meeting toward the end of the eighteenth century, the band meeting was ultimately overshadowed and replaced by the newer prayer meeting, which was much larger and less directly focused on ongoing growth in holiness.

Two key areas of further research have also been identified that would be fruitful to the study of Methodist history. First, there are significant references to select societies in the early Methodist primary source materials. A focused study on the role of the select societies in popular Methodism would further illuminate the role of both communal Christian formation and holiness in eighteenth-century Methodism. Second, there are also significant references to the prayer meeting in late eighteenth- and early nineteenth- century Methodism. A study of the prayer meeting would further the understanding of the decline of the band meeting, as well as provide insight into the changing view of nineteenth-century Methodism regarding the role of communal Christian formation, larger revivals, and growth in holiness.

Conclusion

The lack of a focused study on the early Methodist band meeting marked a significant gap in Wesleyan studies, as the band meeting was the key form of small group formation in the period from Wesley's involvement in the Fetter Lane Society through the advent of the class meeting in 1742. During this period, the band meeting was the lone structure that gathered Methodists together into small groups in order to support one another's efforts to grow in holiness. Outsiders often thought the band meeting was of such value that they would request to join a band before receiving justifying faith or the witness of the Spirit. The fact that many of these requests were granted also indicates the value that early Methodists themselves placed on the potential of the bands to not only sustain those who had experienced the new birth, but to help people who were seeking peace with God find it.

Wesley's development and use of the band meeting marked an important step in his advocacy and practice of "social holiness." In fact, because of the value that Wesley placed on small group formation prior to the advent of the class meeting, scholars should reevaluate Wesley's account of the rise of the class meeting. Given that the "Rules of the Band Societies" contained explicit prerequisites for joining a band, and that these were often ignored when someone was particularly earnest in their desire to join a band, it is at least plausible that Wesley was already looking for an additional form of small group practice that would enable all Methodists to receive the benefits of "watching over one another in love" that Wesley had experienced through his own participation in a band. Perhaps the class meeting, the name of which also has prior precedent in the Moravian approach to communal formation at Herrnhut, was not stumbled upon as accidentally as Wesley suggested. The class meeting solved several problems that Wesley was already looking for solutions to; namely, the need for stricter discipline as something resembling a revival grew and gained momentum, and the need for a structure to provide pastoral support for those who could not meet the requirements for admission into a band itself. This volume, then, has the potential to contribute to a more complete understanding of the origins, development, and significance of the class meeting for early Methodism.

The band meeting also reminds scholars that one of the key aspects of Wesley's theology (holiness) cannot be adequately understood without the context that the band meeting provides. John Wesley consistently advocated for the importance and necessity of holiness in the Christian life. In "Thoughts upon Methodism," written in 1786, Wesley summarized the "essence" of Methodism as "holiness of heart and life."[1] Although scholars have recognized the importance of holiness for Wesley's theology, the band meeting has not been adequately recognized as the central piece of Wesley's "method" that was aimed at helping Methodists who had repented of their sins and received justifying faith to become holy. Wesley's connection of holiness to communal formation means that the success or failure of the bands may have been the most important indicator of Methodism's faithfulness to its own understanding of God's "design" in "raising [them] up," which was "to spread scriptural holiness over the land."[2] Put differently, the band meeting was the most visible example of what Wesley meant when he said that there is "no holiness but social holiness."[3]

A close analysis of the bands also provides an example of the value of paying closer attention to popular accounts of early Methodist experiences. There is sufficient primary source evidence to compare various aspects of John Wesley's conception of early Methodist theology and practice with the popular reception of his ideas. Leslie Church consulted dozens of local histories of British Methodism in his works on the popular Methodist experience in the eighteenth century. And yet, since Church's work from the late 1940s, the abundant primary source materials at the popular level continue to be one of the most underutilized resources in Wesleyan studies and the history of early Methodism. This book shows the value of such materials for the study of the reception of John Wesley's practical theology, as well as the early Methodist experience, which is an object worthy of further study in its own right.

John Wesley's conception of the band meeting and its general reception and appropriation at the popular level provide an initial test case of Wesley's influence within popular Methodism. There are many extant primary sources that attest to the presence and practice of band meetings. These sources also show that both sides of Wesley's synthesis of Anglican and Moravian piety were present in some form in the Methodist experience of the bands. In particular, the band meeting was a place where people particularly anticipated encountering God's grace, and they testified that such encounters often occurred. Popular accounts also evidence that the bands were frequently viewed as a means of

---

[1] John Wesley, "Thoughts upon Methodism," in *Works* 9: 529.

[2] Wesley, "Minutes of Several Conversations between the Reverend Mr. John and Charles Wesley, and Others" (1763), in *Works* 10: 845.

[3] Wesley, "Preface," *Hymns and Sacred Poems*, in *Works*, Jackson, 14: 321.

grace and were a place that reinforced people's commitment to and reliance upon the means of grace.

The band meeting and the general role of communal formation in early Methodism are of further significance for understanding the ways that people adapted to social changes at the beginnings of industrialization. Wesley's conception of "social holiness" was embraced at the popular level because it provided a new kind of social intimacy at a time of important shifts in English society that resulted in the disruption and loss of previous norms of village and urban life. From this vantage point, the experience of early Methodists is a key to understanding ways that English people searched for new forms of social Christianity and the breakdown of the *ancien régime* at the end of the eighteenth and beginning of the nineteenth century.[4]

Though Wesley's conception of the band meeting was influential in popular Methodism, it was not adopted without exception. Particularly in the earliest period of their use, people who would not have been able to correctly answer all the questions that the "Rules of the Band Societies" stipulated that someone should be able to answer *before* being admitted were occasionally accepted. Specifically, people who lacked justifying faith, peace with God, or assurance were allowed to join bands in the early 1740s.

Perhaps the most important exception to Wesley's conception of the band meeting in popular Methodist practice was that Methodists who experienced justification and the new birth did not always take advantage of the band meeting as the prudential means of grace that Wesley was convinced God had specially given to the Methodists.[5] In other words, if there is no holiness but social holiness, and the band meeting was the primary social context in early Methodism that focused on growth in holiness subsequent to the new birth, Wesley's conception of the band meeting suggested that every Methodist who was eligible to join a band meeting should have actually joined one. Wesley's own comments urging traveling preachers to restore bands in various societies evidences that he was aware that band meetings were not as normative as he intended for them to be. Because of the strategic significance of the band meeting as the key structure of communal formation focused on growth in holiness, the decline of the band meeting must be seen as an important indication that Methodism was failing in its efforts to "spread scriptural holiness."[6]

---

[4] The extent to which England was an *ancien régime* society is contested by historians. This transition is generally seen to have happened during the "long eighteenth-century," which J. C. D. Clark's recent work has extended to nearly two centuries, from 1660 to 1832. Clark, *English Society 1660–1832: Religion, Ideology, and Politics during the Ancien Regime*, 2nd ed. (Cambridge, UK: Cambridge University Press, 2000).

[5] Wesley, "Minutes of Several Conversations," in *Works* 10: 857.

[6] Ibid., 845.

One explanation for the decline of the band meeting is the rise in importance of prayer meetings at the end of the eighteenth and the beginning of the nineteenth centuries. After John Wesley's death, most extant accounts of bands appear to be references to what would have been considered band societies in earlier periods, as the accounts appear to refer to all of the members of bands in a particular society and not individual groups of five to seven women or men. In the nineteenth century, it appears that these larger groups eventually replaced the smaller bands and gradually became more and more like prayer meetings, where people were seeking a direct encounter with God through a corporate search for revival. If this is correct, the band meeting is an important context for studying the shift away from small group accountability in early Methodism toward approaches to communal formation (such as prayer meetings and camp meetings) that were larger in scale, less intimate, and lacked the element of personal accountability that both the band meeting and class meeting provided.

Wesley himself was not unaware of the presence and potential of prayer meetings. In fact, there is evidence that at the end of his life, he supported them. In 1788, Wesley wrote to William Simpson: "You did exceeding well to enlarge the number of prayer-meetings and to fix them in various parts of those [places]. I do not know that any means of grace whatever has been more owned of God than this."[7] More detailed study of the rise and development of the prayer meeting is needed to further understand both Methodism's shift away from small group formation toward larger scale revivalism, as well as Wesley's own role in this transition. As such, the prayer meeting is also an important forerunner of the camp meeting, which became a prominent fixture of American Methodism.

Although this book has focused on the history of the band meeting in eighteenth- and early nineteenth-century British Methodism, and as such is primarily intended to be a contribution to the history of Methodism, it also has relevance for contemporary approaches to Christian communal formation. The history of the early Methodist band meeting is of particular importance for members of historically Wesleyan traditions who seek to reclaim the early Methodist commitment to communal Christian formation. However, contemporary interest in Wesleyan communal formation is not always accompanied by well-documented scholarship regarding this history or informed theological reflection regarding small group formation.

The historical study of Wesleyan communal formation should contribute to the conversation about the role of small groups in contemporary Wesleyan communities. Wesley and the earliest Methodists did not embrace a generic, amorphous understanding of small group formation. Rather, they were convinced that the band meeting was valuable, even essential, for ongoing growth in holiness. In other words, the band meeting was valuable because it helped people

[7] Wesley, letter to William Simpson, January 18, 1788, in *Letters* (Telford), 8: 35–36.

become more like Christ, not because it promised to reverse a trend of numeric decline in a denomination. Understanding the theological foundations for the "method" of early Methodism is an important first step for discerning the role of Wesleyan small groups in contemporary Wesleyan communities.

Recent conversations in Wesleyan communities are also too often unclear about the differences between band meetings and class meetings, regarding them as if they were the same thing. The term "small group" is meaningless unless it is being used as a synonym for a particular kind of group that is small. Early Methodists did not use the term "small groups"; instead they talked about their classes and bands. A particular concept of communal formation was in play when Methodists used more generic phrases like "watching over one another in love," which related to mutual support and accountability for growth in holiness. The findings of this book, then, suggest the need for a concrete vision of small group formation and social holiness as key to a legitimate reclaiming of a Wesleyan approach and practice of small group accountability.

To put this even more directly, this volume offers no support for the types of small groups that are most common in contemporary Wesleyan/Methodist communities, which are curriculum-driven and focused on a transfer of information from a perceived expert to a largely passive audience. The most obvious example of this approach is Sunday School. I did not find any evidence that curricula, studies, or books (with the possible exception of Bible passages being read for edification) were used as a way to structure either band meetings or class meetings in eighteenth-century Methodism. In order for contemporary Wesleyan communities to successfully reclaim an authentically Wesleyan approach to small group formation, the first step would be for people to recognize the extent of the disconnect between the eighteenth-century conception of small group formation and that of the contemporary context. Today, the participants in most small groups are passive, and they are engaged in something like studying a book. In the eighteenth century, participants were more active, and the curriculum was their own lives. The topic of conversation was the state of each person's soul.

Wesley was convinced that God had raised up the Methodists in order to proclaim the doctrine of entire sanctification. He was also convinced that this vision would not be actualized without Christian community. The band meeting offered the most effective approach to social holiness that Methodism has deployed to date. It was abandoned not because it was tried and found to be wanting, but because it was laid aside as the early Methodist emphasis on entire sanctification began to be watered down and the understanding of social holiness shifted toward larger scale revivals and away from more intimate and frequent gatherings where people unburdened themselves and shared the burdens of others.

Appendix A

THE RULES AND ORDERS OF
A RELIGIOUS SOCIETY MEETING AT PRESENT
IN A ROOM IN FETTER LANE:
THE MEMBERS CONSISTING OF
PERSONS IN COMMUNION WITH THE
ESTABLISHED CHURCH

Glory to God in the Highest on Earth Peace Good Will Towards Men.
Little Children Let Us Love One Another

May 1, 1738

In obedience to the Command of God by St. James (5:16) and by the Advice of Peter Boehler: (a) It was agreed *by John Bray, Brazier; Shepherd Wolf, Barber; John Edmonds, Poulterer; James Hutton, Bookseller; William Oxlee, Clogmaker; William Hervey, Wine-cooper; Mathew Clarke, Barber; John Shaw (late) attorney, & John Wesley, Clerk—all members of the Church of England.*

1. That they will meet together once a week, to confess their faults one to another, and pray for one another, that they may be healed.
2. That any others of whose Sincerity they are well assured, may if they desire it, meet with them for that Purpose and May 29 it was agreed:
3. That the Persons desirous to meet together for that Purpose, be divided into several Bands or little societies.
4. That none of these consist of fewer than five or more than ten persons.
5. That some *one* person in each band be desired to interrogate the rest in order, who may be called the Leader of the Band

Tuesday Sept. 20.

It was agreed

That John Bray, Shepherd Wolf, John Edmonds, James Hutton, William Oxlee, William Hervey, John Shaw, John Wesley, John Brown and the Leaders of the New Bands meet together at McBray's at 6 ½ every Wednesday Evening. That each Leader then give an Account of the State of each Person in his Band. That a Person and time be then fixed, for doing what may then appear necessary; of which an account is to be given in the beginning of the Next Meeting. That in Particular a Person and time be then fixed, for settling and visiting Female Bands.

Monday Sept. 26

It was agreed

7. That each *of the* Bands meet twice in a week; once on Monday Evenings, the Second time, when it is most convenient for each Band.
8. That every Person come punctually at the hour appointed, without some extraordinary Reason.
9. That those that are present, begin Exactly at the Hour.
10. That every Meeting be begun & ended with Singing and Prayer.
11. That *each Person* in order speak as freely, plainly, and concisely as he can, the Real State of his Heart, with his several Temptations and Deliverances since the last time of meeting.
12. That all the Bands have a Conference at 8 every Wednesday Evening, begun and ended with Singing and Prayer.
13. That whosoever speaks in this Conference stand up, & that none else speak till He is sat down.
14. That nothing which is *said* in this Conference be by any means mentioned out of it.
15. That every Member of this Society who is a Member of any Other, prefer the Meeting with this & with his Particular Band, before the Meeting with any other Society or Company *whatever.*
16. That if any Person absent himself without some Extraordinary Reason, either from his Band or from any Meeting of the whole Society, he be first privately admonished, & if He absent again, reproved before the whole Society.
17. *That such women as have entered their names the Friday before, if there be no objection against them, may meet in the Society Room, every Wednesday from six to eight in the Evening.*
18. *That no men be Present except their Respective Husbands, & the Persons who pray and Expound the Scriptures.*
19. That any who desire to be admitted into the Society be ask'd,

> What are your reasons for desiring this?
> Will you be entirely open?
> Using no kind of Reserve, least of all in the case of Love or Courtship.
> Will you strive against the Desire of Ruling, of being first in your Company, of having your own way?
> Have you an objections to any of our orders?
> The orders may then be read to them.

20. That those who answer these Questions in the Affirmative, be proposed every Fourth Wednesday.
21. That everyone then present speak clearly and fully, whatever objection he has to any Person proposed to be a Member.
22. That those against whom any Reasonable Objection appears, be acquainted with that Objection, & the admitting them upon Trial postponed, 'till that Objection is removed.
23. That those against whom no Reasonable Objection appears or remains, be in order for their trial, immediately formed into distinct Bands, & some Person agreed on to assist them.
24. That if no New Objection then appears, they be after a month's Trial admitted into the Society.
25. That every fourth Saturday be observ'd as a Day of General Intercession, which may continue from 12 to 2, from 3 to 5 & from 6 to 8.
26. That on Sunday se'ennight following be a General Lovefeast from 7 to 10 in the Evening.
27. *That a Collection be made towards a Common Stock, in each Band on Monday Evening at 6 and 8 on Wednesdays, at 8 on Friday & on the General Thanksgiving Day.*
28. *That out of this be defrayed the Expenses of the Love-Feasts, of Letters, & whatever else relates to the Society in General.*

29. That in order to a Continual Intercession every Member of this Society *chuse* some Hour either of the day or night, to spend in Prayer chiefly for his Brethren.
30. That in order to a Continual Fast three of the Members of the Society fast every Day (as their Health permits) Sundays and Holidays excepted, and spend as much as they can of that Day, in Retirement from Business & Prayer.

This document can be found in Whitney M. Trousdale, "The Moravian Society, Fetter Lane—London," *PWHS* 17 (1929–30): 30–32 (emphasis original). The manuscript is at the Archives of the United Brethren in Herrnhut, Germany, Ref: R13.A19.2.

Appendix B

ORDERS OF A RELIGIOUS SOCIETY MEETING IN FETTER LANE

In Obedience to the Command of God by St. James, and by the Advice of Peter Boehler, May 1, 1738, it was agreed,

1. That they will meet together once in a week to confess their Faults one to another, and pray for one Another that they may be healed.
2. That any others, of whose Sincerity they are well assured, may, if they desire it, meet with them for that Purpose.

And, May 29, it was agreed,

3. That the Persons desirous to meet together for that Purpose be divided into several Bands, or little Societies.
4. That none of these consist of fewer than five, or more than ten Persons.
5. That some Person in each Band be desired to interrogate the rest in order, who may be called the Leader of that Band.

And on Monday, September 26, it was agreed,

6. That each Band meet twice in a Week, once on Monday Evenings, the second Time when it is most convenient for each Band.
7. That every Person come punctually at the Hour appointed, without some extraordinary Reason.
8. That those that are present begin exactly at the *Hours*.
9. That every Meeting be begun and ended with Singing and Prayer.
10. That *every one* in order speak as freely, plainly, and concisely as he can, the real State of his Heart, with his several Temptations and Deliverances, since the last Time of meeting.
11. That all Bands have a Conference at eight every Wednesday Evening, begun and ended with Singing and Prayer.
12. *That at nine of the Clock the Names of the Members be called over, and the Absenters set down*
13. *That notice of any extraordinary Meeting be given on the Wednesday Night preceding such Meeting.*
14. *That exactly at ten, if the Business of the Night be not finished, a short concluding prayer be used, that those may go who are in haste, but that all depart the Room by half an hour after ten.*
15. That whosoever speaks in this Conference stand up, and that none else speak till he is set down.
16. That nothing which is *mentioned* in this Conference, be by any Means mentioned out of it.

17. That every Member of this Society, who is a Member of any other, prefer the Meeting with this, and with his particular Band, before the meeting with any other Society or Company *whatsoever.*

18. That if any Person absent himself without some extraordinary Reason, either from his Band, or from any Meeting of the whole Society, he be first privately admonished; and if he *be* absent again, reproved before the whole Society.

19. *That any Person who desires, or designs to take any Journey, shall first, if it be possible, have the Approbation of the Bands.*

20. *That all our Members who are in Clubs, be desired to withdraw their Names, as being Meetings nowise conducing to the Glory of God.*

21. That any who desire to be admitted into this Society, be asked, What are your Reasons for desiring this? Will you be entirely open, using no Kind of Reserve, least of all, in the Case of Love or Courtship? Will you strive against the Desire of ruling, or being first in your Company, or having your own Way? *Will you submit to be placed in what Band the Leaders shall choose for you?* Have you any Objections to any of our Orders? The Orders may then be read to them.

22. That those who answer these Questions in the Affirmative, be proposed every fourth Wednesday.

23. That every one then present speak clearly and fully whatever Objection he has to any Person proposed to be a Member.

24. That those against whom any reasonable Objection appears, be acquainted with that Objection, and the admitting them upon Trial postponed till that Objection is removed.

25. That those against whom no reasonable Objection appears or remains, be, in order for their Trial, formed into distinct Bands, and some Person agreed to assist them.

26. That if no new Objection then appear, they be, after *two* Months Trial, admitted into the Society.

27. That every fourth Saturday be observed as a Day of General Intercession, which may continue from *twelve* to *two*, from *three* to *five*, and from *six* to *eight*.

28. That on Sunday Se'en-Night following be a general Love-Feast from *seven* till *ten* in the Evening.

29. That in order to a continual Intercession, every Member of this Society *choose* some Hour, either of the Day or Night, to spend in Prayer chiefly for his Brethren.

30. That in order to a continual Fast, three of the Members of the Society Fast every Day (as their Health permits), Sundays and Holidays excepted, and spend as much as they can of that Day, in Retirement from Business, and Prayer.

31. *That each Person give Notice to the Leader of his Band how much he is willing to subscribe towards the general Charge of the Bands, and that each Person's Money be paid into the Leader of his Band once a Month at farthest.*

32. *That no particular Person be allowed to act in any Thing contrary to any Order of the Society, but that every One, without Distinction, submit to the Determination of his Brethren; and that if any Person or Persons do not, after being thrice admonished, conform to the Society, they be not esteemed any longer as Members.*

33. *That any Person whom the whole Society shall approve, may be accounted a correspondent Member, and as such, may be admitted at our general Meetings, provided he correspond with the Society once in a Month at least.*

This document can be found in Whitney M. Trousdale, "The Moravian Society, Fetter Lane— London," *PWHS* 17 (1929–30): 32–35 (emphasis original). Trousdale's transcription is from Daniel Benham, *Memoirs of James Hutton* (London: Hamilton, Adams, 1856), 29ff.

Appendix C

RULES OF THE BAND SOCIETIES

Drawn up Dec. 25, 1738

The design of our meeting is to obey that command of God, "Confess your faults one to another, and pray one for another that ye may be healed."
To this end we intend:

1. To meet once a week, at the least.
2. To come punctually at the hour appointed, without some extraordinary reason.
3. To begin (those of us who are present) exactly at the hour, with singing or prayer.
4. To speak, each of us in order, freely and plainly the true state of our souls, with the faults we have committed in thought, word, or deed, and the temptations we have felt since our last meeting.
5. To end every meeting with prayer, suited for the state of each person present.
6. To desire some person among us to speak *his* own state first, and then to ask the rest in order as many and as searching questions as may be concerning their state, sins, and temptations.

Some of the questions proposed to every one before *he* is admitted amongst us may be to this effect:

1. Have you the forgiveness of your sins?
2. Have you peace with God, through our Lord Jesus Christ?
3. Have you the witness of God's Spirit with your spirit that you are a child of God?
4. Is the love of God shed abroad in your heart?
5. Has no sin, inward or outward, dominion over you?
6. Do you desire to be told of your faults?
7. Do you desire to be told of all your faults, and that plain and home?
8. Do you desire that every one of us should tell you from time to time whatsoever is in *his* heart concerning you?
9. Consider! Do you desire we should tell you whatsoever we think, whatsoever we fear, whatsoever we hear, concerning you?
10. Do you desire that in doing this we should come as close as possible, that we should cut to the quick, and search your heart to the bottom?
11. Is it your desire and design to be on this and all other occasions entirely open, so as to speak everything that is in your heart, without exception, without disguise, and without reserve?

Any of the preceding questions may be asked as often as occasion offers; the five following at every meeting:

1. What known sins have you committed since our last meeting?
2. What temptations have you met with?
3. How was you delivered?
4. What have you thought, said, or done, of which you doubt whether it be sin or not?
5. Have you nothing you desire to keep secret?

The "Rules of the Band Societies" are cited with permission from *Works* 9: 77–78 (emphasis original).

Appendix D

DIRECTIONS GIVEN TO THE BAND SOCIETIES

Dec. 25, 1744

You are supposed to have the "faith that overcometh the world." To you therefore it is not grievous,

I. Carefully to abstain from doing evil; in particular,

1. Neither to *buy nor sell* anything at all on the Lord's Day.
2. To taste no spirituous liquor, *no dram* of any kind, unless prescribed by a physician.
3. To be *at a word* both in buying and selling.
4. To *pawn nothing*, no, not to save life.
5. Not to *mention the fault* of any *behind his back*, and to stop those short that do.
6. To wear no *needless ornaments*, such as rings, ear-rings, necklaces, lace, ruffles.
7. To use no *needless self-indulgence*, such as taking snuff or tobacco, unless prescribed by a physician.

II. Zealously to maintain good works; in particular,

1. To *give alms* of such things as you possess, and that to the uttermost of your power.
2. To *reprove* all that sin in your sight, and that in love, and meekness of wisdom.
3. To be patterns of *diligence* and *frugality*, of *self-denial*, and taking up the cross daily.

III. Constantly to attend on all the ordinances of God; in particular,

1. To be at church, and at the Lord's table, every week, and at every public meeting of the bands.
2. To attend the ministry of the Word every morning, unless distance, business, or sickness prevent.
3. To use private prayer every day, and family prayer if you are the head of a family.
4. To read the Scriptures, and meditate thereon, at every vacant hour. And,
5. To observe as days of fasting or abstinence all *Fridays* in the year.

The "Directions given to the Band Societies" are cited with permission from *Works* 9: 79 (emphasis original).

Appendix E

A METHOD OF CONFESSION DRAWN UP BY MR WHITEFIELD, FOR THE USE OF THE WOMEN BELONGING TO THE RELIGIOUS SOCIETIES — TAKEN FROM THE ORIGINAL, UNDER MR WHITEFIELD'S OWN HAND

The Design of our Meeting together is to obey the Command of God; Confess your Faults one to another, and pray one for the other, that he may be healed.

- To this End we intend to meet twice a Week.
- To come punctually at the Hour appointed, without some extraordinary Reason.
- To begin (those of us who are present) exactly at the Hour, with Singing and Prayer.
- To speak each of us in Order, plainly and freely, the true State of our Hearts, with the Faults of Thought, Word, and Deed, and the Temptations we have been in since our last Meeting.
- To end every Meeting with Singing and Prayer, suited to the State of each Person present.
- To desire some Person among us to speak her own State first, and then to ask the next in Order as many and as searching Questions as may be, concerning their State, Sins, and Temptations.

Some of those Questions proposed to every one, before she is admitted among us, may be to this Effect.

- Have you the Witness of God's Spirit with your Spirit, that you are a Child of God?
- Have you Joy in the Holy Ghost?
- Is the Love of God shed abroad in your Heart? If not,
- Have you the Forgiveness of your Sins?
- Has no Sin, inward or outward, Dominion over you?
- Have you Peace with God through Jesus Christ? If not,
- Do you see yourself a lost Sinner?
- Do you know you deserve to be damn'd?
- Do you despair of being sav'd, either by your own Works, or by your own Righteousness, and hope for Forgiveness of Sins, and Justification; only through a living Faith in Christ Jesus?
- Do you desire to be told of your Faults?
- Do you desire to be told of all your Faults, and that plain and home?
- Do you desire that we should tell you whatever we think, whatever we fear, whatever we hear concerning you?

- Do you desire that in doing this we should come as close as possible, that we should cut to the Quick, and search your Heart to the Bottom?
- Is it your Desire and Design to be on this and on all Occasions entirely open, so as to speak every Thing that is in your Heart without Exception, without Disguise, and without Reserve?
- Are you in Love?
- Do you take more Pleasure in any Body than in God?
- Whom do you love just now, better than any other Person in the World?
- Is not the Person an Idol? Does he not (especially in Publick Prayer) steal in between God and your Soul?
- Does any court you?
- Is there any one whom you suspect to have any such Design?
- Is there any one who shews you more Respect than to other Women?
- Are not you pleas'd with That?
- How do you like him?
- How do you feel yourself, when he comes, when he stays, when he goes away?
- The last ten Questions may be ask'd as often as Occasion offers.

These four following at every Meeting.

- What known Sin have you committed since our last Meeting?
- What have you said, thought, or done, of wch you doubt whether it may be a Sin?
- What Temptations have you felt? how was you delivered from them?
- What Comforts or Communications have you had from God, since our last Meeting?

This document can be found in *Gentleman's Magazine* 9 (May 1739), 238.

Appendix F

EXCERPT FROM WILLIAM SEWARD'S MANUSCRIPT DIARY ON THE IMPORTANCE AND METHOD OF BAND MEETINGS

September 14, 1740

- We [Seward and Howell Harris] Exhorted them to Meet in Band, publick & private 5 or 6 in a Band & to have their Love feasts –
- According to the Example of the churches of Xt at London & Bristol the order I was Enabled to leave ym. was to this purpose –
- none to be of the Band but Such who know their Sins are forgiven or are Earnestly Seeking forgiveness
- private Bands to Meet at Some of the Brethrens houses for one hour in a Week—to Confess their Faults one to another to pray one for the other that they may be healed –
- the Leader of the Band to begin with Singing & Extempore prayer then to Confess her own faults & Temptations & also declare wt. Communications she has had from above—then examines every one Singley—& Conclude wth. Extempore prayer wherein every one is desired to Excercise their Gifts & Talents—& to pray as their own & Brethrens States— Require—& no One to be of ye Band who is not willing & desirous to have their Hearts Search'd to ye bottom—& freely to be told of all their faults—that so Sin may not be Sufferd upon them –
- the general Band to Meet once a Week in ye Society Room & to be begun & Ended with Singing & Extempore prayer & then all Cases of Conscience to be decided & all things relating to the Intst. Of Xts. Church then discussd –
- the Love feast to be held once a Month by the general Band to Consist only of Cake & Cheese or Bread & Cheese or Bread & Water—after the primitive pattern of the feasts of Charity— beginning & Ending with Singing & prayer—Singing now & then a Verse while they Eat & talking of the things wch: concern the Ld: Jesus Christ –
- may our Dear Ld. Jesus Bless & prosper this order & make every thing tend to his own glory—amen

This is my own transcription of William Seward's unpublished manuscript diary from September 6–October 15, 1740. The diary is housed at Chetham's Library in Manchester, England, Ref: A.2.116. Cited with permission.

Appendix G

THE METHOD OF MR. WESTLAY BAND MEETINGS, SAMUEL ROBERTS EXCERPT FROM MANUSCRIPT VOLUME

A band is a Company of People joynd to gather in Church falowship (Should be) & when thay Meet together thay Reveal All thare Consarns, Speritual & tempral one to another, thare Desined End is in this to help & Strengthen one another to over come ye World ye flesh & ye Devil. & walk as Xt. walked. til thay Arive to be holy in thought word & Deed. & to have ye Sperit of God to abide with ym. for Ever. In thare inmost Souls ye Same as ye Apostels had: but to be Plainer Stil (The Minester Auder in Uniting & Making of bands) When any Man or woman Say & Spreds it a Broad that thay have found ye Pardon of all thare Past Sins & yt thay Now Can beleve yt thare justifyed by Xt ye Preacher. Puts them into a band. being thought then yt Now thare More Capable of Reseving More Privalegs. in ye Use of ye Means. so thare Put into band & have a Different ticket Given to ym. ye Way of Makeing up bands. is Putting young Men by them Selves & ould Men by them Selves. & young wiming by ym Selves. & ould wiming by them Selves. ye Proper Number of a band. 3 or 4 People. but thare often 5 or 6 becaus of ye Scarceness of leaders becaus ye leader is thought ye Man yt is Got fordest in Grace & now ye Devils Devices More then ye Rest of ye Compeny. So this Compeny of People Meets once Every week. to tel How thare Souls Prospers. & how often thay have Conqurd or been Concerd. by ye World flesh or ye Devil. To tel of worly Consarns. & all joy or Grevance yt Passes in thare mind from one week to another as follows - - - - -

Note yt ye following Descorce is a true & a Clear account of ye Nature of a band Meting. Thearfore lit us Supose yt we Are Now in ye hearing of 6 People Met togather in band, & yt This is ye first time. of thare Meting to gather. since thay was joind to gather in band. Note I Shall Give Every one of ym. thare Name. (as ye Real truth of ye Gospil teach me:) thearfore The Name of ye leader is B hate ye truth. & ye five yt is Under his Care & Dyrections are those Br. knowllittle. Br. Misarable. Br fretful. & Br Slipperry Br. lofty. The Leader Speak furst. My Dear beloved Brethren. I am Glad yt it hath Pleased ye Lord yt we Should be thus joynd to gather in Band of Union. I Confidently hope you will be Sincear in ye ways of ye Lord. & also Sincear & faithful in Declaring ye State of your Souls. & ye Devises & Strattagems of ye Ennemy. togather with all your Worly Consarn. yt all our Greifs & Sorows May be lade open one to another. & yt no longer we may Not be Council keepers for ye Divel, but yt we may all faithfully & in Much love Confess ye hole of what is lodge in our brests. & yt we non of us. May Never to ye Day of our Death Devulg. To Any other Possers. What sover. any thing yt have been Spoken in this our band Meting. Let us Pray. O Lord Most hosly' mot Mity, & infinite God. we thy Unworthy. Children have agrede togather for to Ask in X Name yt thou would of thine Infinite Goodness & marcy Vouchsafe to give us thy blessing at all times when we Meet togather, & yt thou would Unite us More & more by thy Good Sperit. yt we May Declare faithfully ye true State of our Souls one to an other. & whatso ever is a Miss in Any one of Us Good lorde Do thou Remove it from Us. Yt we May Grow from Grace to

Grace. from Strength to Strength from Conkering to [illeg. Word, page folded]. til as last thou hast Made us holy throughout Body Soule & Sperit. for Ever to Prase thy horly Name Amen Our father which arte in heaven - - -

then thay all Sit Down. &: hate ye truth, Speaks First, Of a truth it is a Great wonder, that I am out of Hell. for ye Days of My Youth, have been vary Evil, after I was 14 years of Age. I was Sorely Given to lust after wiming. how to Steal. & Get Money for to go to Get Drunk. alongue with hores was my Constant Studdy As for horse I had Sevarl: yea Mens wives I ust to lye with a Most Every Day. & as for young wiming I had 10 or a Duzen of them. & of a Jentell Sort. but In ye 27 year of My Age. which was 3d years after I was Maried. being led by Severl Accuaintance to hear ye Methodist Preach, it Pleased ye Lord to Pluck me as a brand from ye burnings So I was Struck Under ye word With a Devine Conviction so yt for Severl weeks. I did Nothing but Crye & Rore. & Could Scarce Eate or Drink or Sleep in My bed. being So Destrest in My Mind but at last it Pleased ye Lorde as I was a Coming home one Morning from ye Preaching. all of a Suddon I heard a Voice Speak Inwardly to me. & bad me be of Good Chear my Sins was for Given me: Emedately. by bordding Remoovd my fears vankquisht, away & I was Set at liberty. then Could I bless & Prace God. with a joy Unexpressable & ful of Glory then Could I Say my beloved is Mine & I am his but in a boute a Year after. I Met with one of my Former Misses whom' I Most lov'd. & I was temted by ye Devil to lay her Down. which She frely a Greed to, So yt I was over Come. & Commit yt horrid fact yt I had been so Formily Proon to, then Othen None can tell ye Destress my Soul was in So yt for 3 quarters of, A year ye Lord his his face from me. so yt I began to think ye Day of Grace was Past, but one afternoon as I was a Musing at my work. but all of a Suddon ye Lorde Darted his love into my Soul. Which Came Like litening so yt I found ye Same faith & ye Same confidence. & had ye Same felings yt I had before. O ye Love yt was betwen god & my Soul then. I have had Many fears & Doubts. & I find ye Sperit oft Come in & Goe Oute. but I live in hopes it will one Day take its Everlasting abode in My hart I am In Abled to Stick Cloce to Prayer. & to ye Use of all ye Means: by. I am keep in ye favour of God. I find of late yt I have More Power of My Sins then what I Ust to have so yt my Love to god Daly Increases Whe Saton Coms to tempt my Soul at any time I find ye Sperit Give me a token of it before he Coms so before ye temtation Gets much hould of me. I Goe to Sume Private Place to Prayer. & then I take up a Good book & Reds til ye temter I Can See as it ware Sneek a way. like one yt a Shamd of himself thear is one thing Oftentimes trubels me & yt is I Ough Money hear & theare more then at Preson I Can Pay. So I am forsed to goe in a Poor habit & My Wife. She bears me Many Children. so yt I Am Run Much behinthand in ye World. yt Some times I am temped by Saton, to Run a way. but then A Gain I think what a Sad thing it will be if I Should bring a Reproach upon ye Gospil. but I hope God will keep me & bring me throw all trials & Difficultys. (Br. knowlittle How Doe you Doe: I thank you brother. I hardly know at Present. Hate ye truth, Doe you know wather your a Child of God or no: knowlittle) Sometims I think I am. & then again a little time after I think I am Not. Hate ye truth brother, What Causeth you to Doubt, knowlittle. becaus I find Suchan Evil hart. & yt I So oft fall into Sin, hate ye truth, What do you Never feal ye love of God in your hart. knowlittle yes Sometimes when I am Oft Under ye Word. & yt I have more Power over my Sins & Reed & Pray A Great Deal: then I find my Self vary happy. hate ye truth & Can you beleve in Xt then knowlittle O yes to be shure. I Can feel ye Sperit in me then hate ye truth how longue is it agoe Since you felt ye Sperit of God in you. knowlittle it is now amost a Half a year Since hate ye truth you mite well be in Doubts. I am Ratherly In fear you have greevd ye Sperit or Els' it would Not Stay so longue from you. Do you Not know what it was yt you Greved ye Sperit with. Knowlittle, yess I think is was with over Much agreing with my wife. In ye Marridg bed Hate ye truth, what is you Wife, a vary listful Woman, Now little; O yes She is in Deed. & by yt She oftens Brings me into Great Souls truble hate ye truth Indeed I Can Simpathise with you heare. for my wife when She is with Child Se is never Sattisfyed. but when She is not with Child; then She is quite otherwise well if this is ye Cause yt brings Gilt upon your Contiance. you Can Doe Nothing but Pray to god to alter ye Case. & you Must Strive to Denigh Hor. & Els' Lye Separate. I find brother knowlittle you have Great Need to be upon your Watch; Br. Misarable How do you Doe Alass I Don't know I have just as much Christianaty as Maks me Mesarable. hate ye truth Alas yt is often ye Cace. we are wavring Creatures. Sumtimes up & Sometimes Down. but Br. what is ye Caus of your Mesary. I think I Shall Never hould out to ye End (Why so Br:)

I have Such a Wiced hart. & I Meet with so Many Croses that. I am Every Day in fear of Sinning
Against god hate ye truth; Br. Don't you know yt Xt Says yt my Grace is Sofisant for ye; Why Doe
you Doubt he have Promist yt with ye temtation he will make a Way for your Iscape. Br. misarable a but I find My hart is like tander it Catces ye Divels Bates as fast as he Can Set them. so
yt Many a time I Am forsed to Cry O Reced Man yt I am who' Shall Deliver me from ye body of
this Death, hate Grace. Br. I hope you Don't Sin Wilfully, B Misarable. Sometimes I think I Doe
& Sometimes I think I Doe not, Br. when Did did ye Lord face Shine Upon you, it is now Nigh a
Munth a Goe yt I felt his love. O brother be much on your Gard wach & Pray. & keep Cloce to ye
Means; How are you in your Worly Surcumstance. Many times Hardly food to Eate & when
I have. it is Such as coms from ye foggars. for My wife is a Vary Aling woman & I have 6 Small
Children. & I am often almost Driven out of my wits with ym. hate ye truth. In Deed brother it
is vary hard I Can very well Simphathise with you in those Cases Some People thinks because we
Cannot a Pear jentile & Deasant in ye world We are I Dole laysey fellows but if ye lord was to lay
upon ym what is Lade Upon us. we Should Se ym Like our Selvs. well My Dear brother hould fast
your Confidence a little wile longer. & we Shall see an End of all those Sorows. whear we Shall
land Safe whear Sorrows will be no More! Br Fretful How Doe you Doe. O br. I Doe Sadly in
Deed: why what is ye Matter I think Shuarly yt thare is but few like me for Sometimes I Cannot
help Singing Vain Songues. & Some times Cannot help Swearring. & Some times I am temted to
Corse. god & to kil my Child & to Make an End of My Self., O Strange & what is ye Cause of your
Destress of Mind Br. Why Some times when I let Goe my hould. ye Devil torments me with what
I've Done. & temps me to Hang my Self. & tels me I had better Dye now, then live to Commit
More Sin, & so I am fit to Despare Doe you Never feel ye Presence of god Br. O ye Sum times
when I'm Much Under ye Word & Much in Private Prayer. & by those Means is In Abled Quite to
over Come ye Divil & to live without Sin. O br. Then for ye Lord Sake & for you Soul Sake. kep
Cloce to ye Means. fretful, Yea' I Strive as well as I Can. but Some times I Am of on My Watch &
then ye Divel & my own hart betrays me. then when I am brought Into Sin. then I am a Shamd
to Pray knowing what ye Salmest Say If I Ncline to wickedness with my Hart ye Lord will not hear
me: So I think it Do not Signify me Praying Now I have Sind with my hart. & thearfore ye Lord
will not hear me: hate ye truth, Well my Br. I Can Say Nothing but yt you must Watch & Pray &
keep Cloce to ye Means. & you Must Get ye Brethren to Pray for you & look Up to Jesus. for we
are None of us no longer Safe but whyle our Eye is unto Xt. Well Br. Sliperry How Doe you Doe.
Sometimes Up & Sometimes Down Never at a Sarton Stay. One Day all joy & Gladness & another
Day all Doubts & fears. hate ye truth Alas this is ye Case With Most of us: Sinning & Repenting,
Sinning & Repenting Sumtimes hope & Sumtimes Despart We are Never at one Stay. but we are
Cal'd to Strive. or Elst. Saton Soon will Make his Pray of Us. Br. Slippery How Doe you find your
Self in your Marrig Bed. Indifferant. My Wife has Shortly lade in So I have not lade with hor for
a Mongth. it's true I Cist hor last Nite. But Confiddening Considdering yt it is a Munth Since I lay
with hor. I think. I am Pretty Modrate, hate ye truth how are you In your Worly Surcumstances.
Br Slippery Bless god I Can Make Shift to live; & yt all. hate ye truth, Br I hope you will Strive. to
hould fast to what you have Attaind to. When Did you feel ye witnessing Sperit of God Last
Lords Day. at ye Saryment. hate ye truth & how Did you find you Self thear Why as I was a
Drinking the wine I thought I See Xt Stand with Open Arms. & I thought I See his blood Runing
Down from both his hands & feet. with yt I Cryde lord thou Bleeds for me. hate ye truth, In Deed
Brother yt was a Gloryous Site. I beleve Xt. is Pleasd to Show himself to us Sometimes in yt
Manner. For oure Incorridgment & Soporte. Well Brother I hope you'l Press forwards Well Br.
lofty. how Doe you Doe. O Bless ye Lord I am Vary joyful. I have had Swete Comfort, Since we
met to Gather. Prase ye lord, hate ye truth. how longue Br. have you known ye Lord, lofty 3 hole
years. & I find his ways to be ways of Pleasant Ness, & all his Pasths to be Paths of Peace. hate ye
truth. what Doe you Never find No temtations Br. yes but it is vary Seldom yt thay over Come
me. & when thay do I Doe Not Yeald to them wilfully. hate ye truth But when your overtaken are
you not Sorrow ful then. Yes I am Grevd. but then before I Sleep I Confess my Solt to god. belev-
ing with ye Salmest yt his Marcys is new Every Morning, & yt Xt is ye Propesiation for my Sins.
so ye Next Morning I look on My Self to be in ye favour of God as tho I had Not Sind, so I Goe on
with fresh viggar Watching & Praying keeping Cloce to ye Means. & so I Find yt by so Doing I am
Inabled. to goe on my Way Rejoysing. hate ye truth have you Never no Cloudy Days. when ye

Sperit hides his face. from you. & you find you Soul Could Ded lifeless & barron. O Yes, but Never longe togather. for by. keeping Cloce to ye Means. Praying & watching. & Meditating on ye Promisis of God: Setting ye Crown before. my vue. I goe on Rejoysing. Reckning Every Day yt Goes over my hed, yt I am a Day Nier Everlasting hapyness. hate ye truth. My Br your in a happy State in Deed: but are you Never Cast Down In Worly afares: No, for When I have Nothing but Bred & water. I Can Say with joy. I have all this & Xt besides. & as for Consarnments a boute ye world I let things Goe as thay Come. knowing yt I am but a Pilgrim & a Stranger on ye Earth. & yt hear I have no Continnuing Sitty. but am Seeking a Sitty out of Site Eternal in ye heavens. (hate ye truth.) but Br. are You Satisfyed in ye State your in, Dont you Want to be More Holy. in Inward holyness. Good by inward Goodness. Jentel by in ward jentelness. (that is) Dont You want to be holy throughout body Soul & Sperit O yes. & I beleve I Shall be one Day. before I Depart this life. but this work is ye Lords. & I'll leave it for him to Doe. according to his own Will. hate ye truth But Br. are not you Never in No fear yt you will Never Arive to this Parfict State in Xt. but that one Day you will fall away. & Parish. Yes Somtimes When folishly. I have been looking at a Great length of time yt is yet to Come. then fear have Seesd my brest but this I account to be ye Ennemy. My bisness is to Mind to Day. & Stand my Gard & ye Morrow leve to ye Lord; hate ye truth. & houd Doe you find your Self in your Marridg bed. lofty. formily. ye Ennimy Made a Great Snare of it but by ye blessing of God I have Overcumd him at Last. for I Never lay with my wife after She is with Child. but when She is not. then i Lay with hor. & Use my liberty. but after it appears yt She is with Child, then I lay with my tow boys. & ye Girls lay with thare Mother, & So I Now keep my Contiance in yt Respect. & Br Doe you find Now harty Desier to flye from ye face of all Sin. & to hold fast to all yt which is Good: by Releving ye Destressed & Doing Good of Every Cind. Yes but in those Cases I find my Desiers Increace & Decreace. Acording to ye Measure of love I feel within me. it is my Dayly Prayer More & more to be Establisht in his love. yt I may be more Stedfast in all ye Ways of holyness.!. Well Br. lofty you Have Greate Reason Indeed to Praise ye Lord, he hath Done Great things for you. & also to Pray. for all yt are In faloship with you Aspashally for Br fretful. & Br Sorrowful & Br. Slipperry. & Brother Knowlittle. you se How thare Overpowerd by ye Ennemy of Souls. & go on in leanness. & heaviness. lofty. This one thing I can Experience yt all yt thay Complain of is not ye lords falt. thear is Strength & Comfort Peace & Sattisfaction in Xt. for all yt will Denigh them Selves & take Up thare Cross & follow Xt. but if we Give but way to ye Ennemy. then we Grow faint harted & Misarable hate ye truth. yes Br. what you Say is Rite. but you know we are all frale by Nature, & thearfore ye Strongue ought to bear with ye Informitys of ye weak & Dayly to Pray for them. lofty yes all yt I alow: let us Sing a few verses of an Himn

> Hymn 56 In Doubts,
> My God I Humbly Call ye mine. & will not Quit my Clame
> Til all I have be lost in thine, & all Renew'd I am;
> I hould ye with a trembling hand, But will not let ye Go,
> Til Stedfastly by faith I Stand, & all thy Goodness know;
> When Shall I See ye welcom Hour, yt Plants my God in me,
> Sperit of health & life & Pow'r, & Parfect liberty,
> O yt in me ye Sacred fier, might now begin to Glow;
> Burn up ye Dross of bace Desier, & make ye Mountains flow
> O yt it Now from heaven mite fall, & all my Sins Consume
> Come holy Gost for ye I Call; Sperit of Borning Come:
> Refining fier Go throw my hart. Illuminate my Soule,
> Scatter thy Life through Every Part & Sanctify ye hole;
> Soroh & Sin Shall then Expier, wile Enter'd into Rest,
> I only live my God to admier, my God for Ever blest,
> No longer then my Hart Shall Mourn, wile Purified by Grace
> I only for his Glory burn, & all ways See his Face;
> My Stedfast Soul from falling free, can now no longer move
> Wile Xt is all ye world to me. & all my hart is love;

Lofty Gos'e to Pray first

Most wonderful, Most Amasing, Most Glolyous & a Dorable Lord my God. thou art my Everlasting joy & Porshon & Crown of Reward, thearfore to ye thou king of kings, will I Dyrect my Prayer & thanksgiving, at all times & in all Places will I make my Bost of ye O thou Darling & Delite of My Soul, thearfore o my beloved Savour Now will it Please ye to hear ye Prays & thanksgiving of they blood bought Childdren, offerd up to ye at this time. Now o my Savor ye Darling of all my joy. & Rejoysing will it Please ye to Power upon me thy Unworthy Creature. thy Santifying Sperit, & Cause it to Roote up Every Plant which thy Rite hand hath not Planted. O my Best frend & most Wonderfully beloved. Destroy all yt is Sin in me. yt I may worship ye At all times & in all Places without a Wandring thought. & yt vain & Evil Desiers & thoughts May for Ever Seace from My brest. yt thearby I may Never More be obstructed from always giving thee My hart o thou my Souls Delite. O My beloved will it Please ye Now. to be hould ye Needs & Destresses that My Poor Brethren is in which thay have Declard at this time. O yt Now Even Now thou would bow ye heavens & Come Down Amonguest us, & let them See thy Smiling face. O thou Briter then ye Son. Show them thy butyful Countanance Which are So lovly. O let ym fell ye Kisses of thy mouth yt thay may be inamard with thy love. take ym Up in thine arms & Do thou Norse ym. lay thare heads on thy Brests. wile with ye kisses of thy love. thay may faint a Way, with joy. O my Soul Ravishing Saver. See thy tender lambs. are now Sick with love. O my Soul Sink with a Stonishment & wonder. to Se thy loveing bleeding tenderharted & Compasanate Saver. weping over a few of his Blood bought lams O me thinks I hear ye Say you are ye Purchace of my blood—you are as ye Apel of Mine Eyes, behould I have Ingraven you on ye Palms of my hands. behould I Cover you with my wings. behould I Put Underneath you My Everlasting arms, then fear Not little flock it is your father good Pleasure to give you ye kingdom. thearfore be it According to thy word. thou Neverfailling God but Do thou now Grant. yt from this time forth we May walk Parfectly before ye in thought word & Deed yt we all may Make Our Songs of Prase & addoration to ye for Ever & Ever a Men

Come Holy Gost my hart inspier, Attest yt I am born again Come & bablise us Now with fier, or all thy former Gifts is vain; Whear is ye Sence of Sins forgiven, whear is ye Earnist of my heaven When Shall we hear ye Inward Voice, which only faithful Souls can hear;

Pardon & Peace & heavenly joys attend ye Promist Comforter;

He coms & Riteousness Devine, & Xt & all with Xt is Mine;

Br. hate ye truth. Prayer

Wee Prace thy Name olord for this. & all other opertunitys we have in wating upon ye. we Bless ye yt thou of a truth hast been with us at this time. we beseech ye to answer ye Prayers of our Dear brother. which have been offerd up unto ye o bless thou us according to thy Great Marcys & according to our needs & Nacessatys. yt we thearby may be able to live to ye Prace of thy Great Name. & yt we may Gloryfy ye on ye Earth before ye face of all People. that when ye Messenger Deth Coms to Unlock ye Prisen Dore of this Mortal life we May with thy blest Angels tower away. to thy Blest Relms of Everlasting Joy & Philisaty whear ye Wiced Seace from trubling & whear our weary Souls will be for Ever at Rest. be with o lord in our Unsepperate Plases of a bode, Do thou bless all our familyes. acquaintance & Relations by turning them from all thare Inniquitys. hear us in those Portishons We humbly beg for Jesus Xt his Sake to whome with thy Self & blessed Sperit be ascribd as Ever Due all oner Power Might Magasty & Dominyon both now & for ever More A Men, May ye Grace of our Lord Jesus X be with us all amen - - - - - -

to ye we now togather Came in Singelness of hart. we met o Jesus in thy name & in thy name we'll Part; we part in body not in mind our minds Continnue one & Each to Each in Jesus joynd we hand in hand go on - -

Having Given my Reder a true Account of ye Method & Nature of a band Meting. I would have him Obsarve, yt Some are Not Quite So Strict, in Aczamining into Every Porticalar Matter yt I have treated Upon. (& why so) because Some Do not like to be under So Cloce a tye. as this is thay love to hug thare Durlings Evils, & not Devulg Every thing yt thay Doe amiss. but those are Such yt walk Contrary. to what is Mr Wesltay. Skeam in Matters of this kind. as for my own Parte. ye Preacher one Mr Manners Asked me how I found my Self in my Marridg bed. with All other Cloce Questons yt he Could bethink him Self of & Inded ye band yt I was in, & ye band yt I was leader of Was as Strict as Could be. & in this vary Method, Now ye Leader of ye Bands. of a Sarton Night goes to ye Prechar & Makes him a Quainted of ye State & Condishon. of ye People. yt thay have under thare Care, & this Is Done inauder yt ye Preacher may Now how to Agzort ye People of ye bands, when thay meet all to gather; ye method is as follow. John Westlay. well Br hate ye truth How Doth ye People Doe yt is under you Care. or yt is in your Band I thank you Sor. ye Most of them is in A Poor fretful Misarable way unless one Br. lofty. he Goses on his way Rejoysing, as for ye Other thay are Sorely temted with Divers temtations & seems to me to be in a weak tottering Condishon Westlay how are thay temted Br. Why Sor one is temted to Sing Felle Songs & to Swear, & to kil his Child & to Make an End of him Self. an other is temted with lust. & hard Set to live ye Rest hard Set as it ware to keep thare heds above water. but is a frade yt Saton will overcome ym at Last. & yt thay Shall Parish after all: Westlay & who is yt Br yt is in Destress & want. one Br. Misarable Sor. Br. think me on him ye Next Colection yt is Made for ye Pore. Weslay well Br. Self wise how Dose ye young men Doe. yt is in your band Sor I thank you Some of them Doe Indifferantly well & some of them Vary Porely. westlay What is ye Matter with ym. Bro. one of them is Sorely Burnt up with Lust. & he is in Love with a young woman. & he is Going to be Marrid with hor. & She Do not belongue to us. & thear is an other Sorely temted & is Some times over Come. with lite trifling vain Compeny. which is of a bad Corracter he is led by them a way in taking of Pleasure. & in Going to ye Alehouse. Anothr is over Come with Pride & in wearing Gaudy aparril. Westlay & how Doth you People Doe Br. falshope. yt is in your band, Sor I beleve that ye Most of ym is Striving all that thay Can to Please God. & to obtain to a Parfect State in Xt Jesus vary well Br I am Glad to hear it: & how Doth ye Sisters Go on Sr. Strugel yt you have in your band O lac a Day Sor. Wary Porely. Why so Sr. too trifeling Sor. & Some of ym. is vary wanton. & Provde & vary Cloce & all thay mind is thare Swete harts. & thay keep Compeny with Such Rakes As know not yt Ways of ye Lord. but live in Open Porfainaty. Alas I Am Sory to hear yt Sr we must take some other Corse Amonguest ye Young wiming. You must let me Now Each of thare Names & I Must Speak to them & See what I Can Make of them. Sor I Shall be glad you would for thare a Great truble to me. Sr. bad Grace how Doth ye Sr. do yt is in your band. O Sor Some Do well, & Some vary ill how ill Sr; why Some have Sad Druken husbands. yt follow bad wiming. & live Sad wiced lives. so yt thare bet & a Bused & often keep from hearing ye Word. so yt ye Pore Creatures is oft in Destress & want for food for them Selves & thare Children & other Some is Sorely temted & buffeted by ye foe. & Can Searce keep thare hed a bove water. Some of them is given to Pashon. & Some. are temted to leave thare Husbands & Children. & other Some temted to swear Weladay I am Sory to hear it Sr. & who is She yt is in Such Destress & want one Sr. love no good. O Poor thing think me on; yt She be Relev'd when ye Next Colection is Made for ye Poor - - - This is ye Nature of ye Disscorse between ye Preachers & Band leaders. tho I would obsarve to My Reder. yt I never new this to be Done Every weak. but only Some times when ye Preacher has New Com'd (as thare often Changing) Or When Mr westlay Comes. then ye Clasleaders. & band leaders. is Descorst to in this Meathod. sometimes when thare met alltogather. & Sometimes. Separate. but by this Inquiry ye Preacher knowns. how to Auder his Descorse to ye People ather in ye Private Sociatys. or in ye Meeting of Bands. - - - - -

Mr Westlay's way & Manner of Meting ye BANDS.. .

In ye first Place thay Sing an hymn. & then goes to Prayer, & then Agzorts ye People. In this Method following: My Dear Beloved br. & Srs I look upon you, to be ye Crown & Cause of our Rejoysing. When Assembled before ye Magasty of Heaven. becase you are ye frute of our labours & all yt we Can Show for all our toil yt we have Under ye Sun, What Do you think Brn, Causes me to Refuse Good livings (which I mite have had) & live a toylsum Percuted life. Riding Up & Down all over ye Nations. yea in 7 Nations have I Planted ye Gospil with Good Success. & What have I for all my Pains Do I Get Gould or Gain no Varaly I Do not. what then Do I Get. A Crown of Everlasting Reward this is ye Reward yt I Shall one Day Reseve at My Savours hands when I Deliver up my StuardShip: thearfore my Dear brethren as thear is a Promise of Reward for all those yt Gather in Xt vinyard. be all of you of yt happy Number, Strive to Gather Souls to hear ye Gospil. Pray with ym. Show ym thare Dainger Tel ym of ye Inward Joys of a true Xtan, Set ym a Good Accample by you life & Conduct, & thou O Man yt Can but Gather thy wife, thou wilt in no wise loose thy Reward. & if thou o woman Can gather thy husband. thou will in no wise loose thy Reward. Compel ym. to Come in yt ye house of God may be fild, & by So Doing. you Will have Cause to rejoice

> Hymn
> Move & Actuate & Guide, Divers Gifts to Each Devide
> Plas't according to thy will, Let us all our works fulfil
> Never from our Office Move, Nedeful to ye Others Prove,
> Use ye Grace on Each bestou'd Temper'd by ye art of god,
>
> Swetly now we all agree, Touch'd with Softest Sympathy
> Kindly for Each other care; Ev'ry member feals its Share.
> Wounded by ye Grefs[?] of one, all ye Suffring members groan,
> Honnerd if one member is all Portake ye Common Bless
>
> Many are we now & one, we who Jesus have Put on
> Thear is nather bond nor free, Male nor female lord in thee
> Love like Death hath all Destroy'd, Renderd all Destintions voide
> Names & Seks & Partys fall thou O Xt art all in all; - - - - - - - -

Wach & Pray least ye Enter into temtation. those words Spoke our Lord to his Apostels knowing. if yt was Neglected, that thay would quicly fall into temtation Are Not those word Rit for our Instrucktion & Admonishon yes Varyly thay be. & I Doubt not but Everyone Now yt before god by woful Experiance, yt as Soon as we Seace watching & Praying. but we a Meadeately fall into Divers temtations. Yea My Brethren. & oft vary Grevous ons too. are not Some of you temted to Anger, some to lust, some to Covitteousness, Some to Swear, yea Some to lay voyalant hands on your Selves or Children. some temted to have hard thoughts of God. Why my Brethren are ye So temted Is this ye Cause of your being so temted. because your so Much fild with Love Joy & Peace, in ye holy Gost, No My Brethren no, What then is ye Cause of your Being so temted. Why. Realy it is for ye want of this Love & Joy & Peace. & why Cannot you Rejoyce in ye knowledg of ye love of god & have true Sollid Peace why, why because you have Broke of waching & Praying. & then you have Enterd into temtation. & vary Probably been over Come; & then all, your joy is turnd to Nothing but Misary. then ye Lord Suffers. ye Devil to buffit you. & to make you Greve & lament If you want to. Grow in ye Grace & knowledg of God You Must watch & Pray & that Continnually. & by so Doing you will keep ye Devil at a Distance. & be in abled to Rejoyce over your Ennemy. you'l then thrive in ye ways of God. Increase in Strength & in faith & love & then You be fild with Grace; Glorious & Spesial Grace. so yt all those around you will be Constraind to own yt you liv[?] a Godly Riteous & a Soberlife. Watching is vary Nesary. for if ye Good Man of ye House, had but known, at what time his House, would have been Broken Up. He would Have watch't & Not a Sufferd his house to have Been broken up. So you, if you had but known, yt you would have fallen into temta-tion & have been over come. & so konkerd by ye Devil & a gain become his Subject & Pray., I Say Rather then thus have forfe[illeg.]ed yor favour with God. you would have watced & not a Sufferd ye Ennemy to havd Enterd into ye Dore of your Hart & Rob you of ye favour of God. My Brethren it is for watching. yt all this Mesiry Coms thearfore watch & be Sober, for you Now not ye Day nor ye houer whe ye Lord. Commeth. & blessed Is yt Sarvant home when his lorde Commeth is found watching. you know Br.n yt 5 foolish vorgons was broke of: of thare watch for want of oyle. so yt thay must Needs goe & bye. but ye other 5: Was found watching. & because thay was Ready Watching thay went in to ye Marridg Supper. thearfore my Dear brethren & Sisters as you Prise you Souls Watch & Pray what I Say unto one I Say unto you all Watch & Pray. yt you fall not into temtations An he yt Indureth to ye End ye Same Shall be Saved: therefore if you will be Xt Desiple you must take up your Cross. and follow Xt, Remembring it is annuff yt ye Sarvant be as his Lord. theafore take up your Cross & follow Xt treding in his footsteps. Did Xt Commit No Sin then No More must not you Did Xt Pray hole Nites; So Must you when in temtation Did Xt walk throw Good Report. & Evil Report then so Must you. Was Xt Poor & aflicted & Despised, so Must you.

& Rejoyce yt you are Counted worthy; thearfore my Dear brethren. work out you Salvation with fear & trembling. Remembring yt if you Sufer with him hear you Shall Rean with him hearafter, a few more Days or Munth or Years may See an End to all thy Sorah; thearfore let Patiance have it Parfect Work; yt you may be belt up from one degree of Grace to another. til you are Perfect & holy as Addam was before y efall; O My Brethren Methinks I hear you Say, truly ye Sperit is willing but ye flesh is weak. yet look unto Jesus. Set ye Crown before your vue, It will be a Sad thing if ye Sin of lust Should Caus any of you to Go to hell. it will be a Sad thing if Anger Should Cause any of you to burn In torments, O Denigh Your Selves. & think of ye Length of Eternity. be like Joseph when temted by his Mistress. how Shall I Commit this Great Evil & Sin against God; Remember you Can not Sarve tow Masters. Jesus will ather have all your harts or none thearfore Deseve not Your own Souls. but fly from Sin as you would from ye Devil. for one will hurt you as much as ye other. thearfore my Brethren be in Good Earnist keep ye Prise in vue Pray with out Seasing, & in Every thing Give thanks; then when Death Coms you will be on your Gard. then you will Rest from your labours & your Goodworks will follow you. then Shall you hear your lord Say thou hast been faithful over a few things I will Make ye Ruler over Many things Enter thou into ye Joy of thy Lord; A few more Strugels with ye world flesh & Devil More. A few trials & Conflicts more then all ye Storm will be over. & yt for Ever - - - -

Jesus United by thy Grace, & Each to Each Endeard, With Confidence we Seek thy face & know our Prays is heard Stil let us own Our Common lord, & bear thine Easey yoke A band of Love a threefould Cord Cannot be Easey Broke: there is one thing More I would Speak at this time. I Understand yt thear is Severl heare before god. that have A Mind to be Married. & I Could be Glad yt thay Ritely Understud ye Concyquence of it, St Paul Agzorteth Every one Not to Mary. Unless thay be Constrand by lust. & then it is better to marry then to Born. but If by any Means thay Can Deny ym Selves. it is fare better St Paul hear Considerd ye Croses & Calamatis. People Brought ym Selves into by Marridg: but if thay must be Marred to beware yt that be not Uneakwally Yoak't yt is Belevers not to yoke with Unbelevers. for he was Shure if thay Did this thing, yt thay would Repent it all ye Days of thare lives; but I Understand yt this is a Going to be ye Cace. & if it be. Croses & tryals you will Never want all ye Days of your life. Dont you See Matters of this kind before your Eyes. Yea Even Now in this Place. Some Complaining of thare husbands. & other Some of thare wives. being Poor & aflicted hardly have bred for thare family. or Cloths to wear. O take warning before it be to late. & Doe not Run hedlong into your own Ruing & if you Must be Marred. be Marred to those yt are of ye househould of faith yt you may Live hapily all ye Days of your life. So thay Sing a few verses of a hymn & so Concludes - - - - - -

---

This is my own transcription of Samuel Roberts's account of Methodism. The manuscript is unpublished and privately owned by Dr. John Walsh of Jesus College, Oxford, UK. Used with permission.

Appendix H

OF THE RIGHT METHOD OF MEETING CLASSES AND BANDS, IN THE METHODIST-SOCIETIES

By the Late Mr. Charles Perronet

In general, the method proper for meeting the one is proper for meeting the other. The particular design of the *Classes* is,

To know who continue Members of the Society;

To inspect their Outward Walking,

To enquire into their inward State;

To learn, what are their Trials? And how they fall by, or conquer them?

To instruct the ignorant in the first Principles of Religion: if need be, to repeat, explain, or enforce, what has been said in public Preaching.

To stir them up to believe, love, obey; and to check the first spark of Offence or Discord.

The particular design of the *Bands* is,

To enquire, whether they now believe? Now enjoy the life of God? Whether they grow herein, or decay? If they decay, what is the cause! And what the cure?

Whether they aim at being *wholly devoted* to God; or would keep something back?

Whether they see God's hand in all that befals [*sic.*] them? And how they bear what he lays upon them?

Whether they take up their cross daily? Resist the bent of Nature? Oppose Self-love in all its hidden forms, and discover it, through all its disguises?

Whether they humble themselves in every thing? Are willing to be blamed and despised for well-doing? Account it the greatest honour, that Christ appoints them to walk with himself, in the paths that are peculiarly *his own*? To examine closely, whether they are willing to drink of *his cup*, and to be baptized with *his baptism*?

Whether they can cordially love those that despitefully use them! Justify the ways of God in thus dealing with them? And in all they suffer, seek the destruction of inward Idolatry, of Pride, Self-will and Impatience?

How they conquer Self-will, in its spiritual forms? See through all its disguises, seeking itself, when it pretends to seek nothing but the glory of God?

Whether they are simple, open, free, and without reserve in speaking? And see it their duty and privilege so to be?

To enquire concerning Prayer, the Answers to Prayer, Faith in Christ, Distrust of themselves, Consciousness of their own vileness and nothingness:

How they improve their talents? What zeal they have for doing good, in all they do, or suffer, or receive from God? Whether they live *above* it, making Christ their All, and offering up to God nothing for acceptance, but his Life and Death?

Whether they have a clear, full, abiding conviction, that without inward, compleat, universal Holiness, no man shall see the Lord? That Christ was sacrificed for us, that we might be a whole burnt-sacrifice to God; and that the having received the Lord Jesus Christ will profit us nothing, unless we steadily and uniformly walk in him?

C.P.

I earnestly exhort all Leaders of Classes and Bands, seriously to consider the preceding Observations, and to put them in execution with all the Understanding and Courage that God has given them.

J.W.

This document can be found in Charles Perronet, "Of the right *Method* of meeting *Classes* and *Bands*, in the Methodist-Societies," in *AM* 4 (1781): 604 (emphasis original).

BIBLIOGRAPHY

Manuscripts

Ball, Hannah. Manuscript letter to Patty [Martha] Chapman, August 16, 1776, MAM, Ref: PLP 4/32.1.13.

Bardsley, Samuel. Manuscript diary, MAM, Diaries Collection, Ref: MA BRD 1977/205.

Beecroft, Eliza. Manuscript letter to Mary Fletcher, November 21, 1794, MAM, Fletcher-Tooth Collection, Ref: MAM Fl 1.2/15.

Bennet, John. Manuscript letter to John Wesley, April 25, 1749, MAM, Ref: FL BNNJ (25/04/1749) Clm. Box.

Bourne, Frances. Manuscript letter to Mary Tooth, February 4/5 [1828], MAM, Fletcher-Tooth Collection, Ref: MAM Fl 1.11/14.

Bradnock, Isaac. Manuscript diary, MAM, Ref: 2002/001 MA 9769.

Coke, Thomas. Manuscript letter to John Wesley, December 15, 1779, MAM, Ref: MA 1977/610/48.

Crosby, Sarah. Manuscript letter to Mary Fletcher, March 26, 1787, MAM, Fletcher-Tooth Collection, Ref: MAM Fl 2.5A/18.

Dickinson, Eleanor. Manuscript letter to Mary Fletcher, March 20, 1813, MAM, Fletcher-Tooth Collection, Ref: MAM Fl 2.11/11.

Dugdale, Bennett. Manuscript diary, MAM, Diaries Collection, Ref: MA 1977/216.

"Early Methodist Volume," MAM.

Goodfellow, John. Manuscript diary, MAM, Methodist Diaries, Box 15, Ref: MA 1977/236.

Jenkins, Sarah. Manuscript letter to Mary Tooth, July 5, 1826, MAM, Fletcher-Tooth Collection, Ref: MAM Fl 4/4/25.

Johnson, Elizabeth. Manuscript letter to Mrs Rien [Sarah Ryan], July 3 [ca. 1765], MAM, Fletcher-Tooth Collection, Ref: MAM Fl 4/5/3.

Jordan, Ann. Manuscript letter to Mary Tooth, February 9 1825, MAM, Fletcher-Tooth Collection, Ref: MAM Fl 4/7/7.

Longmore, Rebecca. Manuscript letter to Mary Tooth, November 5, 1828, MAM, Fletcher-Tooth Collection, Ref: MAM Fl 4/13/15.

Marsden, George. Manuscript journal, 1801–20, MAM, Methodist Diaries Collection, Box 21, Ref: 1977/267.

Mather, Isabella. Manuscript diary, 1800–12, MAM, Methodist Diaries Collection, Box 21, Ref: MA 1977/264.

Moore, Henry. *Life of Mrs. Fletcher*, manuscript, MAM, Fletcher-Tooth Collection, Ref: MAM Fl.22.

Oxlee, William. Manuscript letter to John Wesley, April 13, 1739, MAM, Ref: MA 1977/610/106.

Pawson, Frances. Manuscript memorandum book, ca. 1782–ca. 1805, MAM, Diaries Collection, Box 24, Ref: MA 1977/275.

Pawson, John. Manuscript diary, MAM, Diaries Collection, Ref: 1977/276.

Ritchie, Elizabeth. Manuscript letter to Mary Fletcher, December 20, 1787, MAM, Fletcher-Tooth Collection, Ref: MAM Fl 6/6/14.

Roberts, Samuel. Manuscript volume, privately owned by John Walsh of Jesus College, Oxford, UK.

Ryan, Sarah. Letter to my Bands and Classes [n.d.], MAM, Fletcher-Tooth Collection, Ref: MAM Fl 6/9/9.

Seward, William. Manuscript diary, September 6–October 15, 1740, Chetham's Library, Manchester, UK, Ref: A.2.116.

Smith, Mrs. Manuscript letter to Mary Fletcher, September 25, 1782, MAM, Fletcher-Tooth Collection, Ref: MAM Fl 6/10/14.

Stormont, Henry. Manuscript letter to Mary Tooth, October 27, 1823, MAM, Fletcher-Tooth Collection, Ref: MAM Fl 6/12/3.

Thornton, Henry. Manuscript letter to Charles Wesley, November 26, 1741, MAM, Ref: MAM DDCW 8/9.

Tooth, Mary. Personal papers, MAM, Fletcher-Tooth Collection, Ref: MA Fl 33.1.

Valton, John. Manuscript diary, MAM, Diaries Collection, Box 26, Ref: MA 1977/293.

Wesley, Charles. Manuscript letter to Sarah Gwynne, Jr., March 1748, MAM, Ref: MAM DDCW 6/92F.

———. Manuscript letter to [Sarah Gwynne, Jr.], January 16 [1749], MAM, Ref: MAM DDCW 5/20.

———. Manuscript letter to [Sarah Gwynne, Jr.], [January 24, 1749], MAM, Ref: MAM DDCW 5/22.

———. Manuscript letter to Sally, July 9, 1759, MAM, Ref: MAM DDCW 7/18.

———. Manuscript letter to S. W., July 24 [1759?], MAM, Ref: MAM DDCW 5/96.

———. Manuscript letter to Sarah Wesley, March 2, 1760, MAM, Ref: DDCW 7/57.

———. Manuscript letter to S. W., March 17 [1760], MAM, Ref: DDCW 5/108.

Printed Primary Sources

Arminian Magazine. London, 1778–97.

Asbury, Francis. *The Journal and Letters of Francis Asbury*, 3 vols. Edited by Elmer T. Clark. Nashville, TN: Abingdon Press, 1958.

Coke, Thomas. *Journals of Dr. Thomas Coke.* Edited by John A. Vickers. Nashville, TN: Kingswood Books, 2005.

David, Christian. *Beschreibung und Zuverlässige Nachricht von Herrnhut in Ober-Lausitz, Wie es erbauet worden, und mit welcher Gestalt nach Lutheri Sinn und Meinung Eine recht Christliche Gemeine sich daselbst gesammelt und eingerichtet hat*; in *Herrnhut im Herrnhut 18. Und 19. Jahrhundert: Drei Schriften von Christian David, Nikolas Ludwig von Zinzendorf und Heinrich Friedrich von Bruiningk*, 1 Teil. Hildesheim, DE: Georg Olms Verlag, 2000.

Kidder, Richard. *The Life of the Reverend Anthony Horneck.* London, 1698.

"Rules of the Fetter Lane Society." Whitney M. Trousdale, "The Moravian Society, Fetter Lane, London," in *PWHS* 17 (1929): 30.

"Rules of the Original Methodists, 1843." Donald M. Grundy, "A History of the Original Methodists," in *PWHS* 35 (1965–66): 192–193.

Spener, Philipp Jakob. *Pia Desideria.* Translated by Theodore G. Tappert. Philadelphia: Fortress Press, 1964.

———. "The Spiritual Priesthood: Briefly described according to the word of God in seventy questions and answers," in *Pietists: Selected Writings.* Edited by Peter C. Erb. Mahwah, NJ: Paulist Press, 1983.

Stevenson, George J. *City Road Chapel, London and its Associations: Historical, Biographical, and Memorial.* London: George J. Stevenson, ca. 1872.

Viney, Richard. "Richard Viney's Diary." Edited by M. Riggall. *Proceedings of the Wesley Historical Society* (1923–24): 14.

Wesley, Charles. *The Manuscript Journal of the Reverend Charles Wesley, M.A.*, 2 vols. Edited by S. T. Kimbrough, Jr., and Kenneth G. C. Newport. Nashville, TN: Kingswood Books, 2008.

Wesley, John. *The Bicentennial Edition of the Works of John Wesley*. 35 vols. projected. Edited by Frank Baker and Richard P. Heitzenrater. Nashville, TN: Abingdon Press, 1984–. (Volumes 7, 11, 25, and 26 originally appeared as the *Oxford Edition of the Works of John Wesley*. Oxford, UK: Clarendon Press, 1975–83).

———. *The Letters of John Wesley*, 8 vols. Edited by John Telford. London: Epworth Press, 1931.

———. *Original Letters, by John Wesley, and His Friends, Illustrative of His Early History, with other Curious Papers, Communicated by the Late Rev. S. Badcock*. Birmingham, UK: Thomas Pearson, 1791.

———. *The Works of John Wesley*. Edited by Thomas Jackson 14 vols., 3rd ed., 1872; repr. Grand Rapids, MI: Zondervan, 1984.

Wesley, Samuel. "An Account of the Religious Society begun in Epworth in the Isle of Axholm Lincolnshire, Feb:1, An: Dom: 1701–2," in *Two Hundred Years: The History of The Society for Promoting Christian Knowledge, 1698–1898*. Edited by W. O. B. Allen and Edmund McClure. London: Society for Promoting Christian Knowledge, 1898.

Woodward, Josiah. *An Account of the Rise and Progress of the Religious Societies in the City of London*. London: R. A. Simpson, 1698.

Secondary Sources

Albin, Thomas R. "'Inwardly Persuaded': Religion of the Heart in Early British Methodism," in *"Heart Religion" in the Methodist Tradition and Related Movements*. Edited by Richard B. Steele. Lanham, MD: Scarecrow Press, 2001.

Atwood, Craig D. *Community of the Cross: Moravian Piety in Colonial Bethlehem*. University Park, PA: Pennsylvania State University Press, 2004.

Baker, Frank. *John Wesley and the Church of England*. London: Epworth Press, 1970.

———. "The People Called Methodists, 3. Polity," in *A History of the Methodist Church in Great Britain*, vol. 1. Edited by Rupert Davies and Gordon Rupp. London: Epworth Press, 1965.

Campbell, Ted A. "John Wesley as diarist and correspondent," in *The Cambridge Companion to John Wesley*. Edited by Randy L. Maddox and Jason E. Vickers. New York: Cambridge University Press, 2010.

———. *The Religion of the Heart: A Study of European Religious Life in the Seventeenth and Eighteenth Centuries*. Columbia, SC: University of South Carolina Press, 1991.

———. *Wesleyan Beliefs: Formal and Popular Expressions of the Core Beliefs of Wesleyan Communities*. Nashville, TN: Kingswood Books, 2010.

Chilcote, Paul Wesley. *John Wesley and the Women Preachers of Early Methodism*. Metuchen, NJ: Scarecrow Press, 1991.

Church, Leslie F. *The Early Methodist People*. London: Epworth Press, 1948.

———. *More about the Early Methodist People*. London: Epworth Press, 1949.

Clark, J. C. D. *English Society 1660–1832: Religion, Ideology, and Politics during the Ancien Regime*. 2nd ed. Cambridge, UK: Cambridge University Press, 2000.

Collins, Kenneth J. *The Theology of John Wesley: Holy Love and the Shape of Grace*. Nashville, TN: Abingdon Press, 2007.

Colón-Emeric, Edgardo A. *Wesley, Aquinas, and Christian Perfection: An Ecumenical Dialogue*. Waco, TX: Baylor University Press, 2009.

Dean, William Walter. "Disciplined Fellowship: The Rise and Decline of Cell Groups in British Methodism," Ph.D. diss., University of Iowa, 1985.

Foster, J. H. "Bristol Notes," in *PWHS* 3 (1902): 64–65.

Freeman, Arthur J. *An Ecumenical Theology of the Heart: The Theology of Count Nicholas Ludwig von Zinzendorf*. Bethlehem, PA: Moravian Church in America, 1998.

Gollin, Gillian Lindt. *Moravians in Two Worlds: A Study of Changing Communities*. New York: Columbia University Press, 1967.

Goodhead, Andrew. *A Crown and a Cross: The Rise, Development, and Decline of the Methodist Class Meeting in Eighteenth-Century England*. Eugene, OR: Wipf and Stock, 2010.

Halévy, Elie. *A History of the English People in the Nineteenth Century: England in 1815*. Translated by E. I. Watkin and D. A. Barker. New York: Barnes and Noble, 1961.

Hamilton, J. Taylor, and Kenneth G. Hamilton. *History of the Moravian Church: The Renewed Unitas Fratrum, 1722–1957*. Bethlehem, PA: Moravian Church in America, 1967.

Hardt, Philip F. *The Soul of Methodism: The Class Meeting in Early New York City Methodism*. Lanham, MD: University Press of America, 2000.

Heitzenrater, Richard P. *The Elusive Mr. Wesley*, 2nd ed. Nashville, TN: Abingdon Press, 2003.

———. "God with Us: Grace and the Spiritual Senses in John Wesley's Theology," in *Grace Upon Grace: Essays in Honor of Thomas A. Langford*. Edited by Robert K. Johnston, L. Gregory Jones, and Jonathan R. Wilson. Nashville, TN: Abingdon Press, 1999.

———. *Mirror and Memory: Reflections on Early Methodism*. Nashville, TN: Kingswood Books, 1989.

———. *Wesley and the People Called Methodists*. Nashville, TN: Abingdon Press, 1995.

Hempton, David. *Methodism: Empire of the Spirit*. New Haven, CT: Yale University Press, 2005.

———. *The Religion of the People: Methodism and popular religion c. 1750–1900*. London: Routledge, 1996.

Henderson, D. Michael. *A Model for Making Disciples: John Wesley's Class Meeting*. Nappanee, IN: Francis Asbury Press, 1997.

Hindmarsh, D. Bruce. *The Evangelical Conversion Narrative: Spiritual Autobiography in Early Modern England*. New York: Oxford University Press, 2005.

Holsclaw, David Francis. "The Demise of Disciplined Christian Fellowship: The Methodist Class Meeting in Nineteenth-Century America," Ph.D. diss., University of California, Davis, 1979.

Hunter, Frederick. "The Origins of Wesley's Covenant Service," in *PWHS* 22 (1939–40): 126–131.

Kisker, Scott Thomas. *Foundation for Revival: Anthony Horneck, the Religious Societies, and the Construction of an Anglican Pietism*. Lanham, MD: Scarecrow Press, 2008.

Lewis, A. J. *Zinzendorf the Ecumenical Pioneer: A Study in the Moravian Contribution to Christian Mission and Unity*. Philadelphia: Westminster Press, 1962.

Lindberg, Carter, ed. *The Pietist Theologians: An Introduction to Theology in the Seventeenth and Eighteenth Centuries*. Malden, MA: Blackwell, 2005.

Lindström, Harald. *Wesley and Sanctification: A Study in the Doctrine of Salvation*. Nappanee, IN: Francis Asbury Press, 1980.

Lloyd, Gareth. *Charles Wesley and the Struggle for Methodist Identity*. New York: Oxford University Press, 2007.

Mack, Phyllis. *Heart Religion in the British Enlightenment: Gender and Emotion in Early Methodism*. New York: Cambridge University Press, 2008.

Maddox, Randy L., ed. *Aldersgate Reconsidered*. Nashville, TN: Kingswood Books, 1990.

———. *Responsible Grace: John Wesley's Practical Theology*. Nashville, TN: Kingswood Books, 1994.

McCullagh, T. "The First Methodist Society: The Date and Place of its Origin," in *PWHS* 3 (1902): 166–172.

Outler, Albert C. "John Wesley as Theologian—Then and Now," in *The Wesleyan Theological Heritage*. Edited by Thomas C. Oden and Leicester R. Longden. Grand Rapids, MI: Zondervan, 1991.

———. *Theology in the Wesleyan Spirit*. Nashville, TN: Discipleship Resources, 1975.

Platt, Frederic. "The First Methodist Society: The Date and Place of its Origin," in *PWHS* 22 (1939–40): 155–164.

Podmore, Colin. *The Moravian Church in England, 1728–1760*. Oxford, UK: Clarendon Press, 1998.

Poschmann, Bernhard. *Penance and the Anointing of the Sick*. Translated by Francis Courtney. New York: Herder and Herder, 1964.

Rack, Henry D. *Reasonable Enthusiast: John Wesley and the Rise of Methodism*. 3rd ed. London: Epworth Press, 2002.

Ruth, Lester. *A Little Heaven Below: Worship at Early Methodist Quarterly Meetings*. Nashville, TN: Kingswood Books, 2000.

Schmidt, Gottfried. "Die Banden oder Gesellschaften im alten Herrnhut," *Zeitschrift für Brüdergeschichte* 3 (1909): 145–207.

Schmidt, Martin. *John Wesley: A Theological Biography*, 2 vols. Translated by Norman P. Goldhaw. Nashville, TN: Abingdon Press, 1962.

Simon, John S. *John Wesley and the Methodist Societies*. London: Epworth Press, 1923.

———. *John Wesley and the Religious Societies*. London: Epworth Press, 1921.

Snyder, Howard A. *The Radical Wesley and Patterns for Church Renewal*. Eugene, OR: Wipf and Stock, 1996.

Sommer, Elisabeth W. *Serving Two Masters: Moravian Brethren in Germany and North Carolina, 1727–1801*. Lexington, KY: University of Kentucky Press, 2000.

Spurr, John. "The Church, the societies and the moral revolution of 1668," in *The Church of England c. 1689 – c. 1833: From Toleration to Tractarianism*. Edited by John Walsh, Colin Haydon, and Stephen Taylor. Cambridge, UK: Cambridge University Press, 1993.

Stoeffler, F. Ernest. "The Rise of Evangelical Pietism," in *Studies in the History of Religions*, vol. 9. Leiden, DE: E. J. Brill, 1965.

Tappert, Theodore G. "Introduction," in *Pia Desideria*, Philipp Jakob Spener. Philadelphia: Fortress Press, 1964.

Thompson, Andrew C. "From Societies to Society: The Shift from Holiness to Justice in the Wesleyan Tradition," *Methodist Review: A Journal of Wesleyan and Methodist Studies* 3 (2011): 141–172, http://www.methodistreview.org/ (accessed July 10, 2012).

———. "To Stir Them up to Believe, Love, Obey," in *Methodist History* 48 (2010): 160–178.

Thompson, E. P. *The Making of the English Working Class*. New York: Pantheon Books, 1964.

Verney, John H. "Early Wesleyan Class Tickets: Comments and Catalogue," in *PWHS* 31 (1957): 2–9, 15, 34–38, 70–73.

Ward, W. R. *The Protestant Evangelical Awakening*. Cambridge, UK: Cambridge University Press, 1992.

Walsh, John. "Origins of the Evangelical Revival," in *Essays in Modern English Church History: In Memory of Norman Sykes*. Edited by G. V. Bennett and J. D. Walsh. New York: Oxford University Press, 1966.

Watson, David Lowes. *The Early Methodist Class Meeting: Its Origins and Significance*. Nashville, TN: Discipleship Resources, 1985.

———. "The Origins and Significance of the Early Methodist Class Meeting," Ph.D. diss., Duke University, 1978.

Watson, Kevin M. "Forerunners of the Early Methodist Band Meeting," *Methodist Review* 2 (2010): 1–31.

Weinlick, John R. *Count Zinzendorf*. Nashville, TN: Abingdon Press, 1959.

Wigger, John H. *American Saint: Francis Asbury and the Methodists*. New York: Oxford University Press, 2009.

Williams, Colin. *John Wesley's Theology Today: A Study of the Wesleyan Tradition in the Light of Current Theological Dialogue*. Nashville, TN: Abingdon Press, 1960.

Wood, A. Skevington. "Perronet, Charles," in *Dictionary of Evangelical Biography*. Edited by Donald M. Lewis. Oxford, UK: Blackwell, 1995.

INDEX

Albin, Thomas R., 65n98, 67n105, 68n109
Aldersgate Street, 34, 79, 89, 95
Alexander, Disney, 159–160, 164
Alleine, Richard, 54
Allen, John, 166
altogether Christian, 40, 93, 104
ancien régime, 10, 184
Anglican
  growth in holiness, 14, 72
  means of grace, emphasis on, 14, 72, 74, 86, 92, 137, 153
  piety, 14–15, 22, 32, 38, 72, 73–77, 153, 171
  Religious Societies *See* Religious Societies, Anglican
  Restoration Anglicanism, 20
  Wesley's synthesis with Moravian piety, 14–15, 86, 139
Arndt, Johan, 17n3
Asbury, Francis, 6, 8
assurance, 3, 29, 33–34, 38, 72, 73, 78–80, 82, 86–88, 91, 94–96, 99, 101, 104, 108–112, 129–132, 139, 148–153, 184
  Wesley's experience of, 79, 95
Austin, Margerit, 104–105, 108, 109
awakening, 8

backslide, 155–156, 173
Baker, Frank, 35, 37, 58n80, 82n44, 91n80
Ball, Hannah, 55, 56
band meeting, 2–3, 62–71
  Anglican influence, 73–77, 153, 156, 170
  body, 164, 168–169, 180–181
  compared to class meeting, 6, 64–66, 68–69, 160, 182, 186
  difficulty of sustaining, 5, 13, 46–47, 144, 175, 180, 184–185
  focal point of Wesley's approach to social holiness, 2, 5, 14–15, 46–47, 71, 93–98
  format of the weekly meeting, 64, 102–103, 118–122
  importance for flourishing of Methodism, 4, 95, 184

  leaders in, 11, 102–103, 117–121, 133, 139, 142, 144, 147, 149, 154, 162–163
  monitors in Fetter Lane, 73–74, 83–84, 84n53
  penitent bands, 66–67, 70, 173n151
  Pietism influence on, 77–81
  popular Methodist experience of, 13, 107–108, 123–124, 163, 183
  prerequisites for joining, 3, 63–64
  public, 145–147, 164, 167–168, 175, 180
  purpose, 63, 130
  role in the midst of the changes in eighteenth-century British society, 8–9
  rules *See* "Rules of the Band Societies"
  sinews of Methodism, 5–6, 69, 95, 136
  synthesis of Moravian and Anglican piety, 72, 86–87, 139, 170–171, 183
  theological contribution of, 72
  transition to prayer meetings, 177–181
  trial, 144–145
  use throughout Evangelical Revival, 8
  Wesley's conception of, 62–69, 108, 112, 116, 139, 142
Barber, Sarah, 104–105, 109
Barber, William, 114–115
Bardsley, Samuel, 143–144, 146, 148, 153, 159
Beecroft, Eliza, 165
Bell, George, 133–136, 151, 178
Bennet, John, 124–125
Biggs, Benjamin, 136
Böhler, Peter, 17, 27, 32, 34, 35, 36, 37, 49, 77, 77n24, 80, 86n64, 93
Bourne, Frances, 175
Bradburn, Samuel, 160–161
Bradnock, Isaac, 165, 167, 175
Brecht, Martin, 17n3
Bristol, 8n34, 50n46, 52, 57–59, 82, 84–86, 102, 110, 128
  bands, 86
  New Room and beginning of the class meeting, 57, 59
British society, 1, 9